Praise for *East End*

'Jojo is a joy . . . A serious coc
Simon Hopkins

'It is a charming, useful and inspirational book – what people need today'
Claudia Roden

'Jojo writes with great passion and a deep knowledge of the food that she grows. Her family recipes are mouth-watering, simple and show that good food is for everyone, regardless of budget'
Thomasina Miers

'Take one inner-city girl with a country girl's heart and gently fold in the knowledge of a seasoned allotment gardener. Combine with a generous amount of simple yet stunning recipes, and finish with a scattering of relevant and cultural quotes that serve to layer and enrich. Heavenly'
Allegra McEvedy

'Jojo is a cook after my own heart'
Anna Del Conte

THE MODERN PEASANT

BY THE SAME AUTHOR

East End Paradise

The
MODERN
PEASANT

Adventures in City Food

JOJO TULLOH

Illustrations by Lynn Hatzius

CHATTO & WINDUS
LONDON

Published by Chatto & Windus 2014
First published by Chatto & Windus 2013

2 4 6 8 10 9 7 5 3 1

First published in Great Britain in 2013 by
Chatto & Windus
Random House, 20 Vauxhall Bridge Road,
London SW1V 2SA
www.vintage-books.co.uk

Addresses for companies within The Random House Group Limited can be
found at:
www.randomhouse.co.uk/offices.htm

The Random House Group Limited Reg. No. 954009

A CIP catalogue record for this book
is available from the British Library

ISBN 9780701189402

The Random House Group Limited supports the Forest Stewardship
Council® (FSC®), the leading international forest-certification organisation. Our
books carrying the FSC label are printed on FSC®-certified paper. FSC is the
only forest-certification scheme supported by the leading environmental
organisations, including Greenpeace. Our paper procurement policy can be
found at www.randomhouse.co.uk/environment

Typeset by Palimpsest Book Production Ltd, Falkirk, Stirlingshire
Printed and bound in Great Britain by Clays Ltd, St Ives plc

For Beatrice, Hannah and Matilda with love

CONTENTS

PREFACE XV

THE ARCHETYPAL MODERN PEASANT:
In Patience's Kitchen 1

BAKED 17

FERMENTED 65

PLANTED 123

REARED 147

FORAGED 173

PICKLED, PRESERVED, SALTED & SMOKED 199

THE PRACTICAL PEASANT'S YEAR 231

THE ARCHETYPAL MODERN PEASANT:
Recipes from Patience's Kitchen 283

TO END 293

CONTACTS 295

BIBLIOGRAPHY 297

ACKNOWLEDGEMENTS 299

INDEX 301

Good cooking is the result of a balance struck between
frugality and liberality . . . It is born out of
communities where the supply of food is conditioned
by the seasons.

Poverty rather than wealth gives the good things of
life their true significance. Home-made bread rubbed
with garlic and sprinkled with olive oil, shared –
with a flask of wine – between working people, can be
more convivial than any feast.

PATIENCE GRAY, HONEY FROM A WEED

I am convinced that to maintain oneself on this earth
is not a hardship, but a pastime, if we will live
simply and wisely.

To be a philosopher is not merely to have subtle
thoughts, nor even to have found a school, but so to
love wisdom as to live accordingly to its dictates, a
life of simplicity, independence, magnanimity, and
trust. It is to solve some of the problems of life, not
only theoretically but practically.

HENRY DAVID THOREAU, WALDEN

Towns are like electric transformers. They increase
tension, accelerate the rhythm of exchange and
constantly recharge human life. They were born of the
oldest and most revolutionary division of labour:
between work in the fields on the one hand and the
activities described as urban on the other.

FERNAND BRAUDEL, THE STRUCTURES OF EVERYDAY LIFE

LADLE
John Berger

Pewter pock-marked
moon of the ladle
rising above the mountain
going down into the saucepan
serving generations
steaming
dredging what has grown from seed
in the garden
thickened with potato
outliving us all
on the wooden sky
of the kitchen wall

Serving mother
of the steaming pewter breast
veined by the salts
fed to her children
hungry as boars
with the evening earth
engrained around their nails
and bread the brother
serving mother

Ladle
pour the sky steaming
with the carrot sun
the stars of salt
and the grease of the pig earth
pour the sky steaming
ladle
pour soup for our days
pour sleep for the night
pour years for my children

PREFACE

For city-dwellers how to eat is no longer a simple matter. We are cut off from the countryside and the chain of production that served our ancestors so well. In the past, we grew, reared and caught our food or procured it from producers we knew and trusted. Now supermarkets bring the world to our door, in one long, monotonous season. This might seem like a good thing, but when we embraced ease we lost out on taste. It is now quicker and easier to get hold of food than at any time in man's history, but there is a growing realisation that this convenience is a Faustian pact. There is a hidden cost. Aside from the drop-off in taste that comes from eating out-of-season, air-freighted foods, the wastefulness of our current food system is a disaster for the environment. More immediately, our health and our finances both suffer if we lack the skills to make good food for ourselves.

For the first time in history more people live in a city than in the country-side. It is ironic that just as we realise the implications of importing so much food, it seems we can do little about producing it ourselves. Instead, urban-ites sit down nightly to do battle with five squabbling, uninvited guests – time, money, ethics, nutrition and sustainability. We may start the day with high food ideals (and a bowl of virtuous porridge), but all too often the maelstrom of modern life means that we end up falling short of them.

My own solution to these problems lies in rediscovering an earlier trad-ition of cookery – one that reconnects our desire for good food with our ability to make it for ourselves. Once (and not so long ago) food and its preparation were an integral part of daily life, not something to be rushed through; there was a time when the satisfaction of performing practical tasks was valued as one of the ways to give meaning to our lives. It is a style that values good, fresh ingredients prepared with care and simplicity. I have come to think of it as cooking in the style of a modern peasant.

The word 'peasant' is a word worth reclaiming. Used negatively, it describes an uncultured person with a very limited horizon. Its uninflected meaning is a person who works on the land, a person who stays local (the word's Latin root is *pagensis*, from *pagus*, a district) to the earth that they dig and plant. A peasant is a person whose commitment to food production is a livelihood rather than an economic proposition; a person who produces high-quality ingredients. These are used to make sustaining food, cooked with love, skill and a degree of care. It is this sense of the word that modern peasants (and I am proud to count myself one) should reappropriate.

Across the world, in cities as disparate as Detroit and Havana, nature is creeping back in, but this book should really be dedicated to the city I live in. London's thrilling evolution never stops inspiring me. It provided me with the initial impetus to record some of what was going on around me: new businesses were popping up in unexpected places – an artisan bakery in a railway arch, a café on a canal. That the city is always changing is a truism, but somehow this feels different. This time it's not just the look of the place, it's the taste of it that is vital too. Vacant lots are blossoming into vegetable gardens, hives are appearing on inner-city rooftops, and independent producers of everything from bread to cheese and sausages are proving that the traditional can still hold its own in the modern world.

This is a book that celebrates the city as a centre of food production in which old ways and new go hand-in-hand. For the past 200 years there's been a stark choice: move to the country, eat better food, breathe cleaner air and drink purer water, or stay in the polluted, exhausting, maddening, dynamic city and be dependent on imported food. Now things are changing. The smells of bread baking and beer brewing assault me as I cycle through the city, our senses are being reawakened and the city has never been a more exhilarating place in which to live.

THE ARCHETYPAL
MODERN PEASANT

In Patience's Kitchen

This book begins with an act of pilgrimage. When writers die they leave behind their words. When food writers die they also leave behind their kitchens and the pots, pans, plates, knives and chopping boards they used over a lifetime of preparing, cooking and eating food. After their death these items assume the status of holy relics for followers. There was frenzied bidding at the sale of Elizabeth David's kitchenalia, right down to the Tupperware, even though, as her nephew told journalist Michael Bateman at the time, 'these are the dregs'. If a collection of random kitchen implements can create such a furore, then imagine what it feels like to step into the extant kitchen of a writer you have long revered; a writer whose way of life was as much a work of art as the books she wrote about it.

Patience Gray (1917–2005) is most famous for her extraordinary autobiographical cookbook *Honey from a Weed*, first published in 1986 and still in print. This evocative, yet scholarly book has inspired me for many years. In it Gray describes her wanderings around the Mediterranean throughout the 1960s with her lover, the Flemish sculptor Norman Mommens. Together they lived a life of almost prehistoric simplicity, going without electricity, running water and telephones and absorbing peasant culture wherever they went.

Eventually the urge to visit Patience's Salentine farmhouse proved too great for me and, armed with an invitation from her son Nick, the photographer Jason Lowe and I flew to Naples. We landed at lunchtime and hit the motorway, but soon found our bellies growling. We turned off and stopped at a small grocery store, where the owner directed us to an *agriturismo* high up in the hills; it was filled with families in their Sunday best. Consumed by greed and by our excitement at being in Italy, we polished off plate after plate of fried courgette flowers, plump mozzarella, slow-cooked octopus and lemon potatoes. Course followed course, lunch had taken far too long, and now we would have to drive fast through the night if we were to arrive before our hosts, Nicolas and his wife Maggie, went to bed.

Hour after hour we roared down winding roads, moonlit sea on our right, the night growing blacker. We were now in the far south, at the tip of Italy's pointed heel. As our car swung round the corner, stone goddesses leapt up out of the night, caught in the beams of our headlights. In the morning we would see for miles in every direction: we were high up, with a flat plain beneath us, the sea in the distance to our left. But all we could see now was the looming shadow of a line of pines, the glimmer of a wall painted white and the dark smudge of a tower. The building was blind except for a double front door and a small window that showed as a warm yellow rectangle in the deep darkness of the night. We had arrived at 'Spigolizzi', a stone's throw from land's end. For thirty years this farmhouse was the home of Norman and Patience.

On their own journey back into the past, Mommens and Gray spent nearly ten years following a 'vein of stone' from Carrara in Italy, to Catalonia, to the island of Naxos in Greece, before settling here in the south of Italy. This is the journey recounted in *Honey from a Weed*. It is no footloose travelogue. Whether it is depicting mountainous Carrara or the wave-racked shores of Naxos, this is a book that seeks out the ancient heart of each place. Wherever Patience and Norman were, Patience cultivated the locals, especially the women, and enquired into the traditions peculiar to that region, particularly those attached to edible and medicinal plants. She wrote down what she learnt, but most importantly of all she absorbed it practically and unselfconsciously; entering into the area's methods of cooking and preparing food as if she had lived there all her life. Her observation of the simpler ways of living left her in no doubt as to the impact of country life on good food:

> *In my experience it is the countryman who is the real gourmet and for good reason; it is he who has cultivated, raised, hunted or fished the raw*

materials and has made the wine himself. The preoccupation of his wife
is to do justice to his labours and bring the outcome triumphantly to
table. In this an emotional element is involved. Perhaps this very old
approach is beginning once again to inspire those who cook in more
complex urban situations.

The pair settled down for good, south of Lecce in Apulia, where they restored a ruined *masseria*: a one-storey L-shaped farmhouse with a square tower that they painted in smears of pinkish-red. Norman and Patience spent forty years together, thirty of them on their stony hilltop, until Norman's death in 2000. They balanced their creative work (she also made jewellery) with the physically demanding cultivation of their eleven acres. Together, they grew crops of garlic, tomatoes and black chickpeas and made wine. They cleared the terraces and pruned the ancient olive trees, which provided them with all the oil they needed for the year. Norman painted the kitchen walls and ceiling with fantastical horned and feathered figures, figures with undulating arms, serpents and two-faced goddesses, and a double-tailed mermaid who holds out her arms in welcome.

The hilltop wilderness flourished under their care; surrounding the farmhouse is the *macchia* (a wild landscape fragrant with herbs and littered with rough white stone, scrubby aromatics and ancient olive trees), whose fungi and wild herbs were such an important part of Patience's way of cooking. Forty years on, the Spigolizzi *masseria* has a garden full of sculptures, amongst which well-grown quince, fig, olive, citrus and pomegranate trees thrive. Below the garden the terrace of olive trees still provides the household's yearly oil.

Inside the whitewashed kitchen (once a byre) Norman's allegorical figures still dance across the vaulted ceiling. These figures are reproduced as a drawing on the cover of *Honey from a Weed*, and their appearance provokes the disorientating effect of having stepped inside the pages of a book. Yet real people, and not just ghosts, live here. After Norman died, Nick and Maggie arrived to look after Patience until her own death in 2005. Although they had the temerity (in Patience's eyes) to install electric lights and a fridge (though not hot water), the rest of the kitchen is as she left it. Her baskets hang from a rail, her knives are stuck to a magnetic strip on the wall, her earthenware cooking pots still go into the embers to cook beans and mush-rooms. In the ashes of the fireplace sit her two blackened metal tripods.

As this was a pilgrimage of sorts, it seemed right that we had arrived on November 1st, the Day of the Dead, the day after what would have been Patience's ninety-fourth birthday. On the first morning mist clung to the bottom of the valley, snaking through the olive orchards below. The soft orange light of dawn backlit the drifts of wild sage holding withered stalks topped with seedheads, showing sere and brown against clumps of felty grey-green leaves. I picked a handful of wild herbs: *mentuccia* (wild mint), sage, thyme, rosemary and resinous red-berried lentisk (mastic tree).

Whatever fate led Norman and Patience to this hillside, it seems a pecu-liarly perfect habitat for both of them. For the sculptor, there is stone everywhere and the evidence of the various uses to which it has been put for millennia by the hillside's former inhabitants. Contained in small tapestry pouches in the house is a museum-worthy hoard of Neolithic tools collected by Patience over half a lifetime of stooping and working this arid land. There is a smooth black obsidian axehead, and minute polished arrowheads worked with flints. The hillside may be dry, but there is water in the valley beneath and a holy well. The amount of tools found here encouraged Norman and Patience to believe that others before them had found this long flat hilltop a fruitful and productive place. Later inhabitants eked out a living by farming. The hillside is dotted with the rudimentary, one-room pudding-shaped stone houses called *trulli* or *pajare*. Empty and yet intact, their dry-stone walls spiral up to a flat top reached by a spiral staircase that turns around the outside of the dome. Beside each one is a stone bread oven, which was mainly used for drying figs.

This landscape is a living witness to ancient ways of life. Patience anchored herself in it as firmly as one of Norman's large stone figures. She lived on it, and from it she gathered wild chicory and snails, dug out edible hyacinth bulbs and washed her hair in a tonic of water infused with rosemary gathered on the hillside. When we visited this hillside it was parched by a long summer. Patience records in an undated letter to her friend Wolf Aylward (probably in around 1990) that in some years ingredients were more plentiful than in others:

No olives have been picked! They were full of insects. I have just managed to gather some for eating, selected. Owing to the seven month drought, mushrooms are rare, as are other fungi. Or was it because last year there were so many ceps & this year they are sleeping. It may just be a delay. The prataioli come up with brown muddy caps! Half drowned never mind, the other day I picked up the smallest arrowhead I have ever seen.

Lest we think her too heroic, there is evidence in another letter to Wolf of frustration with some aspects of this vehemently anti-modern lifestyle:

Of course while I'm making tisanes for the bronchitic Sculptor the weather has been appalling, wet, damp fig leaves, leaden skies, bonfires that don't burn & sheets that never dry . . .

It is customary to visit the graves of relatives on the Day of the Dead and the cemeteries we drove past were full of smartly dressed Italian families with flowers. We made our own visit to the graveyard outside the nearby town of Salve, where Patience and Norman are buried. Her plaque bears only her dates and place of birth, and an engraving of a writer's plumed quill from which the silvering has faded in the sun. Norman's has the words *maraviglia tutela*, which are elusive, but mean something like 'a capacity to wonder'. They are fitting monuments to these two remarkable people. Norman's talent as an artist seems to have been fed by his ability to fan that spark of wonder. It certainly sustained an extraordinary capacity for hard physical work, while Patience had poetry enough to record their life together in a book that grabs your attention every time you open it. She describes Norman in her last book, *Work Adventures, Childhood Dreams*:

He was 'l'uomo di pietra', the man of stone, 'who long ago handed me not so much a completely new life but more mysteriously a life that is always new'.

When they set out on this life together Norman and Patience weren't trying to live like peasants, they were simply feeding Norman's 'appetite for marble' – this, and not a self-conscious desire for pre-industrial life, 'precipitated them out of modern life'. So it was accident, not design, that put them in the company of craftsmen, living in places where the conditions were primitive. Patience, in a way she could not have foreseen, found her own rich seam, not of stone or marble, but of knowledge, a fact that she reiterates in her most famous book: 'The weed from which I have drawn the honey is the traditional knowledge of the Mediterranean people.' Living on their Salentine hill, they were 'foreshadowing the age to come' as they 'inscribed as artisans' and cultivated 'some acres of stony red earth'.

'Foreshadowing' is an important word, because although *Honey from a Weed* celebrates culinary tradition, there is always an awareness of what our current way of consuming is doing to our world. Patience has no illusions that her way of living runs contrary to the current of modern life. 'Can we be living in a Fool's paradise?' she asks. I think not, and if she were alive today she would undoubtedly be dismayed by much, but perhaps also a little heartened by the resurgence of interest in wild foods and in foods grown near where they are consumed. Her articulation of what really matters when it comes to food seems extraordinarily prescient today:

I am interested in growing food for its own sake and in appetite. The health-giving and prophylactic virtues of a meal depend on the zest with which it has been imagined, cooked and eaten. It seemed to me appropriate to show something of the life that generates this indispensable element at a time when undernourishment bedevils even the highest income groups.

Abstinence, enjoyment, celebration, all have nature's approval; if you practise the first, you maintain what is priceless – enjoyment and its crown, celebration.

I had gone to Spigolizzi to cook in Patience's kitchen and to see at first hand what it meant not just to pay lip service to the ideals of peasant life, but to spend half your life committed to a more traditional way of being. I had read the stories of editors and journalists coming back from Spigolizzi shaken by the lack of plumbing and electricity. Luckily for me, things are not quite as they were in the heyday of Norman and Patience. There is now electricity, although still no heating or hot water, but happily the skies were clear and blue during our stay and the sun heated the water tank on the roof.

The first thing you see on entering the kitchen is the two-tailed mermaid (the original is found in a mosaic in the nearby cathedral of Otranto), who holds her arms out, palms up. A butterfly flies on either side of her. Beneath are written the words *Salve Spigolizzi Ionio*. This is very much a place of welcome – something that Patience's own record of their olive-oil consumption revealed:

> *I had better tell you the worst: a household of two with a good many visitors consumes in a year at least 60 litres of olive oil, using it for cooking salads and for conserving.*

At the end of the long room with its curved ceiling is a low archway leading into a fireplace. I had imagined the fireplace to be the heart of the room, but it is almost like an anteroom. The walls are blackened, as this room doubled as a smokery for hams and sausages. Behind the kitchen is the *cantina*, which once held wine, but now acts as a larder full of preserves and Patience's collection of terracotta cooking pots and tagines. The ceiling in here is low, as this small room doubles as the platform for a mezzanine bed, reached by stone steps running up the outside of this room-within-a-room. This was where Patience and Norman slept.

In her kitchen, Patience cooked with what was at hand, both wild and cultivated, and on our visit to Spigolizzi this was what we tried to do. Over several clear autumnal days, with Maggie and Nick's help, we gathered wild chicory and fennel in the fields around the *masseria* and picked huge deep-yellow quinces in the garden. We used Patience's blackened cauldrons to boil the quinces, and the large copper preserving pan to make the jelly. We went to the fish market for *moscardini* (little cuttlefish), then cleaned them on the large oval chopping board that appears alongside the recipe for that dish in *Honey from a Weed*. We clambered up the steps that spiral round the small stone igloos that dot the hillside and marvelled at the opacity of the Apulian sky and the rigid horizontal line where that sky meets the sea. In back streets we sought out bakers baking bread in ancient stone ovens, bought capers, *puntarelle* (chicory), bouquets of round red peppers, mushrooms and anchovies in the market, and we indulged in Patience's concept of breakfast (damascene plum jam with ricotta and fresh bread). Stepping into the reality of *Honey from a Weed* is like going back in time. Yet it is a journey that throws light on the future too. As Henry Miller says in his book about Greece, *The Colossus of Maroussi*: 'I'm crazy enough to believe that the happiest man on earth is the man with the fewest needs.'

Patience and Norman relished the companionship evoked by hard work done with others, whether it was olive-picking, wine-making or cultivating the fields. There was pleasure to be taken in prolonged physical effort endured, and then relieved by celebration. Modern machinery means one man can work alone, yet there is a loneliness that comes with this efficiency. This was a life in which modern comforts were almost stubbornly refused, but the strength it gave Patience and Norman still lingers on in the house. We might want to romanticise it, but this was no idyll, for the Salento has a harsh climate, hot and dry in summer, freezing in winter. Without electricity, the farmhouse would have been very dark in the winter. The day-to-day life that Norman and Patience lived here was extremely demanding physically, yet it invigorated and sustained their remarkable love affair.

In a letter Patience wrote in October 1990 after a trip to London we get a sense of what this place meant to her:

> It was amazing to get back to cucina mia where we had some kind of merenda featuring bread (real) cheese (Sardinian) own tomatoes, garlic, real olive oil and a bottle of Fano wine, back, to simplicity, love, extravagant space after confinement of streets, people, building. Wonderful.

Simplicity, the deep and wonderful well of collective knowledge that artisans provide and the careful appreciation of the natural world's changing seasons are all things I took both from repeated readings of *Honey from a Weed* and from my visit. The ease with which Patience jumped into a different life led me to examine my own, and in particular the ways in which I procured food. Patience's remarkable ability to live both in the present and in the past got me thinking, as did her propensity for learning from others.

I returned to Hackney determined to eat more weeds (Patience's universal panacea), get bees and seek out those who could teach me their hard-earnt skills. For above all, peasant cookery hymns the traditional skills of the artisan refined over years. I wanted to buttonhole bakers, cheese-makers, foragers, butchers and pastry chefs. I knew I could learn a lot from those who had made food their profession. After all, the greatest part of success in cookery is confidence; for me, watching expert producers at work provided the ultimate in culinary illumination.

In the process of writing this book I have watched my local butcher cutting carcasses into joints, in an attempt to better understand how to cook from the whole animal. I have tried to uncover the secrets of a new kind of English loaf from the master bakers at the bakery that serves the St John restaurants, and I have watched three different kinds of bee-keepers at work, as well as seeking out the green-fingered guerrillas who are turning wasteland into vegetable gardens. All the skills in this book – whether bee-keeping, pickling, preserving, baking or curing – can be mastered by even the most impractical person. I hope the expert tips gleaned from my encounters will help you put simple satisfaction back into the heart of your everyday cooking.

Patience Gray thrived in her remote rural home; as a skilled crafts-woman, she would probably have called herself an artisan, not a peasant, but I am happy to be an urban peasant. I like getting wet and cold planting potatoes, but I don't want to move to the countryside. I crave the fresh-tasting products of country life, not the isolation that goes with them. I want to be where things are constantly evolving. I want to be close to the action. I am awed by the skills of this new breed of food producers and I want to cherry-pick the best of their ideas to use in my own kitchen. From butchering to baking to bee-keeping to vegetable gardens, this book evaluates what the very best modern-day, city-dwelling food producers can teach us.

The first thing to do is assess what we know. How much knowledge have we lost and how do we go about rediscovering it? There are lots of highly practical urbanites, but equally many of us can barely sew on a button, let alone cook, construct or grow things. How did this terrible modern curse creep up on us? For illumination I turned to a book written by a polemicist who was intent on dragging others out of want and into self-sufficiency; a book written nearly 200 years ago, for the bald truth is that we have been losing our skills for centuries.

In 1821 the journalist, pamphleteer and agitator William Cobbett was so alarmed by the wretched condition of the labouring classes that he wrote a manual to teach them how to look after themselves. In this book, *Cottage Economy*, Cobbett proposed to teach the average labourer the means of 'brewing Beer, making Bread, keeping Cows and Pigs, rearing Poultry, and of other matters; and to show that, while, from a very small piece of ground, a large part of the food of a considerable family may be raised'.

Cobbett was an agitator – he liked stirring things up. He delighted in his prickly reputation (his pen name was Peter Porcupine), yet *Cottage Economy* is a charming book: practical, but also overflowing with compassion for those unable to keep the wolf from the door. Here he speaks with great sympathy of the condition of many working people:

> *Yet on men go, from year to year, in this state of wretched dependence, even when they have all the means of living within themselves, which is certainly the happiest state that anyone can enjoy.*

Cobbett wasn't interested in reviving an idealised vision of rural life; he was moved by the desire to free the poorest in society from the tyranny of hunger and want. He aimed to do this by giving them the skills to look after themselves. He wanted to make each one 'a skilful person, a person worthy of respect'. He offers something much more helpful than sympathy – common-sense advice that really works:

> *Competence is the foundation of happiness and of exertion. Beset with wants, having a mind constantly harassed with fears of starvation, who can act with energy, who can calmly think?*

Cobbett truly believed that if you only had a small piece of land and the will to work it, you had the means to feed yourself and your family. As G. K. Chesterton notes in his introduction to the 1926 edition of the book, Cobbett 'had the historical instinct to grasp the great virtues that go with such a small estate. Through all his days he thirsted after freedom. And he understood something that can only accompany freedom, property; and something that can only come with property – thrift.'

Henry David Thoreau, writing thirty years later during his own experiment with self-sufficiency, would echo Cobbett's sentiments:

> *If one would live simply and eat only the crop which he raised, and raise no more than he ate, and not exchange it for an insufficient quantity of more luxurious and expensive things, he would need cultivate only a few rods of ground.*

Cobbett considered practical skills an almost universal panacea, even for angry, disaffected youth:

> *And is it not much more rational for parents to be employed in teaching their children how to cultivate a garden, to feed and rear animals, to make bread, beer, bacon, butter, and cheese, and to be able to do these things for themselves, or for others, than to leave them to prowl about the lanes and common.*

While I don't think growing potatoes will solve the inner cities' problems, reading *Cottage Economy* today I still find a lot that is highly relevant to our current bad food ways and divided society. Above all, the idea that we can free ourselves from the chain of consumption is radical and exciting. It makes me want to sell up, leave the city, buy some land and build a cabin with my bare hands. I fear that my own cabin would be a sloppy affair surrounded by weeds (I am going on the evidence of my allotment), but despite the doubts I have about my own competence, I still find that clarion call to self-sufficiency invigorating. We all have the capacity to learn how to shift for ourselves better and, in doing so, provide food whose provenance and nutrition we can be certain of.

The lessons apparent in *Cottage Economy* are timely; we live in an age of super-consumption, but by producing more food for ourselves or witnessing the labour that goes into food production, or by buying direct from the producer, we will attach more worth to what we eat and will waste less. Being truly self-sufficient requires hours and hours of hard labour that few of us could manage. That said, we can all strive to produce more and consume less. By learning how to bake bread or produce a comb of honey we have, in a small way, loosened the chain of dependence on others that has been winding itself slowly around us for the last 500 years.

For William Cobbett it was the fact that very few villagers made their own beer that really appalled him. He was horrified by their dependence on the 'poisonous stuff served out to us by common brewers'. Our standards are a good deal lower now. Home-brewing is too complicated and too much effort for most of us. But whilst we may not want to start a micro-brewery, there are still plenty of things we can easily do for ourselves.

Today many people are rediscovering the pleasures, and the welcome distraction from daily cares, that come from baking their own bread, making their own marmalade, pickles and chutneys, growing their own vegetables or even keeping their own bees. Even if we only do these things rarely or on a very modest scale, it is still worthwhile, as it adds a level of satisfaction to our lives that can only be appreciated by experiencing it. Not everyone has the time. That doesn't matter; what this book is about is attitude. Start small by making a batch of your own ricotta; plant a seed and savour a home-grown windowsill tomato; or go out and buy a bag of Kentish cherries dripping with dark-purple juice. These things are as achievable as they are satisfying. The first foods I made at home were bread, marmalade and chutney. Now I regularly make yoghurt, sauerkraut, *kimchi* and curd cheese. These foods taste good, they do me good and I enjoy making them. That is good enough for me.

BAKED

Bread and Honey

There is no such thing as cheap bread. The illusion of it is everywhere, but while it may make economic sense, modern methods of bread production have resulted in a loaf that is bad for our teeth, bad for our guts and, in our waste of it, bad for the world. The discovery of the Chorleywood method, a quick chemical way to raise bread, in 1961 led to highly cost-effective, uniform mass production. This meant that we almost lost our connection to handmade bread for ever; with the rapid spread of artisan bakeries we are only now regaining it.

The quality and cost of bread today are probably more varied than they have ever been. There are aisles and aisles of cheap, chemically raised, factory-made breads in the supermarket and there are some really good, reliable artisan bakers producing crisply crusted, chewy, nutty breads. The biggest stumbling block for consumers is cost. A good artisan-produced loaf will cost perhaps three times as much as a supermarket loaf. It will, however, taste ten times as good, last twice as long and every scrap – from crust to crumbs – can be put to use in the kitchen. You will find yourself far less willing to waste handmade bread. Added to this, a handmade loaf is unadulterated, lower in salt, and no chemicals are used during its raising process. Unfortunately we have become so used to cheap food, and cheap bread in particular, that for some the relative cost of a handmade loaf is hard to come to terms with.

Buying a decent loaf of bread isn't always easy, even if you want one. The illusion of good bread (soft, fluffy and sliced) is everywhere, yet highly processed loaves are far from wholesome and strangely unsatisfying. If you don't have an artisan bakery nearby, then making your own bread is the obvious next step. The ability to make a good loaf of sourdough bread

– chewy, elastic, long-keeping and with an excellent crust – takes some time to perfect, but the satisfaction that its production induces is beyond measure.

The frontispiece of Eliza Acton's *English Bread Book* (published in 1857) has an engraving of sheaves of wheat, garlanded with ribbons that read 'Bread strengthens man's heart'. Underneath are written the words: 'In no way, perhaps, is the progress of a nation in civilisation more unequivocally shown, than in the improvement which it realises in the food of the community.'

This is such an extraordinarily modern sentiment, but a heart-breakingly long time has passed since then. We are only just realising how much what we eat actually matters. What prescience to write those words so long ago, and what a pity we have only just begun to heed them. Bread has been a staple of our diet for centuries, yet throughout that time it has been one of the most adulterated basic foods (milk being the other). What better way to serve your local community than by providing a loaf that is guaranteed to be nutritious, wholesome and, above all, tasty.

That the quality of bread eaten in British homes has long been a source of anxiety is revealed by the following quote from Eliza Acton's introduction to her previous book, *Modern Cookery*, published in 1845:

> *It is surely a singular fact, that the one article of our food on which health depends more than any other, should be precisely that which is obtained in England with the greatest difficulty* – good, light and pure bread; *yet nothing can be more simple and easy than the process of making it, either in large quantities or small.*

It is more than 150 years since this wise and witty English cookery writer tried to encourage British housewives that, for value, nutrition, peace of mind and above all taste, they would be much better off baking their own bread; sadly, we did not listen to her advice. Acton felt there was an unjustified repugnance attached to bread baked at home. This dislike was born of repeated failure, which resulted in 'heavy, or bitter, or ill-baked masses of dough' appearing at the table 'under the name of *household or home-made bread*' – a failure that put many people off it for life, and resulted in an over-reliance on bought bread. She never wavered in her firm 'conviction of the superior wholesomeness of bread made in our houses'.

Both in her best-seller *Modern Cookery* (reprinted twice in its first year) and in the less well-known *English Bread Book* Acton provided direct and precise instructions for the preparation of dough and the making of bread. Elizabeth David, no slouch as a recipe writer herself, put it perfectly in *English Bread and Yeast Cookery* when she described Acton's ability to pass on the truly pertinent and useful:

> *There are times when I feel that Miss Acton is too good to be true. An unworthy thought, for so obviously, so transparently, she was utterly thorough, totally sincere in her anxiety to instruct, to pass on the knowledge she herself had acquired through such painstaking experiment.*

Acton knew, and hoped to convince others, that making good bread at home was within the capabilities of all. Perhaps most importantly of all, she had lived in France and knew just what a wonderful thing a good loaf of bread was. Whether or not making your own bread is a worthwhile undertaking is an argument that is ongoing. Many people still find it hard to believe that good bread is easy to make. There is an erroneous belief that making home-made bread is a job for only the most committed cooks, or people with an excess of time on their hands. In fact the time spent actually mixing and baking bread is minimal; the bread rises in its own time, not yours, and only requires that you attend to it at the right moment – this is something that comes easily after the first two or three attempts.

Returning to William Cobbett's *Cottage Economy*, we find that making bread has other advantages too:

> *Give me for a beautiful sight, a neat and smart woman, heating her oven and setting her bread! And if the bustle does make the sign of labour glisten on her brow, where is the man that would not kiss that off, rather than lick the plaster from the cheek of a duchess?*

He goes on to illustrate the best technique for kneading, and its consequences:

The dough must, therefore, be well worked. The fists must go heartily into it. It must be rolled over, pressed out, folded up and pressed out again, until it is completely mixed and formed into a stiff and tough dough. This is labour, mind . . . Let a young woman bake a bushel once a week, and she will do very well without phials and gallipots [pots for ointments].

Cobbett places women firmly in the kitchen, but against my better feminist nature, his assessment of the beneficial effects of hard work still makes me smile. I don't know if I have had my face kissed whilst still red from the oven, but if I keep on baking it may happen one day.

A Tale of Two Bakers

The E5 Bakehouse is an artisan bakery in a unit under the railway arches beside London Fields station in Hackney. Set up by a young and idealistic baker named Ben MacKinnon, it produces sourdough, rye and wholegrain breads. The businesses in the adjacent arches sell second-hand kitchen equipment, used furniture and bric-a-brac; there are joiners and car valets. When the overground train rattles overhead the kitchen shakes (it doesn't affect the dough). Commuters and school children wander past the window on their way to the station, eight arches down.

On the day I was to do my baking there I got up before dawn. I mixed up a batch of dough and left it rising in the airing cupboard, so that I could cook it alongside Ben's that evening. Around 7 a.m. I headed for the bakery on my bike. The space Ben occupies is small (he shares the arch with three other businesses): just an oven, a counter and some racks for storing the bread.

The oven dominates the space. It is a beautiful and homespun thing: cube-shaped, with a big metal extractor sticking out the back, blasting hot, yeasty air out across Hackney. It has a thick lime-washed exterior and the area around the rectangular metal doors is cracked and blackened by the heat. A friend of Ben's welded the hinges and clasps while Ben whittled the oak handles. The oven's pre-industrial exterior is at odds with the strip lighting and the basic, no-frills metal counter of the bakery kitchen.

The owner of this bakery has not long been a baker. Disillusioned by his previous job and inspired by his travels – in particular time spent with Moroccan bakers – Ben took a bread-making course and, still half-afraid to call himself a baker, started making bread. It was a brave thing to do. Like an actor or a musician, all your mistakes are made in public. I asked Ben how he had coped with his early failures. He just laughed and said he had some very understanding customers. The story of how he got his oven and opened the bakery is a rather convoluted tale, but a good one.

To begin with, Ben baked his bread in a pizza oven in Clapham. After a few months he was offered the space within the arch and made this oven. He began by thinking about the arch-shaped ovens he had seen in North Africa. In a Hackney pub he met a man called Jim who smoked a lot of dope and was a self-proclaimed expert on medieval kilns. He talked to Ben endlessly about what form the oven should take, but in the end Ben was too nervous to put Jim's arcane ideas into practice, worried that his historically authentic oven might take hours to heat up. In the end, and with the help of his sister (an engineer working in the Democratic Republic of Congo), Ben came up with a plan to build a simple oven that was popular in the developing world.

The Rocket is renowned for its ability to reach high temperatures quickly, using a relatively small surface area. Ben made his oven using a manual downloaded from the Internet. The materials were begged and foraged. The oven takes forty-five minutes to heat up, fired by free offcuts from a local joinery, and the bread takes about twenty minutes to bake. The heart of the hand-crafted oven is the fire, a crackling bed of embers contained in a hollow space, above two metal shelves that take the trays of bread.

Unlike conventional bakers, Ben does his baking by daylight. He noticed that a lot of his customers wanted to buy bread at the end of the day. On the morning I visited him he had an unusually large (at that time anyway) number of loaves to make: fifty-six in all. The first thing I did was to take the bread baked the night before and stack it up on the shelves. Coincidentally, that day almost all of the people who came in to buy bread were friends of mine, all surprised to see me piling up loaves whilst wearing a floury apron.

To start, we weighed out the 'sponge'; this is a partially fermented mixture of flour, water and sourdough starter. Sourdough bread is made with a natural leaven (raising agent) rather than bought dried yeast. This leaven is called a 'starter' (or sometimes 'mother') and is a combination of natural airborne yeast and bacteria, fed with flour and water. The bacteria make acids that 'sour' the starter. Most bakers keep a bit of starter back from each batch, adding flour to it to keep it alive, but Ben just keeps a sponge (some of the partially risen dough) from each batch. When we lifted the lids, the dough caught, pulling up in strings like pavement chewing gum on a hot summer's day.

We weighed flour and water on electronic scales and mixed them with a carefully weighed amount of leaven. We were making a white loaf with a small amount of wholemeal flour and each batch we made was for four-teen loaves. We tipped the flour, water and leaven into a big metal bucket (part of a professional-sized mixer). We pushed the thick twist of metal that was the dough hook into the machine and ran it for four minutes slow and three minutes fast, then we carried the dough back to the counter and poured it into a big plastic tub; we sprinkled salt over the top and left it for about twenty minutes. Its second mix was one minute slow and six minutes fast. Then we put it back into the tub for forty-five minutes and covered it with a lid.

After this second resting period, Ben took a squeezy bottle filled with olive oil from the windowsill and squirted it onto the counter. He took the lid off the dough – inside the tub, bubbles like the sac in a bullfrog's throat had appeared. He put the dough (a considerable weight) onto the counter and started stretching it out, until it was about the size of a sheepskin. He then folded it into thirds, twisted it round and did the whole thing again, until the dough was wonderfully pliant and elastic; it was sticky, but very smooth and with a sheen on it. It was hard work – you have to be strong, not only to do this, but to lift the metal trays weighed down with their loaves into the blazingly hot oven.

The dough went back into the tub and rested for another forty-five minutes. We mixed up the leaven for the bread that would be baked that night and carried it to the big walk-in fridge.

When the dough was ready we got out the floured proving baskets: small linen-lined wicker baskets that shape the dough as it rises (what bakers call 'proving') and give artisan loaves their characteristic domed appearance. The dough was hefted onto the counter and given one stretch, pull and fold to relax the gluten, then I cut off roughly 850g amounts by eye, using a satisfying metal scraping tool that Ben called the Scotsman. I asked if this was because the tool didn't allow a scrap of dough to be wasted, but Ben had just inherited the name with the tool. I checked and adjusted the weight of each chunk on the scales, and when it was right I passed it to Ben. He had oiled the metal counter a little and pulled the dough out and then in, to form a circle, giving it a good hard crimp at the top; then he pushed down with his hands, twisting as he did so, to form a ball with a good curve and skin to it. When he was satisfied with the shape he turned it over and, holding it by the crease, dipped it into a bowl of flour and then dropped it straight into the wicker proving basket.

After this we switched to making the long *bâtard*-like loaves (short baguettes). These weighed in at 1kg and were rolled slightly differently, as a long sausage. The seam had to stay underneath and a steady, even pressure had to be applied along the dough as you rolled: it was much harder, and I let Ben get on with it as I could see that he wasn't that satisfied with my efforts. The loaves were placed in an old plastic mushroom tray, which had been lined with a piece of floured linen, ridged up to form divisions so that four loaves could be fitted into each tray. They all then went onto a mobile metal shelf unit, which Ben had rescued from a disused bakery.

The trolley was wheeled into a walk-in fridge. Six hours later I came back, bringing with me my eldest daughter and my home-produced dough. The bread was taken out and allowed to come up to room temperature, whilst the oven was lit and reached its optimum heat of 220°C. The temperature inside the oven was checked with an infrared thermometer. When it was hot enough, the catches were pulled back and, using the big floury heatproof mittens, the enormous and very heavy metal shelf was taken out of the oven and placed on the counter. Semolina was sprinkled over the bottom of the shelf and then the loaves were tipped out of their baskets. They had not risen a huge amount, and Ruari, who was baking that night, treated them quite firmly (even quite roughly), using a plastic-handled, serrated bread knife to slash the tops three times, then he placed them in the oven. Each shelf takes between twenty and thirty loaves.

Whilst we were waiting for the bread to bake we got very hungry. The aromas were just too much for us. We took one of the previous day's ciabattas and placed it in the oven's aperture close to the ground, just a few very hot centimetres from the glowing coals. It was soon warmed through. We dripped olive oil over it and gobbled it up. After about twenty minutes the bread was checked, and the oven, being hotter than usual, had cooked the loaves in record time. I had placed my own ball of sourdough, mixed at home that morning, into the oven alongside the E5 loaves. Mine came out more golden and with a better-looking and more professional crust than usual, and was chewy and light when eaten. I left one loaf for Ben and, packing up my basket, took my loaf, some rye bread and my daughter – who had been kept busy stoking the fire – home.

My day at the bakery had been a very happy one. There is no concealing the fact that the urban environs of this bakery are grimy, but the image that stays with me is of a square of fire, a pit of glowing coals greedily eating up the wood that we pushed down the shoot. If you are passing the E5 Bakehouse and the smell of baking bread draws you in, then you will find that the warmth emanating from the oven makes it hard to leave. Local people who have discovered this bakery for themselves love it. Office workers toiling home at around half-past eight can pick up a loaf still hot from the oven.

On top of this there is openness and a desire to meet the people who are buying and eating his bread, which are central to what Ben is trying to do. He wants his bread to be eaten by the people who live and work near the bakery, he wants to employ and train people from that community. Concern for the state of the world, and sympathy with the people around you, might seem to some an odd place to start your journey into bread-making, but I think it is an admirable one. I went home tired, but feeling good about something that was happening in the place where I live – Hackney, a place too often portrayed as a borough rotten with divisive poverty and gangs.

Sceptics might argue that this bread is only finding its way into a certain section of society. On the day I worked there I saw a wide range of people enjoying the availability of a decent loaf in their neighbourhood. Since I visited him, Ben has expanded into his own arch, and has opened a café alongside his bakery. He now uses an industrial electric oven and employs six or seven bakers at a time. The handmade oven has been dismantled and rebuilt and is now used as a pizza oven. The location and the oven may have changed, but the bread is just as good, if not even better. It is chewy and light with a dark-brown top slashed with a cross and marked with concentric rings of flour. They also do the best croissants outside Paris that I have ever tasted.

To get down to more practical matters, as well as uplifting my heart my day at the E5 Bakehouse taught me three very important things: the perfect ratio for a rye loaf (see recipe on page 38); that bread knives are good for cutting slashes in the top of loaves; and, best of all, the secret of autolysis.

AUTOLYSIS

Autolysis is the destruction of a cell by its own enzymes. The word means 'self-splitting'. Without getting too technical, you want to encourage the proteins to blend better. You can do this by mixing your flour, starter and water and then waiting for twenty to forty-five minutes. The flour and water undergo autolysis on their own without kneading.

What is happening during this time? Well, the two enzymes in flour are breaking the starch into sugar and the protein into gluten. If you leave the dough to rest for forty-five minutes without salting it, this process happens automatically without any of the downsides of over-kneading (a sour taste and poor colour) and over-exposure to air. Another advantage of this method is that the flour has time to absorb the water. This helps gluten to form in a more orderly way. Try it and you will find that your dough will be more malleable, and it may rise a little higher; but, most importantly, it will taste better, look better and have a better texture.

Mehdi, the master baker

A baker's reputation is made anew each night. His standing with his public is only as good or as bad as the last loaf he baked. If the baker excels at his or her art, customers – once granted the taste of perfection – take it as their right. They don't care that cold air slowed the rising of the dough down to a standstill, or that a careless hand mixed the dough too wet so that it stuck to the basket. They only expect that, night after night, the baker will perform impeccably. The master baker must take life's least glamorous qualities to heart – those pedestrian traits scorned by poets, rock stars and youth: consistency and reliability.

When bread is handmade, each stage of its journey to completion is fraught with potential failure. The method that transforms the separate entities of flour, water and starter into a finished loaf must be carefully watched over, and a single mistake in weighing, mixing, shaping, proving or baking could spell disaster. It is a hard job, the hours are unsociable and the work is physical. The baker bends again and again, his knees cracking as he crouches before the oven, his face scorched by the intense heat and his nose blocked with the dry dust of scorched semolina. In winter the bakery is freezing; in summer roasting. It requires vigilance too, and the repetitive nature of the work lends itself to error; how to remember if you have done something when you have done it so many times before?

All these thoughts are in my mind as I pedal down the kind of road your mother warns you never to walk down alone at night. But it is late, and lonely, as I cycle down a street in Bermondsey edged on the left by a row of railway arches and on the right by a low-rise housing estate. The road is badly lit and empty, the arches are all shuttered. As I reach a bend in the road, one arch shows signs of life – a door is slightly open and a thin slice of light bleeds out into the night. When I push that door open at 10.15 p.m. the bakery is already working at full speed, there are racks of proving baskets filled with dough and three bakers hard at work. One of them, Luka, is slicing off lumps of dough and weighing it out on scales; the other two, Mehdi and Martin, are rolling fat torpedoes of dough.

The space is deep and brightly lit with a long line of strip lights. It is just a big empty space into which the elements needed to mix, prove and bake bread have been wheeled. It could have been here ten years or ten minutes – it's impossible to say (actually, I know it's only been about four or five months). There is a large metal oven on wheels at the front, and two huge grey humidity-controlled boxes that maintain a consistent environment in which the dough rises. There are a couple of sinks, cupboards and two mixers. This is the new bakery that supplies the restaurants of St John at Smithfield, St John Bread and Wine at Spitalfields and a new hotel in Chinatown.

Mehdi is the boss here, a big square-shouldered man with short black hair and a calm presence; he is immediately welcoming. I am shown into an office piled high with white bakers' trousers and shirts. Baking is a job that requires a bit of muscle, as evidenced by the fact that these duds only come up in XX and XXX large, and I am a small by anyone's scale. I pick some out and put them on. They swamp me, but I pull on an enormous V-necked top and drag the trousers up over my shoes. I have to roll the legs up four times before I can step out into the brightly lit arch. I notice from the jeans hanging on pegs that the other bakers have stripped right down before putting on their uniform, but I keep my jeans on.

Mehdi and Martin are still busy shaping dough, so I join them. Mehdi slaps the dough down on the counter; he is firm with it, and the dough is folded over once and the seal slapped shut, then the package is twisted and slapped down again and the same action performed. Then (and this is the tricky bit) it is simultaneously squeezed with the thumbs and rolled forward with the hands, so that the dough billows out, stretching balloon-like away from the hands. Once shaped, the bread is carefully lifted and placed on the waiting cloth. My own first attempts at rolling the dough aren't up to much. I make several efforts; only one makes it to the floured canvas, where a pushed-up, well-floured fold of cloth separates each fat sausage. My other attempts are reshaped, kindly and tactfully, by Mehdi. By 11 p.m. all the shaping is done.

Then the team splits. Mehdi goes into the office to write out the orders, while Luka starts weighing out the flour and mixing the dough for tomorrow night. He is showing Martin, who is on a trial shift, how to mix the 'mother' (the fermented wild yeast, flour and water mixture) with water and flour, so that the endless cycle of bread-making can continue. Some people are snobbish about the age of their starter (this one is twelve years old), but Luka tells me that once it gets going it doesn't matter if your mother is two weeks old or 150 – it's how you care for it that matters.

The bags of flour are piled up on pallets on the floor. At the St John Bakery they use a mixture of organic stoneground flour and Dove organic flour; the stoneground flour has great flavour, but is not very strong (its gluten content is low) and therefore does not rise so well. What it does do is make a lovely creamy mother. This flour is combined 60:40 with Dove organic flour, which has less flavour, but more gluten.

This is a practical working bakery in which function wins out over design. The bread is mixed in two machines; one is old and characterful with dials covered in masking tape. As it mixes the dough little puffs of flour escape out of the top; it clanks in a friendly way and the silver hook traces soporific spirals in the dough (it is by now almost midnight). Next to it is a larger, newer and much glossier machine; it hardly makes a sound as it works, other than a slapping, squelching noise as the hook sucks at the dough – it sounds like a wellington boot leaving thick mud. It mixes slowly for thirty-five minutes and the dough is then poured out into flat white plastic trays (the kind butchers use) and covered with an ordinary black-plastic bin liner. The countertop is swept down with a nylon brush that is the end of a cheap plastic broom. The starter is kept in a catering-sized green plastic tub that once held olives. The wheeled counter doubles up as a chest full of racks of proving bread.

When the oven is hot enough, this chest is wheeled right up to the oven and Mehdi slides each baguette onto a short plank of wood and then flips them onto a much longer paddle, which looks like a giant cricket bat. He uses this tool to slide the dough expertly to the back of the oven. Later, when he cooks the sourdough, he slaps the balls of dough down hard on to the metal paddle and effortlessly slides them into exactly the right spaces. Mehdi uses a timer, but eye and touch too. He takes some bread out, feels the bottom and then puts it back in. He works steadily; he has a lot of bread to bake, but he is unhurried. All is calm attention.

As the oven cooks the bread, it exudes jets and plumes of steam. The air fills with floury dust and perfect, crusty-looking loaves are taken out and thrown into brown plastic bakers' trays. Mehdi gives us one to eat. In between watching Luka mix the dough and Mehdi bake, I talk to Max – one of the chefs from the new St John hotel – who is rolling out puff pastry for Eccles cakes; he lets me help stretch the pastry over the patties of sugar and raisins that go inside the cakes. We eat Mehdi's warm crusty baguette and chat. It is late now, 2 a.m., and the air is full of the rich and reassuring smell of baking bread.

I look into the oven and see the shadows that the loaves leave behind – circular shapes surrounded by blackened semolina, which Mehdi then sweeps out with a broom. My tired mind flips off in odd directions. The white-jacketed figures bent over little trays covered with cloths suddenly look like mortuary attendants. I shake my head and they turn back into bakers. I watch Martin shape five balls of white dough and place them in an enormous sandwich tin; they rise up, white and shapely above the rim, like some mutant five-breasted woman.

The last loaves are baked and I help Mehdi do the orders – so many raisin, rye or brown loaves for the shops and restaurants that rely on this excellent, chewy bread to impress their customers. Mehdi sells his bread directly to customers only once a week, on Saturday mornings. The rest of the time his purchasers are mainly restaurateurs. Bread is usually the first thing a diner consumes in a restaurant, and first impressions are important; in this case the bread sets a high standard for the rest of the food to live up to.

TIPS TO TAKE HOME WITH YOU

TIME: If you want to control the time of day at which you bake, you can put your dough in the fridge rather than a warm cupboard. This will slow down the rising. The bread at the St John Bakery rises very slowly (the big grey cupboard keeps the dough at quite a low temperature). I find this especially useful on days when I make dough in the morning and only afterwards realise that I am going out in the evening This retarding approach is very useful: you can bake your bread within twenty-four hours, rather than within fourteen hours of mixing it.

STEAM: The oven that Mehdi uses has a mechanism that injects steam into the oven; it is controlled by a black knob that looks like something you see on a church organ. I used to pour water onto a tray in the bottom of my oven, but now (following Mehdi's advice) I spray water using a cheap spray bottle straight onto a hot baking tray in the oven. I also spray the top of the loaf just before I put it in.

BE TOUGH WITH YOUR DOUGH: Mehdi had to pull some of the dough out of the proving baskets (it was too wet and the basket hadn't been floured sufficiently). The dough looked misshapen, but by sprinkling more semolina over the top and deftly twisting the dough up and underneath, he quickly reshaped the loaves into perfect spherical domes.

LOOK AFTER YOUR 'MOTHER': Baking bores may boast about their 150-year-old starter, but they are barking up the wrong tree, according to Luka. It's really not important how old your mother is (it's not a taste that improves with age); rather it's her day-to-day health that matters. Try and remember to add a teaspoon of flour every day to keep her active and bubbling. Keeping your starter in the kitchen rather than the fridge stops it getting too sour.

DON'T LET YOUR BREAD PROVE FOR TOO LONG: The final rising should take place in the oven. If you let your loaves rise to their limit outside the oven, they will probably collapse once inside.

ST JOHN METHOD: For those who want to emulate Mehdi, here is how their baking process breaks down. The starter and water are mixed together. They use tap water; there is a water-softener machine, but as yet no one has been able to crack the very complicated instruction manual. Flour is added and the dough is mixed mechanically for thirty-five minutes. It is poured out into plastic butchers' trays and covered with black bin liners then placed in the dough-retarding fridge. Twenty-four hours later it is weighed out, slapped, rolled and shaped, then placed in floured proving baskets. Three hours later it is baked.

TRADITIONAL OBSERVATIONS

Eliza Acton's bread books contain many excellent 'observations' born of her own patient and thorough experiments. These tips or 'minute useful facts' for better bread-making are repeated several times, because 'many hurried or superficial readers are apt to overlook such small particulars' and some of them 'are really worthy of attention'. This last statement I can confirm. When I returned to my sourdough starter after a two-week absence over Christmas I found it sluggish. The weather was particularly cold, the house chilly, and the dough I made was stiff and unyielding. The dough rose half as much as it usually does and, when cooked, the loaf – though well-risen and still palatable – had a thin layer of unrisen dough at the bottom. The next day I came across the following advice in Acton's bread book: 'Heavy bread will also most likely be the result of making the dough *very hard*, and letting it become quite cold, particularly in winter.'

I have quite often found, for various reasons (lack of attention, too little starter), that my dough is stiff, but adding extra water at the end of the mixing only seems to result in a slippery, wet dough with a solid centre. Now, thanks to Acton, I had the solution: dip the ends of your fingers into hot water and, with your fingers still wet, press them into the dough. Push the dry dough over the wet dough and knead; repeat until the dough is flexible, then put it somewhere warm to rise. To which it should be added that if your dough is heavy, don't be tempted to put it in too hot a spot – slow rising, in heat that surrounds the whole bowl, is the key to good bread. If you overwork your dough, you will find that it is sour in hot weather and bad in any weather.

To test whether your bread is ready to go into the oven, push your knuckles into the dough for a short time. If the impression disappears when you remove your hand, the bread is ready for the oven.

If your dough is too 'lithe' because too much liquid has been used when making the dough, and it spreads about instead of remaining in shape when it has been made into loaves, then bake it in a slower oven, otherwise you will end up with a hard crust and an undercooked centre.

Take your bread out of the tin as soon as it is removed from the oven, or the steam will make the sides and bottom of the bread wet.

All of these are common problems that I have encountered. The sagacity of Acton's advice is equalled only by its often peculiar pertinence. In particular, her definition of why good bread matters is spot-on:

> *In point of fact no bread is so really cheap as that composed entirely of good wheat-flour or meal, because there is none which affords the same amount of pure, wholesome, strength-sustaining nourishment; and a larger quantity will generally be required of any inferior kind to support in equal degree the powers of life.*

Sourdough at home

WATER

The water you use will affect your bread. More rarefied bakers will swear by mineral water. I mostly use horrible, hard London tap water, but I have had good results from experimenting with different waters when baking on holiday. I always try and take a jam jar full of starter with me when I leave home for any length of time. I have made bread in north Devon with spring water collected from a bubbling Exmoor brook, and more frequently in a Welsh valley where the tap water comes straight up from a crystal-clear spring. Every year we go and stay in a borrowed cottage in the Welsh borders and the bread I make there rises high, with a terrific crust and a very light and chewy inside. It may be the water or the fact that I am always happy there, calmed by the heat and crackle of the wood-burning stove, the burble of the stream and the owls hooting at night.

SOURDOUGH STARTER

Sourdough baking is easy – and oh, so rewarding! It's a great way to start your new life as a modern peasant. There are lots of ways to make a sourdough loaf, but I hope you will find the one below fits in with all the other demands in your life.

Before you bake this loaf you need to get hold of some starter. Beg or borrow some (from a friend, a passing acquaintance, a Twitter mate or a baker). Failing that, you can always make your own: do this by fermenting 225g organic raisins with 600ml of water in a bowl covered with a tea towel in your kitchen. When the raisin water starts to bubble, strain it and use 400ml raisin water to ferment 500g unbleached strong white flour. Let this ferment for 24 hours (it should triple in size), then add 450g starter to 400ml water and 500g unbleached strong white flour. Let this ferment for 3 days and you are ready to start your sourdough baking. Maintain your starter by adding a teaspoon of flour a day; you don't have to keep it in the fridge. It should make about 500ml. Discard the excess, use it to make pizza, or give it away.

Whenever you use your mother for baking you must refresh it. Keep the starter at the same strength by always refreshing in these quantities: 1 part starter: 1 part water: 1½ parts unbleached white flour. You can use it again in a day or two. You can also change the nature of the starter by using different kinds of flour (rye, wholemeal, etc.) to refresh it.

Sourdough Loaf

You can't rush this bread. It needs to rise for a long time, so start it either first thing in the morning or in the evening.

Makes 2 x 500g round loaves (one for the freezer)

> *250ml sourdough starter (see page 35)*
> *600ml warm water*
> *50g strong rye bread flour*
> *850g strong white organic bread flour, plus extra for dusting (try to use a good*
> *   local flour; I use Marriage's flour from Essex)*
> *1½ tbsp sea salt, rubbed into fine crystals between your hands*
> *1–2 tsp olive oil*
> *semolina, for baking*

Combine the starter and water in the bowl of a food-processor, or by hand in a bowl. Mix well and then add the flours gradually, stirring well as you do so. If it looks very dry (this depends on how hard your water is and how sloppy your starter), don't add all the flour. The wetter the dough, the more the bread will rise. But be careful: if it is too wet, a large 'attic' will appear in the top half of your loaf. The ideal consistency (not too wet, not too dry) is something you will learn over time.

When you are satisfied that you have a good stickyish dough, cover it with cling film and leave for 20–45 minutes whilst autolysis (see page 27) occurs. You can skip this bit if you are in a hurry; your bread will still be good, just not quite so perfect.

After 45 minutes add the sea salt and knead the dough well. You can do this by hand or with the dough hook on your mixer. Give it a good 8 minutes. Then pour a teaspoon of olive oil onto the work surface and knead your dough again, giving it a vigorous stretch and whack for another 5 minutes or so. You will really feel it working your arm muscles. Finally, shape the dough into a ball by giving it a last stretch, then doubling it over to trap some air inside. Twist the bottom and place it in a very large mixing bowl. I run a line of oil around the rim of the bowl and let it drip down, before I add the dough.

Cover the bowl with cling film and leave it somewhere warm. About 10 hours later have a look at your dough; it should have risen well up the sides of the bowl. Now is the time to release some of your accumulated rage – we call it 'punching the dough baby' in our house. Push the cling film down onto the dough and thump your fist into it – it should deflate spectacularly. Do this a couple of times and then split the dough into two balls.

Flour your work surface. Stretch one of the pieces of dough by pulling all the sides outwards – it should look a bit like a sheepskin. Double it over and do the same again. Then, with plenty of flour on the work surface, push down and away: you are trying to push a swelling ball of dough outwards with a firm seal underneath – it takes a bit of practice. When you are satisfied, push the dough together hard with the flat of your hand and then shape it into a ball, lift it up by twisting up the top of the ball and then pop it gently into a floured proving basket (or well-oiled tin) with the folds underneath. Repeat with the remaining ball of dough.

I usually put my baskets on or beside the hob whilst I cook dinner. If you put the baskets back in a cupboard, you may well forget them. You want to get the bread in the oven whilst the dough is still rising, but before it starts to flop over the side. This should take an hour or two (depending on the heat of your kitchen). I usually put the oven on about an hour after the dough has been proving.

Getting heat into the centre of the bread as quickly as possible is the key to success. Do this by putting a pizza stone or heatproof baking tile in the oven. Preheat the oven to 230°C/gas mark 8. When the oven is hot and you like the look of your dough (or you are desperate to go to bed and just want to get the flaming thing in the oven), take the stone or tile out and scatter a little semolina on top. Roll the bread onto your hand and then flip it gently onto the stone or tile, seam side underneath. Take a bread knife and score the top of the bread – you can do three straight lines in a row, a cross (traditionally to keep the Devil out) or four lines in a rough square (for the real artisan-bakery look).

Spritz the loaves with water. Open the oven door and spritz the oven and then get the loaves in as quickly as you can, without letting out too much hot air. After 15 minutes turn the oven down to 190°C/gas mark 5 and bake for another 35–40 minutes. The loaves should have a good colour and when turned out should sound hollow when tapped on the bottom. Leave to cool completely on a wire rack before attempting to slice or store them.

WALNUT AND RAISIN BREAD

One summer I spent three days with a friend walking on Exmoor. Our object was simple: to leave the car behind and make a journey, on foot, in a wild landscape. We walked from the coast, inland, along four different river systems and back again to the coast, staying in pubs and B&Bs along the way. What to eat when we were out on the moor was a worry. My friend, Lori, brought the three things that had sustained her on the Camino de Santiago, the pilgrims' walk to Santiago de Compostela in northern Spain. These were dried apricots, dark chocolate and raw almonds. I bought a small loaf of walnut-and-raisin bread and a hockey-puck-sized goat's cheese. This small amount of food sustained us during three days of tramping across the moor, through fern-filled ravines whilst skittish Exmoor ponies charged away from us down the valley. We got lost and our legs were sore, but the walk made those few ingredients so memorable that I had to include the bread recipe in this book.

Just follow the regular Sourdough Loaf recipe (see page 36), adding a large handful of shelled and chopped walnuts and some large raisins at the same time as you add the salt.

66% RYE

This is the formula behind the E5 Bakehouse's lighter rye bread, which they call Route 66. It's begun with a starter (or 'leaven'), as is their Hackney Wild sourdough. It's a more involved process as it takes two days to make the leaven, but once you've done that, the proving process is quicker. The stronger gluten in white flour helps the bread to rise a little, for without it the loaf would be very dense indeed. If you like the delicate taste but not the texture of rye bread, then follow the standard Sourdough Loaf recipe (see page 36), adding 50g rye flour instead of wholemeal.

To make the leaven, take 1 tbsp sourdough starter (see page 34) and mix with 120g flour (80g white flour, 40g rye flour). Add 300ml water. Mix well, cover with cling film and leave for a day. Then repeat the process. You now have a rye leaven.

Makes 1 large loaf, or 2 small

> *300g leaven (see above)*
> *700g strong white bread flour*
> *1½ tbsp sea salt*
> *semolina, for baking*
> *a little rye flour*

Weigh out the leaven (keep any excess to make your next batch with). If it seems stiff, add 100–200ml of water and stir well. Mix the leaven with the flour and then knead for 10 minutes. Leave for 30 minutes for autolysis (see page 27) to occur, then add the salt and knead it in well.

Leave for another 30 minutes, then stretch the dough out twice. Flour the work surface and, pushing down hard with the heel of your hand, seal the dough underneath and then make it into a long, torpedo-shaped loaf.

Preheat the oven to 230°C/gas mark 8 and add your bread tile to it. When the oven is hot, take out the tile and scatter it with semolina. Cut three or four diagonal slashes into the top of the loaf (this helps to stop the 'cracking' to which rye bread is prone). Push your hand into the cuts to open them up a bit. Put the loaf on the tile. Sprinkle a little rye flour over the top, then spritz the top of the loaf with water, open the oven door and give that a squirt as well. Put the loaf in and bake.

After 15 minutes turn the oven down to 190°C/gas mark 5 and bake for another 35–40 minutes. The loaf should be well coloured with a good crust. Don't expect it to rise that much.

VARIATIONS

If you like, you can make two smaller loaves and bake them at the same temperature for just 25–30 minutes.

If you want to make a sweet rye loaf, add 150g honey to the mixture at the same time as the leaven.

Sourdough Pizza Bases

If you like the taste of home-made or artisan-baked sourdough bread, then why use commercial yeast in your pizzas? The obvious next step from baking your own sourdough bread is to make your own sourdough pizza. You'll never have to buy a packet of yeast again, and the taste is incomparably better. The process of making the dough could not be easier. Somehow, not having to activate the yeast makes the whole process simpler – it's basically just two steps.

A sourdough pizza is thin, but seems more robust than a pizza made with dried yeast. The dough is easy to work with and has great elasticity. The crust is crisp and filled with pockets of air. It's just a whole different beast from a regular pizza. It holds its shape (you can pick it up like a plate) and the topping doesn't soak in, so there is no sogginess. As you can see, I am an evangelist for sourdough pizzas.

If you already have a sourdough starter in the fridge, then this is easy for you. If not, beg some starter from a baking friend or make your own (see page 34).

The quantities of starter that you need are quite large (I use cups – 250ml, because I hate measuring sticking starter onto the scales and then scraping it off). I refresh my starter by adding some flour and water the day beforehand, to make sure I have plenty, plus enough to keep the starter going.

One batch of pizza dough makes 2 pizza bases

> *375ml (1½ cups) sourdough starter (see page 34)*
> *2–3 tbsp warm water*
> *275g strong white bread flour*
> *25g strong wholemeal flour*
> *1 tsp sea salt*
> *1 tbsp olive oil*
> *semolina, for baking*

Put the starter in a large bowl and, if it looks stiff, add a little water. Combine the starter with the flours and add the salt, mixing well. I chop the dough with a shallow metal serving spoon, cutting the wet mixture into the dry flour at the bottom of the bowl. If it still looks too dry, add a bit more water. After a while get your hands into the bowl and start kneading until the dough begins to come together. If you already make bread, this dough will feel a little stiffer than you are used to.

Add the olive oil and keep kneading. Once the dough has formed a cohesive ball, pick it up and stretch it as far as you can – really give the gluten a workout, then fold it back in on itself. Keep doing this for as long as you can; it's tough work on the hands, but the taste is worth it. You could use the dough hook on a food-processor, but the resulting pizza would not be quite as airy.

Split the dough into two balls and place them in two floured bowls or proving baskets. Cover with cling film or a plastic bag and leave somewhere warm, but not too hot, until the dough has doubled in size (about 2–3 hours, depending on the local temperature).

When it's time to make your pizza, preheat your oven to its hottest setting and put a pizza stone or heatproof baking tile in the oven while you prepare your toppings.

When the oven is hot take one ball of dough and roll it out on a floured surface in a flattish disc about 1cm thick. Rolling it out a bit thicker than usual avoids getting a dry, biscuity crust; the bottom will be crisp and the inside will have a light, airy texture.

Take the stone or tile out of the oven and scatter over a tablespoon or so of semolina. Flop the dough onto it and start adding your toppings. Work fast: you want to get your pizza into the oven as quickly as possible. See pages 43–44 for topping suggestions.

A Spring Pizza of Spicy Sausage and Nettles

Make this pizza in spring when nettles are at their most tender, though autumn rains will sometimes provide a good second crop. Wear thick gardening gloves and take only the tender tips.

Makes 2 pizzas; serves 4 as a snack or 2 as a main course

> 1 batch of pizza dough (see page 41)
> 1 tbsp olive oil
> 2 red onions, finely chopped
> 2 garlic cloves, peeled and crushed with the flat of a heavy knife
> sea salt and black pepper
> 1 carrier bag of nettle tips (blanched tips give approx. 150g)
> 2 top-quality freshly ground coarse pork sausages (ideally home-made; alternatively, I use The Ginger Pig's Old Spot sausages, but you could use fennel-rich Italian or Toulouse sausages)
> 1 tbsp finely chopped fresh herbs (thyme with a little rosemary and sage earlier in the year; basil, marjoram and oregano later on)
> a little Parmesan

Heat the olive oil in a pan and sauté the onions and garlic until soft. Season and set aside (you can do this ahead of time).

Bring a large pan of salted water to the boil and blanch the nettles, in batches, for 1 minute. Spread the nettles out on a clean tea towel to drain.

Skin the sausages and crumble the meat.

Spread half the onion mixture on top of the first pizza, followed by half the nettles, half the herbs and finally half the sausage meat, crumbled over everything.

Bake until crisp (about 15–20 minutes). Grate over some Parmesan and serve. Don't roll out the second pizza until the first is just about to come out of the oven, as the dough sticks to the work surface after a couple of minutes. Get the second pizza into the oven whilst your fellow diners are still blowing on their first scorching-hot slices.

Potato, Sage, Taleggio and Crème Fraîche Pizza

Makes 2 pizzas

> *1 batch of pizza dough (see page 41)*
> *olive oil*
> *200g waxy new potatoes, sliced into paper-thin rounds, washed and dried*
> *150g taleggio, cut into cubes*
> *2 tbsp crème fraîche*
> *1 tbsp finely chopped fresh sage*
> *sea salt and black pepper*
> *a handful of fresh sorrel or rocket*
> *juice of ½ lemon*

For each pizza, roll out half the dough and brush with olive oil. Arrange potato slices so that they are evenly distributed (there should be space around each slice). Scatter over cheese, crème fraîche and sage, then zigzag over a little more oil and season. Bake until crisp (about 15–20 minutes).

As you serve each one, throw on the sorrel or rocket and add a squeeze of lemon juice and some more black pepper.

OTHER TOPPINGS
- Quick tomato sauce with capers, Parmesan and mozzarella
- Gently cooked onions with garlic, or:
- Gently cooked onions, garlic and mixed peppers, with a raw egg cracked on top
- Gently cooked onions with walnuts and anchovies
- Gently cooked onions with blue cheese and rosemary
- Gently cooked onions with anchovies, black olives and thyme
- Gently cooked garlic and pancetta with fresh herbs
- Gently cooked onions with walnuts and griddled radicchio
- Wilted leeks, lemon zest, thyme and goats' cheese

- A 'white' pizza of mozzarella or taleggio garnished with fresh peppery leaves from the salad patch

PIZZETTE

Use the pizza dough to make small pizzas; brush with olive oil and then scatter with either fresh herbs or a spice mixture (experiment with different combinations – I like the Bengali five-spice *panch phoran*, which is equal quantities of fennel, nigella, cumin, brown mustard seeds and fenugreek, but you could do a spicy mix of smoky chilli peppers ground with black pepper and sea salt too). You can serve pizzette before a meal with olives and charcuterie, or soft goats' cheeses and sweet summer tomatoes.

CHEAT'S SOURDOUGH PIZZA

If you are stuck for time, but crave pizza, there is a quicker way. Use 1 tablespoon of dried yeast: get it going by adding 1 teaspoon of sugar and 2 tablespoons of water, mix well and leave in a teacup covered with a saucer to froth up. Make your dough with this yeast mixture, 1 teaspoon of sea salt and 150g strong white flour, but add a cup (250ml) of sourdough starter for flavour. Mix well and add a little luke-warm water to get the right consistency. Knead until supple, then shape into two balls and leave on a floured board covered with a tea towel whilst the oven heats and you get your toppings ready (about half an hour).

Sweet Baking

'The only way to learn to cook is to cook,' says Alice B. Toklas in her eponymous recipe book. Circumstance (in her case, the German occupation of France) turned Alice from a dilettante into serious cook; a cook who could adapt to the strictures of rationing and shortages; one who could also get her cooking done quickly, as there 'were so many more important and more amusing things to do'. When Alice decided to take the art of cookery seriously, she had one big advantage over the average novice. For several years she had been employing and observing a succession of skilful

French cooks. But if you haven't been living with Gertrude Stein on the rue de Fleurus and feeding Picasso a couple of times a week, then where do you start? How do you begin to understand what being a good cook is all about?

You can start with a cookery book of course, but while books are all very well, they only go so far. Trying to learn any language solely off the page is doomed to failure – there are some things you can't get from reading. If you're really lucky, someone in your childhood will have taken pleasure in cooking and preparing food well. Then, over weeks, months and years, as you gradually grow tall enough to see over the kitchen counter, you can pick up all the practical skills you need at first hand. Lots of the best chefs seem to have been handed this happy chance. But what if your mum and dad were both working flat out? Or had a tin ear when it came to cooking? Or preferred ballroom dancing or football or bingo, or just about anything, to making dinner? Maybe your mother was the kind of fabulous, uptight, virtuoso cook who couldn't stand anyone else in the kitchen? I've always felt it unfair that culinary proficiency should be left up to an accident of birth. There are enough inequalities in the world without adding that one to it.

So if you can't learn it all from a book, where do you begin? The easiest way is by getting as close as you can to a really good cook and observing what they do. What the eye sees the hand remembers. The cook I could stand next to for days on end works in the open kitchen of a café beside the canal in East London.

At first glance the Towpath Café doesn't look like much. It takes up four shallow bunkers at the base of a converted warehouse beside Regent's Canal. At night, when the metal shutters come down, it disappears entirely and the towpath returns to bleak industrial anonymity. But by day there is a kitchen, a counter where coffee is served and food orders are taken, and a small dining area with a communal table, under cover. On sunny days the rest of the diners sit on old-fashioned collapsible wooden chairs beside small metal tables on the edge of the towpath or on blankets on a flattened-earth deck. The café is open from 8 a.m. till sunset (5 p.m. on some days). It is run by an American food writer and long-term inhabitant of Italy, Lori De Mori and the husband she left Italy to be with, the food photographer Jason Lowe. It seems like a simple place, but it's the kind of simple that you only get when you've been thinking very hard about something for many years.

That there is an Italian sensibility at work is easy to see. This is a place where you are made to feel welcome, where everything is made from scratch, where the coffee is good – and no, you can't have a paper cup, you have to take two minutes to sit or stand and drink your coffee. It's the kind of friendly, hidden place that you dream of finding, but hardly ever do. The food on offer is prescribed by what is seasonally available. But that fact emerges as a delight, not a manifesto. You might eat a salad of white cabbage and tiny brown shrimps or a plate of orange and crisp *puntarelle*, the bulbous asparagus-chicory of southern Italy. Some of the café's chief delights are its jams and preserves, from the quince jelly that accompanies their door-stopper toasted cheese and spring-onion sandwich to the apricot jam that you can eat with their own home-made yoghurt and granola for breakfast.

The cook here, Laura Jackson, favours pinnies, not whites. These are more like an overall than an apron, and hers come in a variety of vintage prints. They are a world away from a starched chef's coat and provide the first clue that hers is a far-from-ordinary approach, which is not to say that it isn't exemplary – it is. Don't let the pinny fool you.

The first thing you notice about Laura is her focus. She cooks entirely in the present. All her efforts, frustrations and ambitions are focused on whatever dish she is preparing. Her eye is not on the future, but on today, and more specifically on the dish she is cooking.

The second thing you might notice is her precision. Precision is an underrated culinary virtue. I have watched Laura make puff pastry, smearing each dab of softened butter exactingly next to its fellow, or turning each roast potato carefully in fat. It matters intensely to her that the food is as perfect as it can possibly be.

More than any other cook or artisan I've met whilst writing this book, Laura embodies all that a modern peasant should. Not because her food never fails to delight or because her commitment to cooking in season is an instinct, not a fad, but because the pleasure of eating is what governs her life as a cook. She has an old-fashioned capability, whether she is roasting pork for 150 or making the crumbliest pastry shells. Her cooking links the seasons. She takes pleasure in pickling cabbage and onions in winter; in melting quinces down into an amber jelly; or slow-roasting pork until it falls into tiny shreds for rillettes.

It's hard to choose just one area of expertise with Laura, but as I have to, I've gone for pastry. Staying with Alice B. Toklas, I've combined Laura's expertise with sweet pastry with Alice's Tender Tart (of hazelnuts).

A Tender Tart

Alice B. Toklas was not always happy with her cooks. In a chapter of her cookbook entitled 'Murder in the Kitchen' she says, 'Many times I held the thought to kill a stupid or obstinate cook, but as long as the thought was held murder was not committed.' An Austrian named Kaspar was the exception – 'a perfect cook' for whom nothing was too much trouble. Alas, Kaspar was a far-from-perfect man. He had two lovers: an angel and a devil. Eventually he ran off with the devil, deserting both his distraught angel and his employers and leaving only this tart as a souvenir. Alice calls it 'exquisite'. I think you will find it very pleasing. You can prepare the pastry and the nut-meal ahead of time if you like.

Serves 6

Pastry
150g plain flour
70g butter, softened
3 tbsp caster sugar
a scant pinch of salt
1 large egg yolk

Filling
200g hazelnut kernels
2 large eggs
125g caster sugar
zest of 1 lemon
2 or 3 drops of vanilla extract, or the seeds from ½ vanilla pod

Glaze
1 egg yolk
1 tbsp double cream

In a mixing bowl combine the pastry ingredients using a fork to begin with, and then your fingertips. When the pastry has cohered into a mass, scoop it up and knead it briefly against a floured surface, pressing it out with the heel of your hand and gathering it up several times. The pastry will feel stickier than normal pastry. Add a little water if it's too dry. Gather it up in a ball and wrap in cling film. Refrigerate for at least 1 hour, preferably a bit longer.

Butter a 20cm loose-bottomed tart tin and chill in the fridge. Cut the pastry ball in two, one ball smaller than the other (for the lid).

Flour your surface and roll out the large pastry ball quickly to about 3mm thick. You should flour each side well and turn the pastry two or three times while rolling it out, to avoid it sticking. Press the pastry into the tin well, leaving 1cm above the rim. Wrap loosely in cling film and refrigerate for 30 minutes. Rewrap the smaller pastry ball and place it in the fridge.

Preheat the oven to 190°C/gas mark 5. Place a pizza stone or baking sheet in the oven to heat up. Prick the chilled pastry case with a fork, but not too vigorously. Line it with baking parchment and weigh it down with baking beans or dried pulses. Bake for 15 minutes. Remove the parchment and beans and bake again for 5 minutes. Stay close and make sure the pastry does not brown too much. Let it cool in its tin on top of the stove.

Roast the hazelnuts on a baking tray in an oven preheated to 180°C/gas mark 4. They should be a very dark brown and will smell pleasantly nutty (about 15 minutes). Pour the nuts onto a clean tea towel. Rub them together to get rid of as much skin as you can. (Omit this stage if the nuts are already skinned.) Pour the nuts into a food-processor and grind to a fine meal. You could do this ahead of time if you like.

Take the smaller ball of pastry out of the fridge 5 minutes before you want to use it.

Meanwhile, whisk the eggs with the sugar until the sugar has just dissolved. Add the lemon zest and vanilla. Blend in the nut-meal.

Roll out the lid of the pie. Cut a few decorative slashes in the top. Pour the filling into the cooled pastry case. Place the lid on carefully and press the edges firmly to seal. Combine the egg and cream and paint the lid with the mixture. Cook in the bottom half of the oven for 20–25 minutes at 180°F/gas mark 4.

This pie should be served at room temperature. Do not refrigerate it if you make it ahead of time.

TOP TIPS FOR ABSOLUTELY CRUMBLY, CRUNCHY PASTRY

- Always use good-quality unsalted or hardly salted butter.
- Keep everything as cold as possible.
- Cut your butter into tiny cubes and put it into the flour, then put the whole lot back into the fridge to chill.
- Butter your tart tin and keep it in the fridge until you are ready to roll out your pastry.
- Chill your pastry for at least an hour after you have made it.
- When you roll out your pastry and press it into the tin, chill it again.
- Place a baking sheet or pizza stone in the oven to heat up; this will help the bottom of the tart crisp up.

Honey

Can you be an urban peasant if you don't keep livestock? Diehard modern peasants like the urban farmer Novella Carpenter in San Francisco keep goats, pigs, ducks and chickens (see page 134) in their back yard. I suppose I could herd goats on my nearest green space, Well Street Common, but somehow I don't think the locals would approve. Urban foxes wander through our garden daily, so keeping chickens seems like animal cruelty. That just leaves man's smallest domestic creatures – bees. Which is fine by me. I have long been fascinated by bees; bees are eternal beings of myth and legend and, best of all, they make honey.

Honey is magical, a miracle of nature; it captures more than any other preserved food the colour, scent and joy of summer months; as Maurice Maeterlinck, the great Belgian poet, playwright and chronicler of bees, says: 'They are the soul of summer, the clock whose dial records the moments of plenty.' I have wanted to keep bees ever since I opened Maeterlinck's *Life of the Bee* and read his description of 'the rustling, wing-lit hive' and of his own fascination with bees: 'It is with them as with all that is deeply real; they must be studied and one must learn how to study them.'

Who can resist the lure of the deeply real? Added to this is the opportunity to enjoy an ingredient – honey – at its most superlative, something no food lover can ever pass up. Honey taken straight from the hive is at its very best. It is at the peak of its flavour when eaten still warm from the bees, for its delicate bouquet is volatile and swiftly lost. The appeal of bees becomes irresistible when it is described as something that will, according to Maeterlinck, 'teach us to tune our ear to the softest most intimate whisper of the good, natural hours'.

No one would hold up the rigid, pre-ordained society of the hive as a model for mankind. But within the bees' ordered society is much that is admirable. Their selfless industry and ability to work for the common cause are both good qualities. We face an uncertain future due, in part, to our inability to rein in consumption; it is the bee's capacity to store up plenty, in the face of future want, that makes it truly a creature worth observing. 'The god of the bees is the future,' says Maeterlinck, and perhaps it should be ours too?

Philosophical questions aside, what on earth possessed me to want to keep bees? It began with the desire to eat as much very high-quality honey as I wanted; to have jar after jar of subtle, multi-floral, seasonally variable honey ranged along my shelves. I have moved to a house with a garden shaded by an enormous *Robinia* (false acacia) whose pea-like white flowers are similar, although of a different botanical species, to those that provide bee-keepers in Italy and Eastern Europe with a light, subtly flavoured honey. To inherit a garden already dense with bee-friendly flowers and a house with a convenient flat roof seemed like a message from the god of honey that was too insistent to resist.

On top of this, the by-product from all this bee-keeping is wax, from which I can make stacks of thick, sweet-smelling beeswax candles. Beeswax candles burn slowly, smell sweet as they burn, but are expensive to buy. If I can learn to make them myself I can burn candles of a luminous flame at my supper table.

As I began to discover a bit more about bees there came over me the desire to study something complex deeply, to master another skill and perhaps attain the stillness and calm of a good bee-keeper. Inner calm is something that often eludes me. You might get the same effect from yoga, but yoga doesn't give you honey too. As well as spiritual benefits, bee-keeping has physical pluses: there is an old adage that bee-keepers don't get arthritis (something to do with the venom in bee stings). So if I sustain the odd sting I may prevent myself from suffering the arthritis that plagued my grandmother.

All these benefits are in the future, for to keep bees is to enter into speculation. The novice bee-keeper puts up time and money, fear of the unknown (bees) and the risk of pain – Maeterlinck's 'flame of the desert rushing over the wounded limb'. To begin as a conventional bee-keeper you need enthusiasm, but also quite a lot of equipment. To the cost of the bees (currently about £240) you must add that of the hive, a veil and bee suit, a smoker, the foundation (the sheets of wax that the bees draw on to make their comb), plus any syrup the bees will need to survive the winter if you take their honey. Whilst some of these costs are small, added together they all mount up (about £450–600). Against this outlay the optimistic apiarist (and who other than an optimist would embark on such a hobby) can balance the thought of future bounty in the form of jar after amber-coloured jar. A sweet hoard of treasure awaits those with the nerve, diligence and inclination to keep on keeping bees.

But before you get anywhere near eating your own honey, you must weigh up present-day aggravations, in the form of the densely populated city in which you live. Wouldn't it be better and simpler just to move to the countryside and keep your bees (and your being) in tranquil, rural seclusion? Some bee-keepers certainly do; Conan Doyle sent Sherlock Holmes off to Sussex to keep bees in his retirement. And if the novice bee-keeper should need any further encouragement, he or she should take it from the fact that this greatest of detectives and finest of minds (even if fictional) thought bee-keeping a worthy pastime for his retirement. In the real world, the writer Paul Theroux lives quietly in Hawaii with eighty-five hives, but that isn't necessarily the best way. You may get peace and quiet, but the honey isn't any better.

London is a green city in the literal sense, clotted with parks and tree-filled squares. Street after street displays the idiosyncratic marvel that is a

London front garden. Mimosas blaze out against stucco façades, climbing roses hang blowsy, many-petalled heads against the soft brick of Victorian terraces, and wisterias wreath plumes of purple smoke around wrought-iron balconies. From these blooms fly London's bees, drunk with the nectar of a thousand flowers. It begins in spring with the soft down of the pussy willow, the tangled yellow streamers of witch hazel and the hangdog blooms of hellebores. From the modest offering of lovingly tended window boxes to the swathes of floral displays in our royal parks, the capital offers an unparalleled range of flowers untouched by agricultural chemical spraying. With this much choice, the bees make honey with an exceptional taste. London honey has a multi-floral flavour that bees flying over the monocultures of industrial farming such as oilseed rape cannot match. This means that honey from the city regularly wins taste awards.

To keep bees, you must first handle them. There are some things you just cannot learn from a book. I wanted bees, so I needed a friendly bee-keeper, and so far my half-hearted efforts to make contact with one had got me nowhere. Which is how I came to chase a silver-bearded Rastafarian through the back streets of Homerton on my bike. My clue to his profession lay in the conical metal bee-smoker that dangled from his hand. The metal caught the sun, and my eye, as I waited at the traffic lights. The man holding the smoker was tall and lean, his hair packed up neatly into a white turban. He wore his beard twisted in a knot; his bee-keeping uniform was a pair of khaki trousers and a jacket to match, embroidered with lozenges of red, green and gold. My heart skipped a beat as he turned the corner and disappeared from sight. Still the lights held me captive on red.

I chased him down to a bus stop and learnt that his name was Rashi. To my breathless enquiry he politely replied that yes, he was a bee-keeper with about eight hives in the Lee Valley nature reserve. He gave me his card (he was a builder and decorator) and we agreed to meet at a later date. Our conversation was cut short by the blaring horn of the bus trying to park in the bus stop that I was blocking.

Bee-keepers are hard to pin down. So it was with Rashi. After lots of failed phone calls I gave up. But eventually I caught up with him at an open-air meeting of the Epping Forest Beekeepers' Association at their teaching apiary in Wanstead. A bee-keeper for nineteen years, first in Jamaica and then for the last ten in East London, Rashi told me that rosemary is the strongest flavour he can taste in London honey.

That day I got my first look inside a hive. My daughter Hannah, aged eight, and I borrowed some bee-keeping smocks with hoods and got suited up. The hoods have a veil (more like a mesh) that is attached by a zip at the front of the neck.

The inside of the hive is glued together with propolis (a cement-like substance that the bees use for building). Getting into the hive means breaking the seal: to do this, you use a metal tool (a hive tool) with a flat end to jemmy up the comb, using the same motion that a burglar would use on your window with a crowbar.

As you look into the live there is definitely a feeling of violation, a disturbance of their sanctity. The bees have been smoked to subdue them. When the bees smell smoke they panic and instantly eat two or three days worth of honey as insurance, in case they have to flee the hive. They crawl across the surface of the comb, and if you tap them they fall off easily. We took out frame after frame looking for the queen; she is easily recognisable, being bigger and slower-moving than the worker bees around her. I was offered a frame thick with comb, took it and marvelled. It was newly made, a pale waxy lemon-yellow, and felt surprisingly weighty. The urge to scrape my thumb across the wax and release the honey was strong, but I restrained myself. This was the reason then for everything, 'this curious inert substance, a drop of honey' (Maeterlinck again). It was for this that the bees worked themselves to death, on this that 'organs, ideas, desires, habits, an entire destiny' depended.

While I was learning more about bees all the time, I still didn't feel that happy about the way conventional bee-keeping manipulates the bees and disturbs them weekly. I looked around to see how bee-keeping was changing, and met two other bee-keepers at the extreme ends of the craft. The first was Johannes Paul, who, along with his colleagues at Omlet, is responsible for the first redesign of the beehive in more than 150 years. His own beehive is bright yellow and plastic and sits on a flat roof in London's King's Cross.

Bee-keeping is an ancient craft and it is one that has been very slow to evolve. Man has foraged for honey since his earliest beginnings and has exploited bees in mobile hives for at least 10,000 years. But for many thousands of years bee-keeping stayed the same. A variety of materials – clay, cane, straw and bark – was used to construct egg- and dome-like structures for the bees to inhabit. Some communities used hollowed-out trees. The only way to get the honey out was to kill the bees by suffocating, smoking or drowning them. Bee-keepers kept a number of hives, and then chose how many to cull at the end of each season.

The last big jump in bee-keeping technology came with the discovery of what is now called the 'bee space'. In 1851 the Reverend Lorenzo Langstroth (1810–1895) observed that if the same small space (8mm) was left between combs, bees would not build comb to fill that space nor glue it up with propolis (bee cement). This space was just enough for two bees to move around in back-to-back. It could be replicated within the hive between sheets of beeswax in a frame; the bees would then draw out comb on these sheets. This observation led to the invention of a top-opening hive with movable frames and, in doing so, revolutionised bee-keeping. Bee-keepers could now lift out the honey as it was made, without destroying the hive. Langstroth communicated his breakthroughs in a book entitled *The Hive and the Honey-Bee* (1853) and modern bee-keeping was born. Since then very little has changed.

The Beehaus

That is until recently, when a group of young designers decided to reinvent the beehive. Johannes Paul doesn't look like your average bee-keeper. To start with, he is younger by about thirty years. He is also considerably cooler, even in a bee suit. The company he co-owns, Omlet, has dragged bee-keeping away from the world of nineteenth-century clergymen and into the high-tech present. Paul's first adventure in husbandry was with chickens. Along with two other students from the Royal College of Art he came up with the Eglu. This is a small plastic chicken house that comes in a variety of primary colours. After a few years of working with chickens, they looked around to see what else they could improve and decided on the beehive. They talked to wise old bee-keepers and studied the design of current hives. They took ancient skill and combined it with innovative design and new technology, to come up with something totally new – a long plastic hive on legs.

The Omlet Beehaus absorbs some of the current best practice in conventional bee-keeping and combines that with a design that makes life easier for the hobby bee-keeper. The hive is on a stand, so you don't have to strain your back lifting off the top (the super) when it is heavy with honey. It has two ends (it is effectively two hives) so that you can split the hive early in the season to prevent swarming. It is a long hive that enables bees to expand their colony lengthways, as they would do naturally. Conventional beehives stack extra boxes on top as the colony grows, but the bees' natural instinct is to build forward.

The Omlet factory is outside Oxford, but Johannes also has a hive at his house and this is where I visited him. He lives in a tiny brick doll's house behind King's Cross with his wife and new baby. The front door opens straight into their living space. The first thing I see is a comb of honey hung up above the kitchen counter. Johannes doesn't spin his honey; he just scrapes it straight off the comb. We eat some; it is pale and tastes delicately of elderflower. Then we zip up our bee suits and scramble out of the bathroom window. The roof outside is quite narrow, and as well as a hive there are courgettes and tomatoes growing in pots. There isn't that much space. We take the lid off the hive and look for the queen. We don't find her, so we talk about the hive instead. It's plastic, so it won't rot. Instead of being scorched clean at the end of a season, it is cleaned with chemicals. The lid can be moved back bit by bit so that you don't have to expose the top of the hive. Despite the great design and increased functionality, I can't help wishing it wasn't plastic. I know I want to keep bees, but I still don't feel I've found the right way. It's only a year later, after a winter of evening classes in conventional bee-keeping, that I find another way.

TIPS FROM JOHANNES

- Omlet sell canisters of liquid smoke, which are easier to control then the traditional cone-shaped smoker. There is no fumbling with matches as you try to put on your gloves, with your vision obscured by your veil.
- Don't smoke when the honey flow is on. Let the bees get on with collecting as much honey as possible, without disturbing them.
- Don't use a queen excluder (a wire mesh that prevents the queen from going up into the honey stores above), but allow the queen free movement throughout the hive. You can put the excluder in one month before you want to collect the honey.
- Put new foundation (sheets of wax for the bees to build comb on) at the front of the hive, for they naturally want to build forward.
- Take your honey early in the season, and leave the end-of-season honey for the bees to feed on over the winter.
- Eat your honey as quickly as possible. It tastes best still warm from the hive.

ON BECOMING A SUSTAINABLE BEE-KEEPER

On a summer's evening I found myself in the car park of a North London health centre waiting to meet someone I had met on the Internet. My mouth was dry and my stomach fluttery. I was about to take possession of 10,000 bees and I was extremely nervous. I'd had a hive sitting empty in my house for a month now. There had been a number of false starts and I had been wondering if I would ever become a bee-keeper.

In a little while Marilyn, a biodynamic bee-keeper, turned up. She was in her fifties with long hair dyed bright orange. She led me through a padlocked gate and into the long grass of an orchard meadow, which she and other volunteers maintain. It is a wild place full of beauty, thigh-high with long grass and dotted with fruit trees. It was easy to forget we were in the middle of a densely populated city. Marilyn has three hives here, all of which she looks after naturally. Among other things, this means not opening the hive unnecessarily, and letting the bees increase by swarming, collecting them and then rehiving the new colony. There had been two swarms and the bees had been collected and placed in two oblong wooden boxes.

Marilyn introduced me to the bees. We lifted up a piece of wood and had a look. The bees crawled around underneath the mesh at the top of the box. I was not sure which swarm to take, but in the end I opted for the bigger one. We tied the box up with canvas straps and Marilyn plugged the small entry hole with some long grass. We then put on our bee suits, in case the box opened unexpectedly, and carefully pulled it through the meadow on a trolley.

I was a bit scared, but Marilyn is a very calm and encouraging person. She soothed my beginner's nerves and gave me hope. I drove her the short distance back to her house and handed over a bag of vegetables, some jams and pickles (bartered allotment produce was the deal for the swarm). This seemed like a good omen, because according to folklore only living things, and not money, should be given for a swarm. I drove home extremely slowly, constantly checking my mirror to see if the bees had escaped. It was an intense journey, and it felt as if every approaching car was on a collision course. I was very glad to get home. I left the bees up on my flat roof, covered with a piece of wood to keep out the rain, and went to bed.

How did I come to collect a swarm from a stranger? It began when I met a community bee-keeper, Tim Evans, at the Hackney Tree Nursery on the edge of Hackney Marshes. Here, amongst a wild garden and many seedling trees, I stumbled across some hand-built hives concealed behind woven hazel fencing. They were very simple-looking: three small, rudimentary wooden boxes stacked up on top of each other. That day I spent some time watching the bees fly in and out of the hive and did a bit of volunteer work, splitting hazel poles and weaving a better enclosure for the hives, before finding out a bit more about Tim's way of bee-keeping.

A French priest, the Abbé Émile Warré (1867–1951), invented this type of hive in the 1920s. Warré had noticed that the peasant smallholders in his parish had stopped bee-keeping. The old-fashioned straw skep method of bee-keeping was outdated, but the set-up cost of the new kind of bee-keeping was prohibitive. Warré came up with a hive that was simple, cheap to make, bee-friendly and supplied a surplus. He called it 'the people's hive' (*ruche populaire*). In his book, *Beekeeping for All*, the abbé describes the construction of this hive, which anyone with basic carpentry skills can make. Far from being old-fashioned, the Warré hive combines ancient technique with recent discoveries, with an emphasis on a less interventionist, more bee-friendly approach.

Most importantly, the Warré hive is a sustainable beehive. Sustainable bee-keepers attempt to keep bees with a minimum of interference. They try not to use chemicals or feed with sugar, but rather work with the bees' natural physiology to build up strength and resistance to disease. There is a feeling among this kind of bee-keeper that using chemicals with bees has not been helping their plight. Keeping bees in this way means that you can still harvest honey, but you are also helping to create strong, healthy colonies. The number of Warré bee-keepers is growing, and I decided to become one of them. This way of keeping bees is one much closer to the way I grow food – working with nature rather than against it.

If you go down the natural route you have to accept that the bees' well-being is of greater importance than honey production. You will still get some, and probably more than enough, but the Warré bee-keeper leaves the bees enough honey to survive the winter, only taking the surplus. The exploitation element of the beehive has always bothered me a bit. It seems hard that the bees work flat out all summer and then get fed sugar syrup in the winter. Lately research has shown that bees allowed to eat their own store of honey are stronger and healthier than those that are fed sugar. I am not the first person to have misgivings about what we do to bees. In 1923 the Austrian philosopher and social reformer Rudolf Steiner predicted that conventional forms of bee-keeping would cause the mass disappearance of bees within eighty-five years, and in her memoir *As Gypsies Wander*, written in 1953, the great herbalist Juliette de Baïracli Levy bemoaned the use of sugar feeding and recalled her horror when she realised that the bees would have to die for her honey. She refused to sulphur her skep, saying:

> *The bees were more than honey in the garden! They were music in our flowers, patterns in the air and across the grass, comfort and company when one was miserable.*

My highly romantic view of bee-keeping was put to the test instantly. Over the next three days, with Tim's help, I tried and failed to get the bees to go into the Warré hive that we had placed on the flat roof outside our bathroom window. The morning after collecting the box of bees we tipped them out onto a sheet in front of the hive and they sizzled like a bowl of boiling fat. They flew up into the air like a tornado and then started crawling towards the bottom of the hive, but instead of going in, they collected in an enormous flickering beard on the side of the hive. They stayed there all day. It was agonising to see them so close to a perfect home, but reluctant to enter it. I saw scout bees coming back and was worried they might fly off in a swarm somewhere else.

In the night it rained heavily and I was fearful for the colony, exposed to the elements. The next day's attempt (flicking them onto a sheet again and towards a smaller opening) looked as if it was going to work. The bees waggled and danced and scouted in and out of the hive. I went to work feeling good, but when I came back the same terrifying blob of 10,000 bees was still hanging inches from where we brush our teeth. I was sweating with fear and having to change my T-shirt about three times a day. The third day we took more drastic measures. We turned half the hive upside-down and knocked the whole swarm into the cavity and then gingerly put the roof on and turned it the right way up. The queen must have been inside, for they stayed. Soon they were flying back and forth carrying pollen (a good sign). Three weeks later they seem settled, happily buzzing back and forth with supplies of nectar (invisible), pollen (visible as vivid blobs of yellow and orange) and propolis (greyish flake-shaped blobs of resin). It is still very early days in my life as a bee-keeper; it has been a bumpy start, but one that has given me a crash course in bee behaviour.

The clear combs full of honey are still in the future, but somehow they seem less important now. Watching these tiny creatures zooming back out of the sky, homing in towards their hive, is constantly astounding. On windy days they bob like swimmers in a turbulent sea. I sit and watch them and minutes pass like seconds. I now understand the point of homing pigeons – watching a wild creature willingly return to a home you have made for it is an uplifting experience. Bees appear as far-off specks, specks that home in again and again.

The transition between working life and motherhood is often tricky. Now, when our house empties of children and before I sit down at my desk, watching the bees works like an air lock, a space in which to sit still, observe these miraculous creatures and just be.

HONEY IN THE KITCHEN

Things that are naturally delicious should be used in the simplest way possible. So it is with honey. Yoghurt with honey is the everyday pudding of choice in our house, with whatever fruit is in season.

But you can also use honey in place of sugar, in marinades, sauces, cakes and puddings. I regularly make a Moroccan tomato sauce that is flavoured with cinnamon, paprika and honey. You can also use honey whipped with butter and icing sugar to make a cake frosting. But my own particular favourite way to eat honey is on fresh, home-made sourdough bread, with a thick layer of unsalted butter. If the queen *was* in the parlour eating bread and honey, then she must have been a very sensible queen indeed.

Honey Flapjacks

I am not a natural cake-maker. Flapjacks are my reliable teatime treat. If you are faced with having to provide something for a cake sale or surprise visitors, then these very simple flapjacks take only minutes to prepare. They are also a good way of using up honey that has crystallised.

Makes about 20 flapjacks

> 3 tbsp honey
> 150g butter
> a pinch of sea salt
> 75g unbleached granulated sugar
> 250g porridge oats

Preheat the oven to 180°C/gas mark 4. Line a 20 x 25cm tin with baking parchment; or use a circular tin, if that's what you have to hand.

Place a small, heavy-based pan over a medium heat and melt the honey, butter, salt and sugar together until bubbling. Pour the mixture into a bowl with the oats and stir well, until the whole mass is well amalgamated. Tip into the prepared tin and, using a spatula, press the mixture down quite hard, until it is flat and smooth.

Bake for 20 minutes or until the top is slightly browned at the edges – a good flapjacky smell will probably alert you to this moment. Using a sharp knife, score the flapjacks into squares or rectangles in the tin, but leave until cool before turning out. They keep well in a cake tin for several days.

FERMENTED

Yoghurt and Curds

If you want to live for ever (or at least longer), eat a spoonful of yoghurt every day. Even better, eat yoghurt that you have made yourself.

That yoghurt is a food that aids health and increases longevity has been common knowledge in the Middle East for centuries. Its current status as a mass-market health product is down to the work of one man, the Russian-born French bacteriologist and Nobel Prize-winner Dr Ilya Metchnikov (1845–1916). In his classic book of yoghurt cookery, the writer Arto der Haroutunian describes how Dr Metchnikov discovered yoghurt's beneficial influence. Metchnikov had been researching the abnormally long life-expectancy of Bulgarian peasants. Though the lives of these peasants were hard and their diet poor, they were living on average to the age of eighty-seven. Dr Metchnikov laid this fact partly at yoghurt's door, and went on to isolate the two bacilli (*Lactobacillus bulgaricus* and *Streptococcus thermophilus*) found in yoghurt. He found that, if added to warm milk, these bacteria multiply and turn the milk into a sour, semi-solid fermented food product – yoghurt. The longer the fermentation process is allowed to go on, the sourer the yoghurt becomes.

Why would you want these bacteria in your gut? Well, they make you feel better by working as an antibiotic, which helps to maintain your intestinal balance; they also help those who are lactose-intolerant to digest dairy products. These bacteria are particularly helpful for the very young, the very old and anyone who is feeling weak or run down. The surest way to get these bacteria into your body is to make yoghurt yourself (some shop brands have been heat-treated to such high temperatures that all the beneficial bacteria have been wiped out). Home-made yoghurt also tastes wonderful, costs much less than shop-bought yoghurt and is very easy to make. As our ever encouraging friend William Cobbett says, regarding a different matter (that of making yeast cakes):

> *To a farmer's wife, or any good housewife, all the little difficulties to the attainment of such an object would appear as nothing. The will only is required; and if there be not that, it is useless to think of the attempt.*

That is just another of way of saying that success depends on your attitude: if you feel something is worthwhile, then go ahead and try it. It is more a question of being able to focus rather than one of any inherent aptitude.

In Search of the Perfect Yoghurt

One of the creamiest and most delicate-tasting yoghurts I have ever had is made by the Neal's Yard Creamery. This yoghurt is sold in the Neal's Yard Dairy cheese shops (a separate business). So to find out a little bit more about yoghurt-making I went to the Creamery dairy run by Charlie Westhead, located far from London in rural Herefordshire, where they make goats' cheese, yoghurt, crème fraîche, curd and cows' milk cheese. The Neal's Yard Creamery is almost in Wales and about 150 miles from where I live; the working day starts early there, so I arranged to stay with a friend who lives not that far away. I still slept badly, fearful of not waking up in time and having stayed up far too late eating, drinking and talking. But despite the lack of sleep and taking an inadvertent long and muddy detour down a dead-end track, I eventually found the Creamery.

At a little after 6.30 a.m. I am standing in a converted cowshed on top of a hill. I am wearing a white cloth jacket, a little cloth cap and a pair of white wellington boots. Charlie Westhead, the owner, has just dolloped a spoonful of wet, slippery goats' curd into my hand. I am not sure what to do with it. I look at it appreciatively – it is solid enough to hold the shape of the spoon that has sliced into it, but still weeps a little watery whey. Yesterday it was goats' milk. Last night, after the addition of a few drops of rennet and some starter, the process of separating curds from whey began. Now, fourteen hours later, it is ready to be poured out onto nylon mesh balanced on trays of moulds. When enough water has drained out, it will be pushed down into the cylindrical moulds and begin to take the recognisable shape of a log of goats' cheese. I murmur something about it being silky and then, unsure whether or not it is good form to do so, slide the whole lot into my mouth. It is lightly sour and has a fresh, grassy tang; as breakfasts go, it's probably a good substitute for cereal.

Cheese-makers (or at least the ones I have spoken to) are very open; they seem to want to plunge you straight into the process, happy to reveal their working practice, eager for you not just to see, but to touch and taste too. By his own admission, Charlie fell happily into the craft of cheese-making aged about twenty-three and hasn't looked back since. He started out working for the Neal's Yard Dairy but is now his own boss. He is tall and broad-shouldered and, if his general demeanour is anything to go by, cheese-making must be a very agreeable occupation. The hours may be long and a little antisocial, but on a warm June morning it's hard not to be just a tiny bit envious of this industrious creamery – curds dripping, cold stores stacked with cheese.

The daily commute is a short matter, for the Westhead family live next door in a sweet stone cottage with a flower-filled garden and astonishing views. We are on Dorstone Hill, looking out across the Wye Valley, and on a clearer day than today the distant sparkle of Hereford Cathedral spire pricks the middle distance. The hills on either side are rolling and wooded, and massive oaks guided my way up the hill. The hill the Westheads live on keeps on climbing beyond their house, and a little further up the road is a histori-cally important jumble of Neolithic stone, Arthur's Seat, which points towards another uplifting view. This time it's towards Wales, with the impressive curve of the Black Mountains standing out against the sky in sharp relief. The beauty of this position comes with an added cost: the inconvenience of being up a hill. Cheese-making is a very thirsty business, yet water this high up turns out to be a fairly finite resource, and the well quite often runs dry. Charlie's wife Grainne shows me the trickle that comes from the tap of her kitchen.

Charlie has been making goats' and cows' milk cheese for more than two decades now, first in Kent, but for most of his career in this remote and beautiful place. Although I am happy to see goats' cheese being made, my interest is in the two simplest products produced here: curd or lactic cheese and a creamy Greek-style yoghurt, both of which can be made at home. It is this know-how that I am eager to absorb. Thursday is yoghurt-making day, which is why I am here, standing in a light white space full of curds, plastic moulds and stainless-steel trolleys. Even though the equipment and environment have a clinical cleanliness, the sound of water running and dripping evokes a cave – albeit a white, brightly lit cave.

Before I can see anything being made, I go with Charlie to collect the cows' milk from a dairy farm nearby as the crow flies, but separated from us by several large hills. We rattle up and down the hills in a little jeep, pulling a mini-horsebox trailer with a big silver milk tank inside. (This little combo works hard, for later, after the tank has been cleaned, the whole process is repeated with a visit later in the day to the 600-strong herd of goats that supply the dairy's goats' milk.) The trailer's axles frequently wear out. We drive for about twenty minutes before pulling into an organic dairy farm a few miles south of Hay-on-Wye. It's about 8 a.m. and the dairy farmer is hard at work. Most of the cows are still in the parlour, and the farmer comes out to say hello; he is wearing a full-length rubber apron, which is sprayed from top to bottom with liquid green cow shit. Apparently the cows like to evacuate their bowels when they come into the dairy. I've been listening to *The Archers* for twenty years, but somehow the fact that both Ruth and David are knee-deep in liquid shit every morning has passed me by. Dairy farming is definitely not for the faint-hearted.

This farm takes the quality of its milk very seriously. The cows are kept out on grass for all but six weeks of the year, with a very positive effect on flavour. Charlie attaches the pipe from his tank to the milk tank in the dairy and pumps out 400 litres of raw, untreated milk. He scribbles down what he has taken on a little chart in the office; nobody checks to see if he is telling the truth, for it is all done on trust. For the dairy farmer the financial rewards of a relationship with a cheese-maker like Charlie are fairly negligible, as the amount of milk he buys is just too small. Instead the farm gets the satisfaction of knowing where the milk goes. These are very carefully looked-after cows, but when the big tankers take their milk, the farmers have very little idea where it will finally end up. The milk that Charlie takes goes back to the Creamery, where it is made into yoghurt, curd and crème fraîche, as well as the soft cows' milk cheese Finn, the goats' cheese Ragstone, the ash-covered Dorstone and the soft Perroche. Neal's Yard supplies some of the country's very best restaurants and ships a container load of cheeses to New York each week. It may not make these dairy farmers rich, but there must be pride taken from the fact that it is their milk that forms the foundation stone of some of these premier products.

When we arrive back at the Creamery the milk is pumped from the tank straight into a double-skinned stainless-steel cauldron and heated up to 72°C for fifteen seconds or 63°C for thirty minutes to destroy any bacteria. This must be done because, as on all organic farms, the herd is susceptible to TB. The milk is heated up by lighting two gas rings underneath the cauldron. It's a surprisingly low-tech approach. While the milk heats, Haydon, who has worked at the dairy since Charlie moved it up here, mixes dried milk powder with double cream. The smell is rich and tangy. This will be added to the yoghurt while the milk is warming up. It gives a better set and makes it delicious, with a thick, creamy 'top-of-the-milk' layer on top. Once the mixture has reached the right temperature it is left to cool down a little and a skin forms. Haydon does not share the Armenian love of this by-product of yoghurt-making and bins it.

When the vat is cool enough for me to hold my hand against the side with ease, Haydon adds the yoghurt starter. This is a culture made by mixing yoghurt and a particular strain of bacteria into a pot and letting it ferment. If you use the same yoghurt over and over again you will find that it becomes sour over time. In the same way, when making yoghurt at home it is probably a good idea to use a small amount of commercial yoghurt every second or third batch to prevent your yoghurt becoming too thin and sour. The mixture of milk, cream and starter is pumped up into a glass cylinder above the vat. A nozzle squirts the soon-to-be yoghurt mixture into individual pots. Ellen, one of the three full-time dairy workers, labels it with a sticker and seals the lid down with a satisfying double click. The yoghurt is then incubated for half an hour, or until the poured liquid breaks cleanly when leaving the pot. We test the yoghurt once or twice. When it's on the way to a firmish set, it is put in the fridge to stop it separating. Too long an incubation means that a bright-green liquid separates from the whey; it is still edible, but not that saleable.

Watching Haydon make this cream 'Greek-style' yoghurt (a title the Creamery claims to have invented) has added a little to my understanding of what would make a better home-made yoghurt. I decide to try adding single cream and milk powder when I get home, as I like the rich layer of thick, yellower yoghurt on top; and to refresh my starter more often with commercial yoghurt.

Cheese-making involves periods of waiting, so it lends itself well to multiple lines of production. Whilst the yoghurt is incubating, the curds for the goats' cheese are being pressed down into moulds, smaller cows' milk cheeses (Finn) are being brined (washed in a salt-water bath) and we begin to make the curd cheese (see page 92 for the recipe).

Plain Yoghurt

Makes about a litre of yoghurt

1 litre semi-skimmed or whole milk (whole milk gives a creamier yoghurt)
1 tbsp commercially produced plain yoghurt

Heat the milk slowly in a saucepan, stirring it occasionally until you see bubbles appear on the surface. As the froth rises, take it off the heat immediately. Pour the milk into a basin and allow it to cool (the temperature should not fall below 32°C). You can speed this bit up by putting the basin into a larger bowl filled with cold water. It is cool enough when you can hold your finger in the milk without wincing in pain.

Fill a large glass or earthenware jar with hot water; in this way the temperature of the milk will be maintained when you pour in your yoghurt mixture.

Whisk the plain yoghurt into a cup of the warmed milk, then pour it into the bowl of milk and whisk again. Discard the hot water and pour all the yoghurt into the jar, then seal and wrap it in a towel or blanket and place it in a warm spot for 8–12 hours (the longer you ferment your yoghurt, the stronger it will taste). Don't jostle the pot or your yoghurt may not set.

An alternative to the blanket method is to use an insulated coolbox. I find that this guarantees success every time. Take a small coolbox and heat it by filling it with hot water, then pour the water out and put your jar, wrapped in a tea towel, inside. This will make the yoghurt snugger and imitates a commercial yoghurt-making machine. And it's harder to wobble a jar that is held tightly inside a box.

After it has set you should refrigerate the yoghurt. It will keep in the fridge for about a week, after which time you can still eat it, but it will start to taste unpleasantly sour.

In some recipes you are advised to stir the milk as it cools to prevent a skin forming, but in his definitive book on the subject Arto der Haroutunian has a different approach. For him, the skin is the thing – it is the cream and should be removed, mixed with sugar and spread on bread. According to Haroutunian, this cream (known as *ser* or *kaymak*) is 'one of the great luxuries of life', and is served throughout the Middle East for breakfast.

TIPS: WHY DIDN'T MY YOGHURT SET?

- The milk wasn't the right temperature.
- Too much or too little starter yoghurt was added.
- The 'nest' was insufficiently feathered (this latter failing could be said to account for about 90 per cent of life's disappointments).

Greek-style Yoghurt

At the Neal's Yard Creamery they make 'Greek-style' yoghurt by adding buckets of thick yellow cream to their cauldron of whole milk, with the addition of some French freeze-dried semi-skimmed milk powder. By adding cream or crème fraîche and leaving the yoghurt to set for a little longer you can achieve (nearly) the same result at home. This yoghurt has a lovely creamy texture and a jelly-like set; if you are lucky enough to eat the first few spoonfuls, you will notice a thin layer of yellow cream on top – delicious!

Makes about 1.25 litres of yoghurt

> 1 litre whole milk, preferably organic
>
> 250ml double cream or, for a tangier yoghurt, crème fraîche
>
> 2 tbsp dried semi-skimmed milk powder (optional, but it will make your
>   yoghurt very creamy)
>
> 1 tbsp commercially produced plain yoghurt

Whisk the milk together with the cream (and the milk powder if you are using it) and place in a large pan. Heat slowly until the milk just froths up, then allow it to cool to 32°C or a temperature at which your clean finger can happily stay in the milk for a few seconds without making you wince.

Whisk the plain yoghurt into the cooled cream and milk mixture and pour into a warm jar or other vessel, and seal well. Wrap the jar in a blanket or place it in a warmed coolbox, as in the previous recipe (see page 73). Leave for at least 12 hours and up to 16.

This will keep in the fridge for a week or so.

WHAT TO DO WITH YOUR YOGHURT

You can use yoghurt as an alternative to double cream in many recipes. It is particularly good with beetroot soup, adding a welcome creaminess and a sour note that complements the beet's sweet flavour. It is also an essential condiment alongside dhal or any vegetable curry. And a breakfast of muesli, compote and yoghurt is one of my favourites. If you want to do something specific with your yoghurt, you can use it to make *labneh*. This very basic cheese is simply yoghurt drained through a bag or cloth so that it forms a ball. After that you can add your own flavourings, traditionally mint, dill, chives or spring onions. It's a dish at its best in spring when milk is creamiest and herbs are at their most verdant. I eat *labneh* sprinkled with fresh chopped onion tops, mint, marjoram and chives from the allotment, and with sourdough flatbreads sprinkled with chilli flakes and salt.

Pour about 500ml of home-made yoghurt into a sieve lined with muslin or a clean J-cloth. (If you really get into making *labneh*, you can sew a little drawstring cloth bag and hang that up over a bowl.) What you are aiming to do is let the liquids drain into a bowl for 5 or 6 hours, then turn the cheese out onto a plate. If you wish, you can form it into little balls or mix it with herbs and spices to your taste. Allow about 4 tablespoons of fresh herbs for *labneh* made with 500ml of yoghurt.

Cheese

When the kettle was boiling, the old man put a large piece of cheese on a long iron fork, and held it over the fire, turning it to and fro, till it was golden brown on all sides. Heidi had watched him eagerly. Suddenly she ran to the cupboard. When her grandfather brought a pot and the toasted cheese to the table, he found it already nicely set with two plates and two knives and the bread in the middle . . .

He commanded her to eat the large piece of bread and golden cheese. He sat down himself on a corner of the table and started his own dinner. Heidi drank without stopping, for she felt exceedingly thirsty after her long journey. Taking a long breath, she put down her little bowl.

'How do you like the milk?' the grandfather asked her.

'I never tasted better,' answered Heidi.

'Then you shall have more,' and with that the grandfather filled the little bowl again.

Johanna Spyri, *Heidi*

Cheese is proof of human civilisation. It was partly man's ability to transmute milk that raised us up from mere existence to something a good deal pleasanter. Happy chance separated the curds from the whey, just as it brined the olive and fermented the grape. As with wine and olives, the exact moment of cheese's discovery is obscured in myth. What is known is that what began as a piece of luck developed into an art, an alchemy in which a readily available, but perishable ingredient – milk – is transformed into something durable, storable and dense with protein: cheese.

The quality of a cheese is dependent on the skill of its maker, the time of year and the quality of the raw materials. Most of us were raised on mass-produced cheese, but lately there has been a resurgence in the making of hand-crafted cheese. This ancient process of artisan production takes us straight back to a more pastoral existence. Bite it and you are back in the meadow or on the mountainside. The taste of the cheese you are eating depends on the wild herbs or grasses that the cow, goat or sheep has eaten; the quality of the milk depends on the breed of animal that has been milked, and on the time of year that the milking was done. Is the cheese made from the rich, creamy milk available from May to September from animals pastured outside? Or is it factory cheese, produced year-round from animals that never see the sun? Good farm cheeses are, according to the French cheesemonger Pierre Androuet (author of *Guide du Fromage*), 'true to the soil from which they spring'.

The taste of any cheese is further affected by the type of coagulation induced, the temperature to which the milk is heated, the way the curd is cut and pressed, the technique of salting and shaping, the length of curing and the place in which it is cured. It is dizzying to consider the number of processes that are necessary before we can enjoy a simple piece of cheese – none of which the majority of us ever stop to think about. Perhaps, for once, we should put adoration aside and give cheese and its production some thoughtful consideration. Cheese is one of the most ubiquitous ingredients of the modern kitchen, yet beyond the bald fact that all cheese is made from milk, we take it pretty much for granted.

As James Joyce observed, 'Cheese is the corpse of milk.' Or as the horticulturalist and writer Edward Bunyard put it less gloomily, 'Cheese is milk that has grown up.' Here is further evidence (if any were needed) of the illuminating power of literature. The Joyce quote (from *Ulysses*) is odd, jarring, but also apposite in that it reveals the most important part of the cheese-making process. Cheese is the result of the careful husbandry of the solids that form in milk as it ages. Milk is an extremely perishable foodstuff, and decay is a vital part of this process. Cheese-making evolved as a means of using up milk that would otherwise go off. Excess milk was no longer left to sour, but instead was transformed into cheese and left to mature. The cheese-maker is triumphant in the face of spoilage; he even hastens milk's decay by encouraging bacteria to flourish in fresh raw milk. In his novel *The Debt to Pleasure* John Lanchester quotes Joyce's 'corpse of milk' and provides further illumination by adding, 'dead milk, live bacteria'. He goes on to explain that:

> *The process of ripening in cheese is a little like the human acquisition of wisdom and maturity; both processes involve a recognition, or incorporation, of the fact that life is an incurable disease with a hundred per cent mortality rate – a slow variety of death.*

So now, to cheese's greatest attributes – taste and smell – we can add that it is also a philosophical tool, one that reminds us of the futility of human existence and gives us some perspective as we face life's day-to-day annoyances.

Once the Dr Frankenstein-like cheese-maker has combined life with death (the addition of live bacteria in the form of a starter to the milk), he encourages coagulation (the separation of the watery whey from the thick curds) by adding rennet. This is the first stage of making cheese: curdling. The lactic-acid bacteria present in raw milk can be left to flourish unaided, but pasteurised milk has been heated to kill all bacteria and so needs help in order to sour. The souring process can be helped along by the addition of lemon juice or buttermilk. A curd will form when raw milk is soured in this rudimentary way, but a firmer curd (and more reliable cheese-making) can be obtained by the use of rennet.

In order to discover how to make a cheese I had first to discover a bit more about its evolution. Rennet is a digestive enzyme found in the stomachs of suckling mammals. It is a key element in cheese-making, but its helpfulness in the transformation of milk into cheese was probably discovered by accident around 4000 BC. Although this date is hard to confirm, Alan Davidson notes in *The Oxford Companion to Food* that there are cave paintings in the Libyan Sahara dating from 5000 BC that show milking and what may also be cheese-making. As there is no hard evidence to suggest exactly where cheese-making began, we can only guess backwards as to what actually happened. It might have gone something like this: a prehistoric herdsman would have used an empty calf's stomach to store milk (it is a handy ready-made bag), and as that stomach also contained rennet, the enzyme would have caused the curds to separate from the whey. When the herdsman came to drink his milk, he found it had curdled and separated; he then noticed that the new substance lasted longer than milk, and so rudimentary cheese-making was born. Cheese was a popular food in the ancient world as it was easy to transport and high in protein (curds are made of coagulated casein, the primary milk protein, and the fat that the casein enfolds).

Once curds have formed, the cheese can be pressed and then eaten as a soft cheese or aged to become a hard cheese that can keep for years. Keen as I am on autonomy in the kitchen, I would rather leave more complex cheese-making to the experts. I lack the necessary hygiene standards (proper cheese-making involves an awful lot of very careful sluicing and sterilising) and the patience, plus I don't have access to raw goats', sheep's or cows' milk. I did contact Hackney City Farm to see if I could milk one of their goats, but both were suffering from phantom pregnancies. That doesn't mean that I gave up on the whole idea of cheese-making. Curd or lactic cheese is the most basic form of cheese – it is simply milk in which bacteria have flourished for a few hours, separated with rennet and then drained.

These soft cheeses are relatively easy and quick to make. In the past farmers' wives all over Britain made them. Such cheeses (with names like Slip-cote, Cambridge and Colwick) were perishable and hard to transport, but as they were intended for friends and near-neighbours this did not matter. Their production is appealingly rudimentary. Slip-cote was produced by being left to drain in the concavity of a small plate and then wrapped in a cabbage leaf.

The simplest process of cheese-making – taking the curds and letting them drain through something porous (in the case of the simple curd cheese recipe on page 92, muslin) – helps explain how cheese got its name. In classical times woven baskets were used, and in Greek these were called *formos*; from this word comes the French for cheese (*fromage*) and the Italian (*formaggio*). In Latin the word was *caseus* (basket), from which comes Spanish *queso* and English *cheese*. But words can only explain so much. The best way to understand what cheese is, and how best to use it, is to make a simple cheese yourself. A good one to start with is goats' curd. It is easy to produce and gives a delightfully tangy soft cheese. You can use it in tarts, soups and salads or simply spread it onto bread. It is also low in calories, despite being delicious. If you think about how cheese is made, then it's easy to work out why a cheese like ricotta (a loose collection of curds drained, but hardly pressed) is low in calories, whilst Parmesan (a dense conglomeration of cheese proteins and fats pressed together over months or even years) is one of the highest-calorie cheeses.

Good cheese, like good wine, is linked to its *terroir*. Its taste and quality are dependent on the individual geography and geology of the place in which it (and the ingredients that constitute it) is produced. It is all about the breed of animal, the grass, the soil and the water. This is one reason why cheese from the south-east of England has always had such a bad press, for the grazing there is poor, and consequently so are the milk and the cheese. In 1661 Samuel Pepys recorded the following in his diary:

> . . . *and so home, where I found my wife vexed at her people for grumbling to eat Suffolk cheese, which I also am vexed at. So, to bed.*

Up to a fairly recent point the history of British soft cheeses was a narrative of loss, of local specialities rapidly becoming extinct, with the advent of motor transport and increased industrialisation. It is sad to read about these lost British cheeses (especially as our lack of traditional soft cheese is in great contrast to Europe, where historical, small-sized local cheese-making concerns can still be found in great numbers). But for once it is a sad story with a happy ending. We may have lost a lot of varieties, but at the moment Britain is experiencing a boom in artisan cheese production. The wine merchant and gourmet André Simon, writing in 1936, called upon cheese lovers to 'foster proper pride and increase honest gain' in British dairy farming. And to lay the foundations of classed cheeses in Britain, by asking for cheese to be described with as much care as wine. Simon wanted the name of the farm from which the cheese came to be named, along with the person who made it and the type and date of production. He felt that curders lagged behind vintners in their inability to advance beyond broad regional classifications. Simon also showed great forethought in stressing that consumers bear some responsibility for the standard of their food. Unless a better product is demanded, none will be supplied:

> *By finding out the best and asking for it again and again we may, despite the cheesemakers' coyness, lay the foundation of classed cheeses in England.*

Amazingly, Simon's desire for better, demand-led cheese production has now come to pass, thanks in part to Randolph Hodgson who set up Neal's Yard Dairy, the London-based cheese shop, in the 1980s. This shop (which once also owned the Creamery of the same name) champions traditional methods of cheese production and continues to support individual cheese-makers as they develop their products. Hodgson has helped stop the decline of traditional British farm-cheese production and has encouraged generations of new cheese-makers. If you are interested in knowing more about Britain's native cheeses, then Neal's Yard Dairy is a good place to start; it's a unique and satisfying place to visit, a temple to artisan cheese production.

The Bermondsey Friar

I love the city, but I have always daydreamed about living in a remote and picturesque cottage, keeping a few goats and a hive or two of bees, and making money by selling honey and soft cheeses at the gate. In this idealised life there would be plenty of time for lying in a hammock reading novels, or deadheading the roses around my front door. But any wistful notions I had about giving up the rat race and becoming a cheese-maker were swiftly dispelled by the hard facts that I encountered, one wet and windy Sunday morning. My understanding of the daily work involved in cheese-making had been a bit hazy. The cheese-maker William (Bill) Oglethorpe soon put me straight.

To be a cheese-maker you must rise before dawn. Before you can make any cheese you must first fetch your milk – and not just any milk. The French cheesemonger Pierre Androuet talks about cheese having a *cru*, or growth, just like wine. Instead of the quality of the grape, it is the quality of the milk that is the first (and possibly the most fundamental) thing a cheese-maker must get right. If you want to make a unique and inimitable cheese you must find a reliable source of raw, organic milk within an hour or so's drive of your dairy. This is not something an alpine shepherd ever had to contend with; traditional cheese-makers lived with the livestock that provided the raw materials for their product. Things are a bit more complicated for the urban cheese-maker. Around 4.30 a.m. each morning Bill leaves his flat in Streatham and gets behind the wheel of a white van with a big plastic tank on top. He drives for fifty minutes to an organic farm just outside Sevenoaks in Kent. Here begins the process of transforming milk into a round wheel of cheese.

When Bill arrives at the farm the cows have just finished milking. He unloads his scrupulously clean, squat aluminium churns and pours a little of his fermented milk starter into the bottom of each one; the last churns get a bit more as they will have a little less time to ferment. The milk comes straight out of a tank in the milking parlour, through a pipe and into the churns at the temperature at which it leaves the cow's body: 30°C. Bill fastens on the lids, heaves the churns into the back of the van and then ties them down securely with a canvas strap and a ratchet and drives off. He then heads off to Bermondsey, the milk already acidulating. There Bill makes cheese in an arch that he shares with a brewer and a mozzarella-and-Parma-ham salesman. It is early now, but in just a few hours the milk sloshing around in the churns will have been transformed into five fat wheels of cheese. Bermondsey Hard-pressed cheese goes from udder to a recognisable cheese in a little over seven hours. But that is getting ahead of ourselves – right now it still looks like curdled milk.

William Oglethorpe sounds like a very English name, but this cheese-maker is a Frenchman raised in Switzerland and Tanzania. The method Bill uses to make his cheese was gleaned from time spent working in the Swiss Alps. The simple way in which cheese was made there (by heating raw milk) appealed to him, as did the relatively small amount of equipment needed. The cheese is similar to a Tomme de Montagne: a cheese of the high alpine meadows, where the sweet green grass of the mountains is the key to its taste. The crisp, clean air of viridifloric meadows is about as far removed as you can get from this arch hedged in by low-rise tower blocks. Bill's decision to work in the city is linked to his other source of income: on Thursday, Friday and Saturday he runs a stall at Borough Market selling grilled-cheese sandwiches and mountains of new potatoes, raclette and gherkins. This enterprise funds his cheese-making.

To someone who has spent years in the mountains, this space (despite its other advantages) must seem rather grim. There is not a scrap of green to be seen anywhere. Lassco, the architectural salvage firm, stores rusting radiators, flooring, tiles, planks and oddments in the space surrounding the arches, and stuff is piled up everywhere. Today it is dripping and sodden; the trains rattle overhead. On a Sunday morning in the rain, with every arch blind and the blue metal shutters pulled down, it is a bleak and menacing place. Nature seems far removed.

I have come to see the alchemy of cheese-making in person. Nothing fixes a process in the mind more securely than watching it actually happen, but on this Sunday morning I am a bit late and the doors that I knock on remain resolutely closed. Eventually I find the right arch and bang hard on the metal shutters. I peer through the letterbox in the shutter door and eventually see a ponytailed figure in blue plastic clogs and a white coat coming towards me. The door finally opens and I go in. The dairy is sealed off, a hermetic, temperature-controlled block with a picture window for nosy visitors. The super-bright cheese-making room is below; upstairs is a cool, dark cheese-storage room. If you look up to the long vertical window above you can glimpse the shadowy shapes of cheeses.

I have managed to miss the first two steps in the cheese-making process and as Jennipher, Bill's assistant cheese-maker, kindly informs me, I have in fact arrived to disturb the cheese-makers at a vital moment: the cutting of the curd. What I have missed is the pouring of the fermenting milk into the cauldron, the adding of the drops of rennet and the setting of the curd. This last process takes about half an hour, after which it is time to get physical.

The cheese-making room is brightly lit, with white tiled walls and metal sinks; there is a long trolley with a deep-sided tray on the top. The thing that stands out is the huge copper cauldron hung from a black metal handle. When I walk in a little after 8.30 a.m. Bill stands bent over the cauldron. He is a compact figure, round-shouldered but strong-looking. The sound of Bach's St Matthew Passion and the sight of Bill's balding head bent reverently over the cauldron add a monastic air to the process.

Bill is wearing a white coat, blue rubber shoes and has put on a little white cloth cap, with the brim jauntily flipped up. He is slicing the curd with an implement called a 'harp'. This is a long-handled piece of wood with eight metal strings strung from two metal bars. He swings the tool back and forth in a figure-of-eight. He makes it look easy, but he has the assured strength of someone engaged in habitual exercise. As the consistency of the curd changes, Bill focuses intently on the state of it, and spreads out his fingers so that the small pieces of curd catch between them. He squeezes out the moisture and the curd holds together; on pulling it apart, it is fibrous and there is, as he says, a 'chicken-breast quality to it'. He sweeps back and forth, switching the harp for a squatter-handled implement, with metal wires curved in circles like a gyroscope at one end. His movements are small and efficient, and slowly the curd crumbs to a finer texture. Now, instead of swooping, he appears to be paddling up a choppy river. He is careful – there is no slopping of the milk. When he is happy with the result, electric metal paddles are clamped to the top of the cauldron and the curd is scalded (in an alpine dairy a fire would have been lit under the cauldron) for half an hour.

Cheese-making is all about timing, but physical strength and dexterity are of equal importance. The next stage involves a long piece of coarse cheesecloth being wrapped around a curved metal pole; this is pushed under the curd and pulled up, to form a round pouch of curd. Cheese-makers need thick skins; the milk can sometimes be so hot that they must first immerse their arms in ice-cold water before plunging them into the cauldron. The cloth bag is lifted up and squeezed of as much liquid as possible. Then the whole lot is dumped into a round wooden frame, a bit like an embroidery hoop, with a thin circular metal tray underneath. All these frames have been rinsed with hot water, as have the thin metal discs underneath them. The curd is in a fragile state and must not suffer any thermic shock by coming into contact with anything cold. Water sluices off the tray and onto the floor, and a bright-red squeegee is used to sluice it towards the drain. We are making food, but the bright lights and the water on the floor remind me of a swimming pool.

Cheese-making today combines scientific process (precise temperatures, timings and pH levels) with elements more often associated with craft (tasting, smelling, precise observation and instinct). A good cheese-maker must be able to do all these things well. The frames are stacked up on top of each other and then clamped into a metal press; the mixture is pulpy and unformed, but over the next hour or so the frames will be unclamped repeatedly, the curds lifted out, the cloth peeled off and the curd packed down again. Each time the curd gets smoother, denser and rounder and looks more like a cheese. So far, so traditional. But now the pH of the cheese must be taken with a digital probe and a protein label made of casein bearing the date and EU identification number must be pressed into the top of the cheese. On the final round of pressing a thin sliver of rubber, with the letters 'Bermondsey Hard-pressed' in relief, is pushed between the cheese and the frame. The milk is no more; this is now a cheese – and a named cheese at that.

There is no rest for the cheese-maker whilst the cheese is pressing. Bill and Jennipher go outside and start sluicing out the churns with a high-pressure hose. The whey left in the cauldron after the curd has been lifted out must also be got rid of. It cannot go down the drain, and there are no pigs to eat it, so it is pumped into the tank on top of the van and taken back to the farm, where it is drained into the slurry pit. It is a pity that this rich source of nutrition cannot be given to a city farm, but strict regulations prevent this.

When the cauldron has been scrubbed and the churns rinsed, we go upstairs to taste cheese. The cheese-storage room is like a chapel. The only light comes from a long vertical window and from the blue glow of the fly-zapper. The shadowy outlines of about sixty cheeses sit on planks of untreated spruce, held up by rows of scaffolding poles. The shelves are on either side of the room, with a space in between; the planks can be slid across the space so that Bill can reach the cheeses, flip them and wash them by hand. The cheeses are heavy (about 6kg, each) and Bill must crouch down to reach the lowest shelves. Flexibility and a good back are as essential as patience when it comes to making cheese. After rinsing comes the tasting. Using a tubular boring tool, Bill takes small cylinders from a variety of cheeses, plugging up the holes with a little tube of liquid plastic. We squeeze small amounts of cheese between our fingers – the youngest cheeses are bland and rubbery, but as they age the flavours become more and more complex, and the older cheeses have a pleasant pineapple tang. At four to six months the taste becomes interesting; at eight months lovely.

Cheese-makers need to be resilient, for the early days of cheese-making can be fraught with disappointment. The time involved, and the possibility that so much work may go to waste if a batch is spoiled, is chastening. I wonder at the fortitude and perseverance that it takes to succeed as a cheese-maker. The process of improvement never ends, but it seems to suit someone like Bill, who has an enquiring mind, open to change and possibility. Our conversation strays from cheese to the human mind, memory palaces and Nietzsche. The day's tasks, however physically arduous, are approached with humour, and I will always remember the process of making this cheese against the soundtrack of Bill's high-pitched giggle. Children learn through mistakes, and so must the cheese-maker; in this case failure can be a force for good.

Our Lady of the Thistles

One night an email pings into my inbox. It's from an old friend called Fred, who now works at Neal's Yard Dairy as a cheesemonger. The subject reads: 'we have an amazing pig that needs divvying up'. A stranger to capital letters, he goes on to say:

Our pig comes from mary holbrook – doyenne of goats cheese tymsboro, cardo, sleightlet and old ford for neals yard and pigs for st john and great queen street amongst others. mary pigs are lops who munch their way thru her meadows at sleight farm near bath. They feast on the whey from the cheesemaking. She's been makin cheese and sidelineing in pigs for around 30 years. I have it regularly and it is a real treat.

I can't resist, and a week later I am collecting £75 worth of bagged-up, frozen pig bits from the back of a pickup truck parked outside Mary's London flat in Bethnal Green. Roasted, the pork is so good, with a creamy taste and texture that are hard to describe, but mesmerising, with absurdly crisp crackling. Fred's description of the farm, and of Mary, intrigues me so much that a month or so later Fred, my eight-year-old daughter Hannah and I are hurtling down the M4 in our antique Volvo estate towards her farm.

Sleight Farm is only a few miles outside Bath in Somerset, yet it feels far more remote. It almost seems to exist outside time. The feeling of unreality begins with the entrance. It's easy to miss, and there's no sign; just a white five-bar gate set back from the road. Craning our necks, we wonder if we have come to the right place; the tarmac drive curves away round the hill, but no house is in view. On the left of the drive a herd of kidlets (weaned goats born this year) ebb and flow across the field like starlings in a winter sky. The frisking kids are the only clue. We follow the drive up and at the top is a grey stone house with mullion windows, pointed gables and a farmyard teeming with piglets and goats. We have arrived at Sleight Farm. We park behind a Land Rover and look for Mary.

Mary Holbrook has lived here since 1967, first with her husband and, since his death, alone, although a succession of would-be cheese-makers come to work alongside her and learn the craft she has been perfecting for more than thirty years. She makes four different goats' milk cheeses, three soft and one hard: Cardo, Tymsboro, Sleightlett and Old Ford. The two soft goat's cheeses – Tymsboro and the fluffy ash-covered Sleightlett – evoke France with their creamy, nutty lemon taste, while Cardo's cracked orange rind with its yielding, moreish interior (which is a little like Brie, but also totally unique) is Mary's take on the Portuguese cheese Queijo da Serra.

The grey-skinned Old Ford (named after the road off Bethnal Green in East London where she spends part of the week) evokes the smooth, waxy, hard cheeses of southern Europe. Fred and I are here to watch Old Ford being made; Hannah has come to play with the newly weaned piglets.

Today some cheese-makers are definitely a hybrid of artisan and scientist, combining centuries-old technique with the latest technology. But Mary is an artisan right down to her cheese-maker's plastic clogs. 'Recipes are prescriptive,' she says. 'This is really a peasant way to make cheese.' You can tell that, to her, this can only be a good thing – a fact underlined when I learn that Mary's recipes were taken at source from Sicilian shepherds or Portuguese artisans, methods that she has transplanted to a Somerset farm with great success.

Mary began on a small domestic scale, making feta with milk from two goats. Her interest soon grew, leading her to research recipes first in France and then in Sicily and Portugal. This way of making cheese, by keeping a flock (of sheep or goats), milking them and then feeding the excess whey to the pigs that she breeds for meat, is eternal.

She did not begin her working life as a cheese-maker; she trained as an archaeologist and spent some years working in Greece. These years seem to have been formative. She may now live on a hill overlooking rolling, green West Country fields, but it is immediately apparent that her heart (and her palate) lies somewhere far hotter and sunnier. The trees and plants that grow up around her home are by no means native; nor are the types of cheeses she has chosen to make. When Mary and her husband first came here they planted a white mulberry, a fig tree and a vine; today these engulf the farmhouse, with the mulberry and the fig pressing up against the windows. We head off to our rooms to drop off our sleeping bags, and at the back the vine sprawls, blinding the windows and giving a cool green underwater light to the upstairs corridor. The interior of the house, which is whitewashed throughout, has an equally Aegean feel.

Outside, the feeling of being somewhere other than Somerset persists. Goats hop up onto ledges in the farmyard, straggle down in a crowd towards the barn and, most of all, stare with their knowing, black-irised eyes. It is a purely quizzical gaze, without malice. Mary's goats are a mix of Saanens,

Nubians, Boers, Alpines and cross-breeds, and they graze freely (if pickily) in the fields above the farm. Goats are fastidious eaters – they won't eat just anything, but nibble selectively, choosing the tips of the sweetest herbs, flowers and grasses, as well as the tender parts of weeds such as nettles and thistles. When we walk through the fields we see the seedheads of rye grass and the tips of nettles bitten down to a uniform height. The goats also strip the bark from trees (they need double the fibre of other milk-producing animals to keep their guts healthy and their immune system strong). These goats are especially fond of wild flowers; it has been many years since Mary glimpsed a cowslip on the farm. At milking time she gives them each an oatcake to munch. All of which goes to explain the fantastic quality of her herd's milk.

At night the goats come into the barn and so begins the circle of perfection. In the evenings the goats eat the sweet, home-grown hay cut in the farm's meadows. The next morning they are milked. The milk goes straight from the dairy through a pipe into a vat in the cheese room. Half an hour after the goats are milked the cheese-making process has begun. An hour or so later the whey, which has been siphoned off into plastic kegs, is taken away and fed to the pigs. This rich liquid makes for exceptionally sweet, tender pork. That this diet creates some of the best pork in the country is not just my opinion, but is backed up by the restaurateurs who choose to serve it. Mary's pork is served at London's most famous meaty restaurant, St John, and at the many restaurants that have absorbed the St John ethos of serving the very best-quality British ingredients, cooked simply. Mary also sells her kid meat to the acclaimed Moorish restaurant Moro in London's Exmouth Market.

On the summer weekend that we visited we began the day by drinking strong black coffee with fresh goats' milk in Mary's kitchen. There are shelves full of interesting-looking recipe books and jars of spices, all of which bear witness to Mary's culinary curiosity. We then went through to the cheese room to watch Mary and her assistant Ross making Old Ford. Whilst they stirred the curdled milk in a huge silver vat on one side of the room, racks of Tymsboro ladled out the previous evening wept their weepy, watery whey on the other side. The vat contained 400 litres of morning and evening milk combined. This is cultured with whey from the previous day's Tymsboro production. The curd is set with 2ml of rennet for every 10 litres of milk.

When the curd has begun to set (about ninety minutes later), 80 litres of whey are drained off and replaced with 80 litres of hot water; Mary was shown this hot-water method of heating the curd in Sicily. When the curd has set still further, Mary and Ross then break it up using their arms rather than a metal harp. This reminds me of Heidi and her grandfather:

Sometimes the grandfather would make small round cheeses on those days, and there was no greater pleasure for Heidi than to see him stir the butter with his bare arms.

Mary and Ross swish their hands gently through the curds, slowly grabbing and releasing handfuls, occasionally squishing up the bigger bits with their fingers. When the curd is small enough, it is scooped out of the vat and pressed down into circular moulds lined with sky-blue nylon cheesecloth.

At this point it looks nothing like its smooth, waxy future self, but instead resembles mounds of cottage cheese. The cloth is then folded over and the curds are pressed down into the mould. After ten minutes they are flipped over. Inside, the curds are already cohering – this way of making cheese simply encourages what is already occurring. The process continues, using the weight of the cheese itself to expel the rest of the whey. No added pressure is applied. When the cheese is hard enough it is taken out and washed in brine, before being aged in a temperature-controlled cheese room at the Neal's Yard Dairy storerooms in Bermondsey.

Mary may live and work according to rules of production laid down centuries ago, but she markets her cheese cannily. She has a close relationship with Neal's Yard Dairy. She works in their cheese room one day a week, but, while they sell her cheese, she has always promoted her products herself. Sitting over lunch the next day, Mary describes how she got her cheese into Harrods Food Hall soon after she started making it in the early 1970s. The buyer tasted the colander-shaped cheese that Mary was making then (called Mendip) and instantly agreed to stock it. Early success is one thing, but it's Mary's staying power that awes me. That she has a natural ability for cheese-making is evident, but it has been backed up by the dedication to keep doing a demandingly physical job for decades. Her hardiness and commitment to her work are humbling. It may not be obvious, but I wonder whether her early career in archaeology – which requires patient, careful attention, repetition and plenty of back-breaking bending – was not such a bad preparation for cheese-making after all.

Simple Lactic Cheese or Cows' Curd

This simple lactic cheese is one of the easiest cheeses to make. It's currently very popular with chefs. This is partly due to the subtle taste and texture, but also to the fact that it fulfils the same role as goats' cheese, but at one-third of the price.

At the Neal's Yard Creamery in Herefordshire they make the curds when the cows' milk comes in from the farm first thing in the morning, using 40 litres of milk that are pumped out into two plastic drums. A little starter is added to each drum and a few drops of rennet (for cows' milk products they use calves' rennet, and goats' rennet for the goats' milk cheeses). The milk is allowed to ferment for a few hours and then poured onto mesh to drain. The consistency is that of very thick yoghurt. My visit to the Creamery set me up as a home cheese-maker, as I took back with me not just the sour-milk tang, but also a sheet of plastic mesh, a little starter (cheese culture) in a pot and some rennet. With these few ingredients I could be making curd cheese for the next year.

The first few times I made cheese in the kitchen I copied what they did in the Herefordshire dairy and placed a big piece of plastic mesh over a baking tray, but after I had tipped whey all over the kitchen floor (and my shoes) for the fourth time I decided to use a colander.

Makes about 500–600g curd cheese

2 litres whole milk, preferably unhomogenised
a pinch of freeze-dried cheese culture (I used Flora Danica)
1 drop of rennet
sea salt

Bring the milk up to blood temperature (put a clean finger in; it should feel pleasantly warm but not too hot). If you are using raw, organic milk, then you will need to raise the temperature to above 120°C to kill off any bad bacteria, before letting the milk cool and adding your good bacteria (culture).

Add the freeze-dried culture and stir well before adding the rennet. Leave to set for about 6 hours, then tip the mixture into a colander lined with clean muslin or a new J-cloth and leave to drain over a bowl for another 4 hours (you may need to drain off the whey from the bowl intermittently). Don't put the whey down the drain as it is very nutritious and can be fed to animals or used as a plant fertiliser.

When the curds have drained, tip them into a bowl and add salt to taste. You can use the curd as part of a cold plate, or as an ingredient in a tart of curd, cream and whipped egg whites. (This recipe can of course also be made with goats' milk or, in the unlikely event you have access to it, sheep's milk.)

Kid Cooked in Goats' Milk

'Thou shalt not seethe a kid in his mother's milk'– or so it says in Deuteronomy – which is a pity because it's a very good way to cook goat. We don't eat much goat in Britain, but when eaten young and properly cooked it is really very tasty. Mary Holbrook sends a proportion of her kids for slaughter every spring. One of the restaurants she supplies is Moro, where the chefs seal the meat by browning it in a pan and then cook it very slowly in sherry.

I took some convincing. Raw kid is not gastronomically promising in appearance. The loin and leg that came out of the freezer on Saturday night seemed all sinew and bone and no meat. The next morning Fred put it in a roasting tray with some goats' milk straight from the dairy. Into the tray also went a couple of roughly sliced onions, a few scrapings of nutmeg, some fresh sage, a few curls of lemon peel, garlic, fresh ginger, salt and pepper. The goat was then cooked very slowly for four hours.

Donna, who milks Mary's goats each morning in the small parlour next to the cheese room, was not pleased when she found that Fred had used all the milk that had been put aside from cheese-making, leaving none for her mid-morning tea break. The only milk left to use already had rennet added to it. When we went back for a second cup of tea half an hour later, the milk had set hard.

Serves 4

1 leg and loin of kid
3 strips of lemon zest
4 or 5 whole garlic cloves, unpeeled
4 or 5 fat coins of fresh ginger
a few scrapings of nutmeg
fresh sage
1 bay leaf (Mary uses dried bay leaves from Qatar, available in her local East
*   End grocery store)*
2 medium onions, peeled and roughly chopped
3 carrots, peeled and roughly chopped
1 litre goats' milk

Preheat the oven to 120°C/gas mark ½.

Put the meat in a roasting tray that just fits it. Scatter over the aromatics, herbs and vegetables and pour over the milk. Move the whole lot around with your hands so that the flavours get to mingle a little.

Roast the kid slowly for 4 hours, turning the meat over after 2 hours. For the last half-hour turn the oven up to 150°C/gas mark 2, but keep a close eye on the meat so that it does not brown too much.

Serve with a dish of plain boiled rice or mash, or a gratin of potatoes, as you wish.

Simple Goats' Cheese

Makes 1 small goats' cheese

1 litre goats' milk
a pinch of freeze-dried cheese culture (I use Flora Danica)
1 drop of rennet
sea salt
small cheese mould

In a large heavy-based saucepan or preserving pan heat the goats' milk up to not more than 28–32°C. If you have no suitable pan you can put the milk in a bowl suspended over a larger pan and half-fill the latter with water. When the milk has heated up, add the freeze-dried culture and the rennet. Stir well. Leave to set. This will take about 8 hours, although it may set sooner. When you tip the pan, the edge of curd should fall away from the side of it in a clean line. You will know when you see this.

What you do next depends on the shape of cheese that you want to make. I use a pyramid-shaped ricotta mould, but you could just as easily tie up the cheese in clean muslin and suspend it over a bowl with string (if your curd seems sloppy, this is the best option, as the curd has less opportunity to pour out).

Place your mould in a deep tray or gratin dish. Using a spoon, carefully ladle the curds into the mould – the less you break them, the moister and more delicate your cheese will be.

Allow the curd to settle, and then top it up until the cheese fills the mould. You will be surprised at how much whey continues to pour out. After about 12 hours it should be ready, but if you want it to be a little firmer, wait 24–48 hours. Then salt the bottom of the cheese and tip it out onto a saucer.

You can eat the cheese straight away, when its flavour is freshest, adding herbs or cracked black pepper. If you want to refrigerate it, it will keep for two or three days.

CHEESE-MAKING TIPS

- There is no need to buy lots of expensive moulds. You can make your own by piercing the sides of a yoghurt or ricotta pot with holes to allow the whey to drain out. At Neal's Yard they use grey plastic drainpipes drilled with holes to make the long, white goats' cheese called Ragstone.
- If you can find it, use raw milk (farmers' markets sometimes sell this) to make cheese and yoghurt and you will be amazed at the delicacy and superlative taste of your dairy products. In contrast, if you use goats' milk from the supermarket you may find it has an unpleasantly 'goaty' taste when made into cheese.
- Add herbs to your soft cheese. I mix it with 1 tablespoon of freshly picked and finely chopped borage leaves, which add a light cucumber note.

How to make your own Ricotta

You can of course buy perfectly good ricotta from a cheese shop, but you will be astonished by how easy it is to make your own. It requires ingredients that you probably already have in the fridge, and no more specialist equipment than a sieve, muslin and a little forethought.

The word *ricotta* means 'recooked' – this refers to the fact that it is usually made with whey left over from the cheese-making process. Few of us have ready access to whey, but you can easily fake it by mixing milk, yoghurt and a little lemon juice. The souring agent (in this case, lemon juice) causes the milk and yoghurt to separate into curds and whey. (Those familiar with Little Miss Muffet and her tuffet may feel pleased that they finally know what curds and whey look like.)

Makes about 300g

> *1 litre whole milk*
> *250ml yoghurt or thick cream*
> *½ tsp sea salt*
> *2 tbsp lemon juice*

Rinse out a heavy-based pan with cold water (this will stop the milk from scorching). Mix the milk, yoghurt or cream and salt together in the pan and slowly bring just to the boil. Stir occasionally. When you see steam on the surface of the milk and the odd bubble, add the lemon juice. Simmer for a minute or two and the liquid will curdle and separate into curds and whey. Turn off the heat and leave to rest for about 30 minutes (or up to 2 hours). It will look very unappetising – like sour milk.

When you are ready to drain the cheese, line a sieve or colander with damp muslin, place it in a deep tray and gently spoon in the curds. Leave to drain for 1–2 hours (the longer you leave it, the drier it will be). Lift up the cloth and squeeze gently – the liquid should run out a little milkily (if it runs clear, leave it a bit longer).

Cover and refrigerate the ricotta until you are ready to go on to the next stage of your recipe. You don't need to bake it; it is delicious eaten fresh with salad and good olive oil, or as a pudding.

If you want to eat your ricotta as a pudding, replace the yoghurt in the recipe with thick cream, and serve the drained cheese with cinnamon and a swirl of honey alongside baked figs or apricots.

Baked Ricotta with Herbs

Serves 2 as a main course, or 4 as a starter

300g ricotta (see page 97; if you are using shop-bought ricotta, drain it in a
   sieve lined with kitchen towel before you use it)
2 eggs
1 tbsp very finely chopped fresh thyme or marjoram
1 tsp lemon zest
2 tbsp freshly grated Parmesan
1 tbsp olive oil
sea salt and black pepper
butter, for greasing

Preheat the oven to 180°C/gas mark 4.

Place the ricotta in a small bowl, then break in the eggs and mix well. Stir in the herbs, lemon zest, Parmesan, oil and seasoning.

Butter a small ovenproof bowl and spoon in the ricotta mixture. Bake in the oven for about 20 minutes, until the top of the ricotta is golden and it smells fragrantly cheesy. Serve with a good garden salad of mixed leaves and herbs.

Watercress Soup with Ricotta 'Dumplings'

Home-made ricotta keeps for at least three days; if you have any left over, you can use it to make the herby dumplings in this smooth, green, velvety soup.

Serves 2

>   1 shallot, finely chopped
>   1 tsp butter and 1 tbsp olive oil, for frying
>   1 floury white potato, peeled and cubed
>   500ml chicken stock or water
>   leaves from a bunch of watercress (reserve a few for garnish)
>   75–100g ricotta (see page 97; if using home-made cheese, you may need to
>   add a beaten egg if it is too dry to hold together in a ball)
>   1 tbsp freshly chopped mint
>   1 tbsp finely grated Parmesan
>   a little grated nutmeg
>   sea salt and black pepper

Sauté the shallot in a little butter and olive oil. Add the potato and sweat for 10 minutes over a low heat. Add the stock (or equivalent amount of hot water from the kettle) and simmer until the potato is soft.

Heat a small knob of butter in a heavy-based frying pan. Sauté the watercress for a few minutes, until tender.

In a small bowl, beat the ricotta with the mint and Parmesan. Add the nutmeg and season with a little salt and pepper.

Add the sautéed watercress to the soup and blend with a stick blender. Add a little more stock or water if it's too thick. Check the seasoning.

Ladle the hot soup into individual bowls. Use a tablespoon to take a curved dollop of ricotta and place it gently in the centre of each bowl. Add a few reserved watercress leaves and a grinding of black pepper. Serve with thin crusts of toast.

Tofu

'There is a rose in Spanish Harlem' – or so sang Mama Cass. In that song, a red rose bloomed against the asphalt. In my version, a soya-bean plant slides open its bright-green leaves between the cobbles of a courtyard off London's Brick Lane. It may be an odd and discordant sight, but it's a neat way of summing up the cross-cultural transplantation that is going on here. I am in Taylor's Yard, which leads directly off Brick Lane, just north of the Old Truman Brewery. This long street is still a jumble of different businesses, some on the wane, others on the up; there are a few of the original Jewish-run wholesale cloth houses, shops selling leather goods with workshops behind them, Indian supermarkets, curry houses and confectioners and the newer vintage-clothes shops, design shops and bars. Strange as it may sound, I've come to see an artisan tofu-maker at work. For here, in an industry of one, Neil McLennan produces his organic tofu, which he sells under the apt name of Clean Bean.

The small outer office leading to the workshop is packed to the ceiling with brown paper sacks of organic soya beans, the paper stamped with Chinese characters. I put my coat down on a stack of sacks and look through to the windowless concrete-floored room where Neil makes the tofu. What was once an old leather workshop is now filled with a collection of unusual-looking boilers, cookers and tanks, some of them connected with pipes wrapped in tin foil. If the machines weren't running you would never guess what is being made here, until you see the soya beans caught in the drain cover – a spiral of chalky-beige and silver.

Tofu and cheese-making share a basic method – in both cases milk (soy or animal) is heated, curdled, drained, squeezed and turned from a liquid into a less-perishable solid. The most obvious and immediate difference between the two processes is the noise. Tofu-making is hot, steamy and loud. The pressure cooker clanks as it steams another batch of beans. A high-decibel crushing and whirring noise comes from the machine that sucks those cooked beans up a pipe, mashes and then steams them, and pushes them through a filter using centrifugal force. Excess whey is sluiced out of a cauldron and onto the floor. Pressurised air hisses out of the hydraulic press that squeezes the curd into blocks of tofu. The milk – and it really does look like creamy, frothing milk – shoots out of a pipe into a cauldron, whilst on the other side the dry pulp (*okara*), which is all that is left of the beans, is sprayed out into a bin.

Cheese-making rooms are usually still and quiet, the silence broken only by the sound of whey dripping out of moulds. For the artisan tofu-maker, the dairy and cheese room are one. On a farm, for obvious reasons, these two places must be kept separate, and all the bleating, mooing and shitting that accompany milking happen either in a different building or (if cheese-making and milking are separate operations) miles apart. The tofu-maker doesn't have to drive to collect milk or keep his animals healthy and milking: instead he must import and then unload pallet after pallet of heavy sacks of dried beans. Sometimes the sacks split and the beans are spilt; in Neil's case, they lie between cracks in the cobbles outside his workshop and, if the weather is warm and wet, they germinate. Soon small green fronds push up through the compacted earth.

Once or, on busy weeks, twice a week, these sacks are cut open. The beans are poured out and then soaked, cooked, pulped and spun, all in the same small room. When I arrive at Clean Bean's workshop to watch the tofu being made, the din is as intense as the humidity. Despite the cacophony, Neil and his co-worker of ten years, Dean, move around the congested space calmly. Jazz is playing loudly and they each get on with the job in hand (about five processes, all running at the same time). It could almost be a noisy piece of performance art.

Neil is wiry and pale with reddish-blond hair and a goatee; he is wearing a hair net and a blue boiler suit. Dean is tall and black and has a diamond stud-earring. He is wearing a blue hair net too and a black-and-purple T-shirt that says 'Florida', which seems quite appropriate given the temperature inside the workshop. The pair exude a calm, focused energy. It is obvious that they like working together and can anticipate what has to be done without the need for words. It might look simple, but good tofu-making takes years to perfect. There are so many variables in the process that a momentary lapse of concentration can ruin a whole batch. Far from finding the work boring, Neil and Dean both seem to relish the calm focus that is required. Tofu-making days are good days.

Neil and Dean have been working since 6 a.m., but the tofu-making process began last night. The beans were poured out into a rectangular steel box (about the size of an old-fashioned water tank) and then soaked overnight. It is now around lunchtime and Neil and Dean have already made about four batches of tofu. To start the next batch, Neil takes a tin jug, scoops up the beans and pours them into the pressure cooker. The beans are cooked for twenty minutes before they are mashed and turned into milk.

As the milk pours into the cauldron, a thick frothy scum appears. This is scooped off and tipped into a tray on the floor. Spraying out of another funnel is *okara*, the by-product, which looks and feels a bit like desiccated coconut. In another parallel with the cheese-making process, in China, Korea and Japan tofu workshops are often found near farms so that excess *okara* can, like whey, be used to fatten up pigs or cows. In Japan it is used to make a porridge-like dish and as baby food. If UK rules regarding waste disposal were less strict, Neil could feed it to the pigs at the city farm just behind his workshop.

Neil discovered the flavour of handmade tofu whilst living in Sichuan province in China. He got a taste for *ma po doufu*, an oddly named spicy-bean, pork and tofu dish that translates as 'pockmarked-faced old woman's tofu' and is a regional speciality. When he came home he was so underwhelmed by the quality of the tofu available commercially that he began making it himself. He started out in a friend's flat on a small scale, using everyday kitchen equipment. He bought and burnt out a different Argos blender each week, which he returned to the shop again and again, filthy and broken, but under warranty. Argos acted as unwitting sponsors of his fledgling business – a business that has grown steadily through word of mouth.

Basic tofu-making is simple to learn, but like any craft it takes years to hone. There was no one to teach Neil, so he had to learn everything by himself, starting with books, and in more recent years aided by the connective power of the Internet. Artisan skills are hard to uncover, and if you ask a Japanese tofu-maker how to make tofu, he or she will respond with the briefest of directions.

I watch Neil slowly drip *nigari* into the soya milk to set the curd. *Nigari* (meaning 'bitter') is a super-concentrated brine; it is the lye left over after the process of crystallising sea-salt flakes from salt water. I dip my finger in and taste it. It's so salty that I instantly gag. 'It's taken as a cold cure in Japan,' says Neil. I take his word for it, whilst vowing never to try it again.

Neil adds the *nigari* using a jug – dripping it in slowly helps the curd to set evenly. Once the milk starts to curdle, he stirs the mixture using a specific technique that he picked up after spending a day with a master tofu-maker in Shanghai. Like cheese, tofu-making relies on precise, repetitive technique refined over many years. A small adjustment can make all the difference to the final product.

When the whey has separated and clumps of curd have formed (a few minutes later), he tips the cauldron (which is conveniently fixed to a spinning axis) and pours the excess liquid straight out onto the floor. The remaining curds are scooped up using a steel bowl with a handle, and poured into square moulds lined with muslin. The curds are fluffy and clumpy like cottage cheese. Neil carefully folds the cloth over the curds and puts a plate on top, before adding a weight and then the pneumatic press. Once the curd has reached the edge of the mould (about half an hour later) it is taken out and sliced into rectangles. These are then washed in small tanks of moving cold water, before being put in the fridge. Later on he will seal them into water-filled boxes.

Clean Bean tofu has a unique taste that is as far removed from the plastic cubes sold in health-food shops as a processed-cheese slice is from a subtle, tangy piece of artisan Cheddar. In the same way that an artisan cheese-maker creates an individual cheese, so an artisan tofu-maker stamps his tofu with his own personality, experience and skill. Raw materials play a big part too. Neil uses Japanese techniques (setting it with *nigari*) and organic Chinese soya beans. The resulting tofu has a firm texture, is good for frying or roasting, but soft enough to eat in soup, and has a clean, fresh, tangy taste. In the beginning Neil was both producer and seller. He sold his tofu on a stand at Spitalfields organic market and later at Borough Market. He talked to his customers and found out what they liked best. He believes that properly made tofu is a food with a wide appeal. You don't have to be vegan or even vegetarian (Neil is neither) to like the taste.

I asked him what Chinese customers thought of his tofu. 'To the Chinese,' says Neil, 'it tastes Japanese, and vice versa. Most aren't impressed when I tell them I make tofu, as it's a low-status profession in China, the fallback job for any peasant who has lost his land and had to move to the city.'

Neil's Quick Clean Bean Tofu Soup

Serves 4

1 block of Clean Bean or other good-quality tofu (approx. 350g)
1 tbsp vegetable oil
a bunch of greens (chard, spinach, etc.) or long-stemmed broccoli or pak choi
3 tbsp miso paste
*a few julienned carrots, sliced mushrooms or tomatoes, or whatever good-
    looking fresh vegetables you have to hand*
a bunch of spring onions, shredded
*a few shiso, basil or mint leaves, thinly sliced (shiso is a Japanese herb
    related to the nettle)*

Cube the tofu. Heat the vegetable oil in a pan and fry the tofu until slightly crispy on the outside. Remove and set aside.

Bring a pan of salted water (about 1 litre) to the boil and plunge in the greens. Boil briefly, until tender. Take a ladle of the water and dissolve the miso in a small bowl, then return it to the pan (off the heat).

Ladle the broth, chosen vegetables and the greens into bowls and distribute the tofu evenly among them. Scatter over the spring onions and the herbs.

Serve at once.

Tofu and Tomato Salad with Shiso

I can't claim this dish as my own. It's a slightly less labour-intensive version of a recipe in David Chang's very entertaining *Momofuku* cookbook, which also details his hard-scrabble rise to the top of the New York restaurant scene. Chang peels and then chills cherry tomatoes in an ice-bath, but unless you are feeling very fancy, simply slicing the tomatoes is fine. I am also not too sure about chilling something as sun-loving as a tomato, but Chang is right when he says that the creaminess of tofu does the same as mozzarella in an Italian *caprese* (tomato and mozzarella) salad, with *shiso* standing in for basil.

Serves 4, as a starter

> 1 block of Clean Bean or other good-quality tofu (approx. 350g)
> 500g ripe tomatoes
> sea salt and black pepper
> 6 shiso leaves or Thai purple basil, very finely sliced
>
> Vinaigrette
> 4 tbsp sherry vinegar
> 1 tbsp soy sauce
> 1 tsp sesame oil
> 125ml light olive oil or grapeseed oil

Slice the tofu in half horizontally and then into cubes.

Core and slice the tomatoes, or if you are using cherry tomatoes, simply halve them.

Mix the vinaigrette ingredients in a bowl and then add the tomatoes and toss to dress well.

Pour the tomatoes onto a large platter and scatter over the tofu cubes. Season with salt and pepper and sprinkle over the *shiso* or basil.

BETTER TOFU WAYS

In Britain tofu has a reputation for being bland and rubbery. It's too often associated with an old-school style of vegetarianism that put ethics and nutrition way ahead of taste. I had absorbed some of these prejudices, and tofu was definitely not an ingredient that I was confident with. Even with a slab of Neil's beautifully hand-crafted Clean Bean tofu in the fridge, I still wasn't sure what to do with it. I ate half of it chopped up in miso soup, but to my shame, whilst I dithered about what to do with the rest, it went off and I had to throw it away.

In Japan it's very different, for tofu is a versatile and prized ingredient. Japanese cookery is the opposite of other Asian cuisines, for instead of creating effects through blending, the tastes and properties of individual ingredients are singled out and made a virtue of. The texture of tofu is one of its strengths: when raw, it is malleable and can be used to makes pastes and sauces; when fried, it adds crunch followed by a soft curdiness inside. The subtlety of its taste is another virtue.

Koya

To find out just how good tofu can taste I went to Soho, to visit the Japanese restaurant Koya. Koya specialises in a kind of robust and heartening country-style food that isn't often found outside Japan, and which I hoped would prove enlightening.

Koya takes authenticity of taste very seriously – so seriously it almost seems too good to be true. It specialises in doing one thing – *udon* noodles – simply, beautifully and with great care. The noodles are even kneaded in the traditional way, using the pressure of human feet. Most importantly, Koya serves properly tasty food that is also healthy, heartening, authentic and imaginative. It's almost the epitome of modern peasant food: staple ingredients rooted in tradition, made with care to sustain and nourish those who spend their lives in the denaturing bustle of a modern city.

Say 'Japanese food' to most Westerners and they think of sushi. But in Japan noodles, and in particular *udon* noodles, are just as popular. Street stalls and no-frills restaurants specialising in *udon* (made on the premises) are common. Going by the Web comments left by visiting Japanese travellers, Koya is probably as close to a Japanese experience of *udon* as you are going to get outside Tokyo. The noodles at Koya are thick and chewy, like super-sized spaghetti. They are made in the restaurant's basement with imported Japanese wheat flour, and served in dark glazed bowls of steaming broth based on *dashi* (stock) made in the traditional way. The Koya method of making *udon* comes from a very specific place: Sanuki, a remote island off the south-west coast of Japan, which has its own *udon* culture and a very refined approach to making it.

In the way that London delightfully forms bizarre-sounding but successful working partnerships, these wonderfully authentic *udon* noodles are cooked by a Japanese chef in a restaurant owned by an Irishman and kneaded by a pair of Polish feet. The large pair of black-socked feet belongs to Michael, who shuffles back and forth across the dough (protected by a plastic sheet) several times daily and takes huge pride and satisfaction in his work. It is a job whose repetition, lack of natural light and relative isolation, he cheerfully admits, would drive others potty, but it seems to suit him perfectly. Each day a dough is made of semolina, wheat flour and salty water. It is mechanically mixed, before being pressed and rolled into fat, squat cylinders. Several of these are pressed down into a metal tray, trodden on, rolled up and trodden on again twice more, before being left to rest for twenty-four hours, then pressed and cut into fat noodles by a machine.

The *udon* noodles offered here are a successful example of the modern city's ability to absorb traditional skills. The smooth cream-coloured dough is appealing, but it's the side dishes on the menu at Koya that really make my mouth water. The small bowls of pork belly in cider are cooked for so long and so slowly that the fat, skin and meat can be eaten in one sweet, tender bite.

The chef here, Junya Yamasaki, is a head taller than any of the chefs in his kitchen. He has black hair pulled back into a bun, broad shoulders and very high cheekbones. He smiles frequently when talking to his staff. When I arrive at about ten he is busy, but calm, making decisions about that day's menu, talking to his staff and bringing ingredients up from the downstairs larder. I take a look around. In the doorway hangs a traditional split-cloth door curtain (*noren*). Opposite is a karaoke bar – a coincidence, but the aptness of the view seems to add another layer of verisimilitude. The restaurant itself is a narrow, plainly decorated room with a mosaic-tiled floor and boards on the wall describing the menu. The daily changing specials are chalked up on a blackboard. Yesterday's (including the appetising-sounding Watercress and Egg *Udon*) are still there. The kitchen is at the back, with a low wooden counter with a bench directly in front of it. It's the best seat in the house: a place for lone diners to sit and feel at their ease or, as the waitress charmingly puts it, 'not feel lonely'. It's also the perfect spot for those who, like me, want to observe a kitchen at work.

In the kitchen, steam rises from the large, constantly boiling water tank used to cook the noodles, and what looks like a prawning net hangs beside it. On the stove three huge vats of stock bubble. The three chefs are busy prepping the day's dishes. One of them is frying slices of Clean Bean tofu. The tofu is sliced about 3mm thick and deep-fried to form a crisp, wrinkly orange skin. Junya tells me that in most Japanese restaurants the fried tofu is usually bought ready-cooked. This is what he did himself until he started using Neil McLennan's tofu. He takes the postcard-sized slab of fried tofu and washes it with hot water to get rid of the oil, before popping it under a grill to crisp up again. 'Japanese people don't like too much oil,' says Junya.

This way of serving fried tofu with spring onions on top (*kizami*) is on the menu every day, but today I am watching Junya use tofu as a dressing for vegetables, ground up in a paste with sesame and miso. He uses a Japanese mortar (*suribachi*). This is an earthenware bowl, glazed on the outside; the inner surface is ridged with fine lines. You could use a food-processor instead or a traditional pestle and mortar. In Japan, Buddhist monks start the day's cooking by using a *suribachi* to prepare sesame-seed pastes. I watch Junya spin the pestle around the edge of the bowl; it takes time to change the sesame from seed to paste, but is an absorbing, satisfying and meditative task. The paste forms the base for the dressing in the following recipe using vegetables and fruit.

Kaki Fruit Salad with Spinach, Tofu and Shiitake Mushrooms

Serves 4 as a small plate

approx. 150g tofu
3 kaki fruit (persimmons) (you can substitute roasted cubes of squash or
*   pumpkin at other times of the year)*
2 bunches of spinach
2 tbsp toasted sesame seeds (buy them toasted, or toast them yourself)
1 tbsp aka (red) miso paste
100ml vegetable stock, to dilute
6 shiitake mushrooms
slivers of fried tofu, to serve

Take the tofu out of its box and wrap in a tea towel. Compress with a weight (a stack of small plates, or a tin of something on a plate) to get some of the water out.

Peel the *kaki* fruit, slice into quarters, then core and slice into eighths. Chop into non-uniformly shaped pieces. Place the fruit in a bowl of salted water.

Blanch the spinach by holding it as a bunch, stems down, in boiling water for 1–2 minutes, and then briefly immerse the whole bunch in the pan. Drain and leave to cool in a bowl of iced water. This particularly Japanese method removes the tacky-mouth feeling that you get when biting down on spinach. Leave to chill for 30 minutes whilst you make the sauce.

Pour the sesame seeds into the bottom of a bowl. Using a pestle, work the seeds until they start to break down and release their oil. The mixture should look like damp sand. Break the tofu up in the bowl and then grind with the pestle – it should look clumpy, like over-whipped cream. Add the red miso, mix and taste again, adding a little more miso if necessary.

Dilute the mixture slightly with half of the vegetable stock (Koya vegetable stock is made with *kombu* (kelp), shiitake and sun-dried tomatoes). Add more stock as necessary. When the consistency is that of a thick, pourable dressing, set it aside.

Toast the shiitake mushrooms until dry and nutty-smelling, either under a grill or in a very hot oven. When cool, slice thinly.

Drain the spinach and squeeze out the water, then chop.

Combine the *kaki* fruit, spinach, mushrooms and sauce and mix well. Serve with a few slivers of fried tofu on the side.

Fermentation at Home

Good cooking is the best and truest economy, turning to full accountancy wholesome articles of food, and converting into palatable meals, what the ignorant either render uneatable, or throw away in disdain.

Eliza Acton,
Introduction to Modern Cookery for Private Families.

Fermentation is one of the oldest magic tricks in the kitchen. For almost as long as humanity has existed we have been using bacteria to preserve and enhance the flavour of our food. Fermentation is an ancient art, one with complex flavours and health-giving properties, and occurs in different forms (using grains, dairy foods, vegetables and beans) in every society around the world. Try to imagine your kitchen without yoghurt, vinegar, bread, cheese, coffee, chocolate or pickles. All are foods that require fermentation at some stage of their production. Fermented foods use microscopic bacteria and fungi to transform basic ingredients into something that has a longer shelf life. Milk is turned into cheese; cabbage into sauerkraut; and grapes into wine. This process allows us to eat fruit and vegetables out of season when green things are scarce, by preserving them through the alchemy of fermentation. It is also a wonderful way of avoiding food waste. Aside from the great taste and utility, the lovely thing about fermented foods is that they are so good for us.

In America the fermented-food movement today takes in disparate groups (from techno-peasants to dumpster-diving punks) whose common link is a reaction against over-processed, industrialised and chemically engineered food. The American food writer Sandor Katz describes himself as a 'fermentation fetishist'; his book *Wild Fermentation* is the bible of the movement. The history of fermentation would run to volumes, and this section is just a brief foray into the world of fermented foods. Katz's own journey into fermentation began by accident when he found an old crock buried in the barn of the gay commune he is part of, situated in the hills of Tennessee. He makes great and convincing claims for the health-giving power of fermented foods, and shares his knowledge with a grace and enthusiasm that are invigorating.

According to Katz, who goes into a lot more detail, fermentation makes food more nutritious. Eating fermented foods is healthy because, by consuming them, you are 'lining your digestive tract with living cultures essential to breaking down food and assimilating nutrients'. The main reason to make fermented food yourself is that commercially available options are often pasteurised – heated up to the point where beneficial microorganisms die. With this many pluses (taste, health, the satisfaction of making something yourself), the fermentation movement deserves all the attention it gets. This book includes a few of the easy-to-make fermented foods (such as sauerkraut and *kimchi*, sourdough and yoghurt) that you can concoct at home. All of them are great places for the would-be fermenter to begin. Katz's book is an enthusiast's volume that is part-memoir, part-cookbook, part-scientific analysis – an essential addition to the kitchen shelf of any would-be modern peasant.

The biggest shift for us would-be fermenters to make is in our attitude towards bacteria. We are taught to fear bacteria and the danger that lurks in unpasteurised cheese, raw eggs, pink undercooked chicken or pork. Antibacterial soaps and sprays are marketed in a way that plays on that fear. TV adverts show ugly cartoon microbes being chased away by a glistening swipe of cleaning spray. However, bacteria can do both good and ill, and by eating fermented foods we take more good bacteria into our guts, where they help to break down food and aid our digestion. Refrigeration and food-processing mean that fermented foods have fallen out of our diet and need to be rediscovered.

MAKING GINGER BEER

Fermented food is very much alive, and fermentation can be a volatile process, as I found out when two bottles of home-made ginger beer exploded in my laundry cupboard, with a force that shattered the bottle into shards of glass and filled the room with a sticky miasma. I gingerly (ha-ha) carried the remaining bottle outside and uncapped it; it had a good fizz and a deep gingery, quite beery taste, but the splintered glass and sticky mess were less appealing, as was the lecture from my husband who had told me on the morning of the explosion to move my stash of bottles outside to the garden shed. It was a good lesson in the power of naturally occurring yeasts, and luckily no one was hurt. If you still want to make ginger beer, be sure to use a plastic bottle for at least one of your beers, and in that way you can keep an eye on the level of fermentation. If it looks bloated and stretched out, release a little of the gas. Don't do what I did and just put it back in the cupboard!

You can of course make ginger beer with commercial yeast, but then it wouldn't be a wild ferment. The following method uses a ginger beer 'bug' (starter), or what the social historian Dorothy Hartley calls a 'bee' in the charming introduction to her extraordinary book *Food in England*. As well as compiling what must be the most exhaustive and entertaining collection of popular English recipes, Hartley (who had been both an art student and later an art teacher) illustrated all her own books with really delightful line draw-ings. They have great clarity (witness the cross-section of a country privy) and charm; the woman in a bun glimpsed in some of them looks a bit like Mrs Pepperpot. The book begins with a description of her first kitchen, in a house high on the Yorkshire moors, and a picture of a cat watching 'the ceaseless activity of the ginger beer"bee" going up and down, buzzing faintly "like a bee in a bottle"'. As well as the cat and the bubbling jam jar, the wide stone windowsill holds red geraniums in pots, a Christmas cactus, a jumble of knitting, a hastily thrown-off apron, a wooden doll, a book and a coffee cup. It's a comforting picture for someone like me who worries that my scattergun approach to garden, allotment, work, kitchen, children, husband-wrangling and the odd bit of crochet means that I end up doing none of these things particularly well.

One of the most heartening things about these age-old domestic processes is their tolerance of imperfection. Whether you are nursing a crock of bubbling sourdough or mixing cream with milk to make yoghurt, you can be sure that no two results will ever be exactly the same. Some days your bread will rise; some days your yoghurt will have a firmer set. Getting better through practice is the key, and from it comes deep satisfaction; instant success has nothing to do with it.

TO STERILISE JARS AND BOTTLES

There are two methods of sterilising jars, bottles and lids. The simplest is to put them through a hot cycle in the dishwasher. Alternatively, carefully wash and dry them and place in a roasting tray (the lids sitting beside the jars). Put the tray in a cold oven and heat at 160°C/gas mark 3 for 20 minutes. Turn off the oven, leaving the tray inside. Fill the jars or bottles while they are still hot.

Ginger Beer

Makes about 2 litres

a large thumb of fresh root ginger, grated
400g granulated sugar
250ml water
juice of 2 lemons, strained

Put 2 teaspoons of the fresh root ginger into a bowl with 2 teaspoons of the sugar and all of the water. Stir well and pour into a Kilner jar. Cover the top of the jar with muslin or kitchen towel, but don't seal the jar. You want to keep dust out and the air in. Put the jar on a warm windowsill à la Dorothy Hartley and leave for several days until the mixture starts to ferment: you will hear the ginger-beer 'bee' start buzzing. (I will admit to disappointment here, getting a crust that lifted up gassily rather than a 'bee', but it was a little chilly when I attempted it.)

When you are satisfied that fermentation has occurred (the surface should look gassy and bubbly), bring 2 litres of water to the boil and add the remaining grated ginger and sugar. Stir until the sugar has dissolved and then allow to cool.

When the sugar water has cooled, strain it into another bowl and add the lemon juice. Strain the fermented 'bee' mixture, reserving 1 tablespoon of it, if you wish to keep on making ginger beer, and pour the rest into the bowl. Using a jug and funnel, pour the beer mixture into sterilised bottles (see page 115), seal tightly and leave in a warm place for a couple of days. Transfer them to the fridge and leave for up to 1 week before drinking. Keep checking to make sure that too much gas is not collecting in the bottles. Let a little out if you're worried.

Elderberry Shrub

A 'shrub' is a tart fruit-and-vinegar syrup that is mixed with water, tonic or soda to make a refreshing drink. It's a soft drink of the past, an American colonial concoction that was pretty much wiped out by the mass production of carbonated drinks. The unusual name comes from the Arabic for 'drink' – *sharab*. You can make a shrub with any fruit or berry, but I chose to make mine with elderberries. The sight of abundant crowns of wine-dark berries hanging over the garden wall and going to waste had been oppressing me. A shrub, which requires no further initial effort than steeping the berries in vinegar, seemed like a good solution.

Before I harvested the berries I first asked forgiveness of the tree. The elder is historically known as a sacred and magical tree, and Gypsies and woodsmen will not burn its wood. If you do, the Devil is supposed to come down the chimney. To avoid annoying the spirit of the elder you should always offer thanks first, before taking the fruit or flowers. In his ever-illuminating *Englishman's Flora*, the writer and naturalist Geoffrey Grigson records the folk names of this sprawling, stinking and weedy-looking tree, which reveal its doubtful reputation. Although prized by herbalists, the elder is notorious not only for being the tree from which Judas hanged himself, but also the wood upon which Christ was nailed. In Dorset the old name for it is 'God's stinking tree', in Kent 'Judas tree' and in Cumbria 'Devil's wood'. The diarist John Evelyn wrote that it was a 'Catholicon against all Infirmities', which is a lot more than you can say for cola.

Grigson also maintains that, despite its often sprawling appearance, elder can, with age, become a tree of great charm and beauty: 'Old Elders against limestone are as lovely as old olive trees on the Karst.'

Makes approx. 750ml shrub

250g elderberries or other fruit (quinces, apples, blackberries, redcurrants, etc.)
500ml red-wine vinegar
sugar, to taste

Dust off the berries or fruit and, if necessary, give them a quick rinse. Dry them and pack them down into a large sterilised glass jar (see page 115).

Pour over the red-wine vinegar and screw on the lid tightly. Place on a shelf somewhere cool and out of the light. From time to time shake the jar. After a couple of weeks strain the liquid into a pan and heat gently, stirring in as much or as little sugar as suits your palate and complements the fruit you have used. When the sugar has dissolved, bring the liquid up to the boil and simmer for 2–3 minutes. Skim off any scum. Strain the shrub into a bottle and seal with a cork.

Dilute to taste with fizzy water or, if you prefer, lemonade, tonic or soda water and serve over ice. You can also use the shrub as a cordial or as a base for spritzers and cocktails. In the nineteenth century it was often spiked with rum and brandy.

Sauerkraut

Traditional sauerkraut is made with cabbage, but you can add lots of roots too. Radishes and carrots add colour, as does the red cabbage in this recipe, which makes for a deep red-coloured brine and pink-tinged kraut.

Makes 10–12 servings

2 hard white cabbages
1 red cabbage
1 tbsp juniper berries
1 tbsp caraway seeds
roughly 3 tbsps sea salt per 2kg of vegetables

Peel off and discard the outer layers of the cabbage and shred the rest very finely. Take a large clean bucket with a lid (or a pottery crock if you are lucky enough to find one) and layer the shredded cabbage in it, sprinkling on the spices and salt evenly as you go.

Weigh the cabbage down using a plate and a couple of jam jars filled with water. Wait 24 hours; the cabbage should have exuded enough water to cover it. If it hasn't, make a brine by adding 1 tablespoon of sea salt to 1 litre of water and pouring it over. Weigh the cabbage down again – the water should now cover the vegetables. Cover with a lid or muslin to keep out the flies and dust and leave in an out-of-the-way corner or cupboard.

Check your sauerkraut every day or two. If there is any bloom (mould) on the surface, skim it off. Taste your kraut after a week – it should be ready now. Eat some of it with lots of smoked sausage. You can refrigerate the rest to stop the fermentation process, or just take a little at a time, noticing how the longer fermentation produces a softer, tangier kraut. When it starts to fizz, stop eating it. The kraut liquid is a complex mix of healthy bacteria and, as such, is a powerful tonic.

Kimchi

Kimchi is the national Korean dish of fermented cabbage and chillies. In a surprising bit of cross-cultural serendipity, it goes remarkably well with hot dogs and makes very good grown-up party food. It's a lighter take on the American chilli dog, a frankfurter topped with a spicy concoction of mince and beans that I learnt to love when I lived in Los Angeles.

I multiplied this recipe by four and, along with eighty hot dogs and eighty delicious potato-flour finger buns (baked by the London bakery of Flour Power) fed a party load of adults, who jostled – elbows out – to grab their *kimchi* dogs. I started out using a big plastic drum with a lid, but such is my love of brined pickles that I have now graduated to a glazed terracotta kraut pot with earthenware weights.

Makes 6–8 servings

Vegetables in brine
4 tbsp sea salt
1 litre water
1 cabbage, with the tough outer leaves discarded (traditionally Chinese napa
*   or pak choi, but I used 'January King', grown on my allotment, with*
*   good results)*
1 long white radish (known as daikon or mooli) or several red radishes,
*   sliced or julienned*
2 carrots, peeled and julienned

Spice mix
50g fresh root ginger, peeled and finely grated
a small bunch of spring onions, finely chopped
6 garlic cloves, peeled, crushed with the flat of a heavy knife and finely
*   chopped*
4 fresh red chilli peppers, peeled, seeded and finely chopped
2 tsp chilli flakes, or whole dried chillies ground in a mortar

Mix the salt and water together to make a brine.

Chop the cabbage roughly and add the radish and carrots. Put in a large plastic tub or pan and mix well. Pour over the brine and, using a plate, weight the vegetables down so that they are submerged beneath the brine. Leave to soften overnight.

The next day mix together the ginger, spring onions, garlic, chilli peppers and chilli flakes.

Drain the vegetables, reserving the brine. Taste them and if they are overly salty, rinse them; add a few pinches of sea salt if you think they need a bit more.

Mix the vegetables with the spice mix and pack them down into jars (or a big plastic container or pottery crock) until the brine rises. If the brine does not cover the vegetables, add a little of the reserved brine (if you don't need it, you can now discard it). Fasten the lids tightly.

Over the next 4–7 days let the *kimchi* ferment at room temperature. Each day open the lid to allow the gas to escape, and push the vegetables back down under the brine. This is a very smelly ferment, so you may want to do this by an open window. Don't let this put you off – the *kimchi's* flavour is far more subtle and tasty than the pong would indicate.

Move the *kimchi* into the fridge, where it will keep for several weeks. You can eat it on its own with rice and yoghurt, or stir fry with cooked rice and spring onions and top with a fried egg for kimchi fried rice.

PLANTED

Urban Vegetable-Growers

Our current food system is criminally wasteful. Keeping supermarkets fully stocked with perishable goods means that a lot of food gets thrown away. So if you think growing your own vegetables and going to farmers' markets is just a lifestyle choice, think again. There is a cost to the choices we make when we source fruit and vegetables. I don't mean money; I mean the true cost – the cost in energy, rural jobs and environmental impact. This cost is hard to see, and most of us don't worry about it too much. We know enough not to buy strawberries and tomatoes in December, but beyond that it's a case of: it can't go on like this, but what am I supposed to do about it?

Take a bag of pre-washed supermarket salad leaves as an example. If we could see the supply chain that brought each salad leaf together, we would throw up our hands in horror. Common sense tells us it's wrong to fly in leaves from five continents for a simple bowl of greens; but while we know it, very few of us are sufficiently engaged to do anything different. I thought I knew a bit about this issue, but it took a visit to a group of inner-city salad-growers to really wake me up to the wastefulness of our current food system.

Growing Communities was set up in 1993; to say they are doing tangible good feels like an understatement. Their premise is simple: as consumers, our connection to small-scale local producers that we can trust has been lost. Growing Communities bring consumer and producer face-to-face again, by running a fully organic veg-box scheme and holding a farmers' market each Saturday in Stoke Newington, North London, that sources all of its organic produce from within 100 miles of Hackney. In doing so, they have thrown a lifeline to small-scale organic farmers struggling to get a fair price for their goods, and have given consumers the chance to eat better-tasting vegetables that have not travelled thousands of miles.

In the end it may be that common sense is the most powerful weapon for change. We want real alternatives to the bad food ways we've got ourselves into, but right now they are thin on the ground. Which is why it's so wonderful to find an urban vegetable growing initiative that goes beyond mere tokenism. Window boxes full of tomatoes and herbs are attractive and uplifting, but in the face of climate change and rising oil prices London's millions of inhabitants need more than just green window-dressing. Through trade we can re-establish the links between cities and the agricultural land that surrounds them. By offering farmers a fair price we can keep small-scale farms alive and maintain the countryside we love. Understanding this strips away the aura of indulgence that is unfairly attached to organic produce.

The plain fact is that sourcing fruit and vegetables from these farmers has reinvigorated rural communities, many of which have high rates of unemployment. By encouraging organic food production we are also ensuring the health of that land for future generations. The cleverest thing of all is that this political and environmental propaganda is aimed directly at our stomachs. When I visit the market in Stoke Newington there is a good mixture of people, and the atmosphere is a happy one. Most importantly, what's on offer is tempting: there are wild and cultivated mushrooms, great-looking sausages, damsons, plums, apples, and raw milk sold by the cup and the pint. This is real food that really makes you want to cook. Buying vegetables in this way enables customers to reconnect to really tasty seasonal produce. Regulars report that though the initial cost of some vegetables may seem higher, they save money because the freshness of the produce means it lasts much longer. The striped green-and-red tomatoes and mottled peppers that I buy and make into a thick sauce of roasted vegetables cooked with black pudding, chorizo and waxy potatoes make a densely flavoured, meaty stew that tastes great, not worthy.

CHANGING THE WORLD ONE LEAF AT A TIME –
RECIPE FOR A POLITICAL SALAD

The other side to Growing Communities is the one that really interests me: their network of inner-city market gardens and micro-plots where they grow salad leaves for the box scheme and some local restaurants. Potatoes, onions and other main-crop vegetables cannot be grown in the city, for there isn't the space and it doesn't make sense financially in terms of labour and land. What can be grown are leafy greens of every kind: chicories, sorrel, lettuces of every stripe and hue, cabbages, kale, Brussels sprouts, fresh herbs and chard. These quick-growing mineral-filled leaves are also the vegetables that lose their nutrients fastest after they are picked. So if you can grow and deliver them within a few miles of a city you are winning on taste, health and environmental grounds – not bad for a bag of salad.

Greens that really taste of something make cooking easy. If you have access to shiny beet leaves, lemony sorrel, red-ribbed dandelions, pepper-hot fresh rocket or spicy giant red mustards you can serve an omelette or a steak, or even just make a sandwich, that is really special. As a political act, growing gourmet greens might seem gentler and less effective than more headline-stealing forms of direct action, but in the end its impact may be far longer-lasting. The winning formula that Growing Communities has come up with is to link the salad habit to a veg-box scheme for maximum impact, and reach thousands of people each week. It is a great model and one that they are trying to roll out countrywide through a start-up scheme. So far six different schemes based on the Growing Communities model are running in Burnley, Margate, Moffat, Herne Hill, Kentish Town and Manchester.

When I visit it is open-house day, and the first thing I see is a white milk float with cow horns on top, painted with black-and-white Friesian-style patches, parked outside one of the scheme's three plots. This is in the middle of Clissold Park in North London. Maisie the milk float is the delivery vehicle used to drop off the bags of organic fruit and veg boxes to 750 households each week. A table loaded with leaflets and maps of the scheme's drop-off route informs people what Growing Communities is all about. When I push my bike through a gap in the railings I find five raised beds and a large polytunnel. In terms of husbandry, both of the earth and plants, it's an impressive sight. The orderly plot bristles with healthy-looking greens of every variety – attractive enough to charm the most recalcitrant, vegetable-averse meat-eaters. Cut out of a small section of Clissold Park, what was once a butterfly tunnel has been re-covered with plastic and now shelters seedlings of 'Bright Lights' chard, coriander and 'Bull's Blood' beet, all of which grow faster under cover, protected from the weather and the birds.

I've come to meet Kerry Rankine, one of the people behind Growing Communities. Kerry is six foot tall, with long blonde hair and an unabash-edly frank take on the faults of the current organic movement. She has a history in Green activism and brings with her a forceful and highly politicised attitude to the world of organic fruit and vegetables. It's not hard to imagine her chaining herself to a plutonium reactor in her past life with Greenpeace. Kerry makes it clear that Growing Communities are serious. There is a real sense of urgency to what they are doing: trying to wake people up to the long-term effects of our food-purchasing habits by creating what they call a 'community-led alternative to the current damaging food system'. Kerry is far from being a wild-eyed Green zealot. She is a working mum (her son arrives from football practice whilst we speak) who has to struggle with the same balancing acts of ethics, time and money that we all do when feeding ourselves and our families.

The truth is that you have to make it easy for people. Growing Communities does the shopping for you, then bags up the fruit and veg and uses the milk cart to drop it off at various spots near your house, where you can pick it up from padlocked wooden lockers. All it takes is a short walk. After my tour of the polytunnel and a chat with Kerry, I arrange to visit one of their inner-city micro-plots – what Growing Communities call the Patchwork Gardens – and see how one of their apprentices is getting on.

The Patchwork Gardens are tiny plots that use land that is generously made available by the community (from plots in vicarage gardens to spare land on inner-city estates). These micro-plots (10 x 15m) are run by appren-tices who are trained by Growing Communities, and then given land, seeds, tools and support. I visited Ximena, an ex-textile designer, at one of her gardens on the edge of Hackney Marshes. In six beautifully tended raised beds are a variety of very healthy-looking greens protected from the weather and pests by horticultural fleece. I interrupt Ximena, who is patiently hand-weeding the beds, to find out a bit more about her journey to becoming an urban salad-grower. She volunteered at one of GC's market gardens before getting herself a City & Guilds qualification in allotment gardening and joining the apprentice scheme last year.

Here are some of Ximena's favourite salad leaves:
- The green-and-red mottled leaves of the colourful and tender lettuces, 'Marvel of Four Seasons' (so named because of its hardiness throughout the year) and sweet-tasting 'Flashy Butter Oak'.
- 'Bull's Blood' beetroot, sown purely for its dark-red leaves, which add colour and a beety taste to the salad bowl.
- The startling and eye-catching 'Bright Lights' chard, which has a vivid variety of red, green and yellow leaves and adds flavour and a splash of much-needed colour to a winter vegetable bed. The leaves are picked small to use as salad, or left to grow bigger and then cooked.

TIPS ON GROWING SALAD FOR YOUR TABLE

- Grow under cover. If you can't afford a polytunnel, getting some kind of cover (even if it's just a small one-metre-high tunnel on hoops) will extend your season and increase your yield dramatically. If you want reliable salad crops throughout the winter months, this is the key.
- If you can't be bothered with a plastic tunnel, then a small piece of horti-cultural fleece thrown over your salad bed will protect it from the worst effects of the weather and wildlife.

ROTATION

Whether you decide to cherish a single pepper plant on your windowsill or plant an entire garden's worth of vegetables, you will find that growing your own food revolutionises your approach to cooking it and deepens your connection to the natural world.

If you do decide to grow a plot's worth of vegetables in the city and don't have a huge amount of space, then rotation is the key to growing organic vegetables successfully and controlling pests without chemicals. To make short work of a complex topic, you need to grow a wide variety of plants, broadly split into four main biological families (see below). Doing this helps to keep plants and soil healthy by means of variety.

Rotation is a key part of organic vegetable-growing, and is not that complicated when you get the hang of it. At Growing Communities they work their leafy green growing beds on a four-year rotation (which, with the addition of manures, equals five years). To make it easy they have come up with a neat system of classification.

They start with green manures. These are crops that are sown, grown and then cut down to rot into the soil. They include red and white clover, rye, alfalfa, mustard and *Phacelia tanacetifolia*. Many of them are highly bee-friendly, but also fix nitrogen in the soil and act as a living mulch. After the crop is cut down three or four times in the year, it is dug in. Later on a layer of rich compost is also spread over the bed.

Following this feeding year come the brassicas (kale, cabbages, mustards), then plants in the aster family (all kinds of lettuces), then what are charmingly called 'goosefoot plants' (with leaves roughly shaped like a goose's foot), including spinach, chard and red orach. The last group is umbelliferous (parsley, coriander, celery and coriander) and is a bit of a catch-all, so includes sorrel too.

Within each year a spring- and winter-sowing are made. Two different plants from the same family follow on from each other, so that a spring sowing of chard might be followed by an autumn one of perpetual spinach.

Parathas: Indian Bread Stuffed with Winter Greens, Chilli and Coriander

Even the most committed vegetable-eater has days when they can't face another bowl of winter greens. Whether you use kale, beet leaves, mustard greens, chard or spinach, this northern Indian stuffed bread feels like an indulgent way to get your fix of iron-rich vegetables. You can eat it as a snack with a cup of tea and some yoghurt, or make a thick spicy dhal with pumpkin for a main meal

Makes 8–10 parathas, depending on how big you want them

Dough
200g chapatti flour, or half sifted wholemeal, half plain flour
200ml warm water
a few tablespoons of melted ghee or vegetable oil

Filling
150g greens (kale, mustard leaves, spinach, chard, beet leaves or sorrel; if you
    are using sorrel, don't blanch it – just cut into ribbons and add it raw to
    the dough)
1 tbsp dry fenugreek leaves (optional)
4 hot slim green chillies, split, seeded and chopped
4 tbsp roughly chopped fresh coriander

Make the dough by putting the flour in a mixing bowl and gradually adding the water until you have a fairly sticky mixture (you may not need all the water). Knead the dough until it is smooth and elastic (about 10 minutes), adding a teaspoon or two of the ghee or oil as you knead.

Leave the dough to rest for around 15 minutes by placing it in a clean bowl and covering it with cling film whilst you get on with making the filling.

Bring a large pan of salted water to the boil and plunge in the greens. Let the water come back up to the boil, then remove the greens and drain. Refresh under cold running water and leave to drain again. When cool, chop the greens roughly and mix well with the fenugreek (if using), the chillies and coriander. Set aside whilst you roll out your dough.

Roll the dough into a cylinder on a lightly floured surface. Cut the cylinder into 8 equal discs, shape them into balls and cover with a tea towel. Take 1 ball at a time and roll into a disc about 10cm wide. Place a heaped tablespoon of greens mixture in the centre, brush the edge of the circle with ghee or oil, then pull the edges in to enclose the mixture. Pinch or twist to seal it well. Add a bit more flour to the surface and roll the little parcel into a flat round patty. Brush half the circle with ghee and fold it over. Brush half the semicircle with ghee and fold again. Roll it out again so that you have a pennant-shaped bread, with two sides approximately 14cm long. Don't worry if a little mixture pokes through.

You can roll out all your breads before you start cooking; just don't stack them up, or they will stick together. As it is usually late when I start cooking, I roll them out whilst I am frying the first breads in the pan, but you may find this too frenetic.

Heat a cast-iron frying pan or, if you are lucky enough to have one, an Indian *tava*. Shake off any excess flour and place a *paratha* in the pan. Cook for about 3 minutes, until the underside of the bread has a good, mottled brown appearance. Brush the top of the bread with a little ghee or oil and turn. Cook for another 1 minute or so. Brush the top side with oil, turn and fry for another minute. Place on a plate wrapped up in a clean tea towel whilst you make the rest of the breads.

Parathas Stuffed with Potato and Chilli

Makes 8–10 parathas

paratha *dough (see page 131)*

potato filling
250g potatoes, unpeeled
4 hot slim green chillies, seeded and chopped
1 tbsp fresh ginger, peeled and finely grated
4 tbsp roughly chopped fresh coriander
a good pinch of cayenne pepper
a squeeze of lemon juice
a good pinch of sea salt

Put the potatoes into a steamer and cook until tender. Whilst the potatoes are hot peel off the skins and mash roughly. You can do this ahead of time.

Mix the potatoes with the chillies, ginger, coriander, cayenne and lemon juice. Season and taste. Then proceed as in the main *paratha* recipe on page 131.

Two urban farms in San Francisco

When it comes to being a modern peasant, Northern California is decades ahead of us. I knew I had to visit it when writing this book. It's not just the taste and variety of what is on offer, it's the innovative, open-minded approach to food production. For years farmers, fishermen, cheese-makers, wine-producers and restaurateurs have been showing the rest of the world how to live in a way that is connected to nature, earth-friendly and, most importantly, downright tasty. Pioneering restaurateur Alice Waters helped to forge the bond between growers and eaters before most of us were even born. I found my way to San Francisco via her Chez Panisse cookbooks, whose simple, seasonal approach relies on the very best ingredients, but does not skimp on technique, either.

Nowadays the food scene in San Francisco evolves with dizzying speed. There are Catalan-style tapas bars combining Barcelona's best ideas with the Bay Area's finest produce; roadside taco trucks that tempt you with mind-bogglingly appetising mini-tacos of braised pork; and super-trendy lunch counters that pop up in disused warehouses selling baguettes of braised steak, griddled pear and *kimchi*. For some, it goes beyond mere cooking – the process of food production becomes a political act and defines the way they live.

In Oakland, California, there is a farm on a dead-end street beneath the freeway. This part of the Bay Area's second city is poor and off-limits to tourists. Martin Luther King Jr. Boulevard is a wide and unlovely street. It takes four lanes of traffic past the end of this urban farm, while overhead is the freeway and the rail carrying the electric BART trains. It's very far from being anyone's pastoral ideal. But in direct contrast to the criss-crossing concrete and acres of asphalt, this vacant lot on the corner of 28th Street and Martin Luther King Jr. Boulevard has one of the most beautiful and fertile vegetable gardens I've ever seen.

The sky was blue and springtime had already arrived when I visited one morning in late January. Peas and beans were flowering, scrambling up through twiggy supports; fruit trees were lined up in tubs waiting to be grafted; bees flew in and out of hives; and in the corner a hand-crafted mud-and-straw cob oven smoked gently. Beds of lettuce, broad beans and dark-purple and golden mustards flourished beside the arching, silvery leaves of artichokes; a banana fluttered its great green flag-like leaves. All this on what was once wasteland on a dead-end street in a ghetto. Every leaf, flower and scrap of compost owes its existence here to one woman: the self-styled urban farmer and writer Novella Carpenter.

As I walked down the street Novella drove up and started unloading bins of sawdust from the back of her white pickup truck. In real life she is gruffer and scruffier than her book cover would lead you to believe. I wasn't fooled by the pinkly-scrubbed picture on the back of Novella's paperback, in which she wears a gingham shirt and holds a cute-looking goat; I am happy to find that, in the flesh, she looks far more like a real farmer. She hefts the tubs of sawdust out of the back of her pickup truck dressed in a pair of baggy jeans, the cuffs spattered with mud, dusty boots and a baggy T-shirt. She is friendly enough as she peers through black-rimmed spectacles at me (she was expecting me, after all), but not effusive. Her book, *Farm City*, was a best-seller, and I suspect uninvited visitors like me are the downside of its popularity.

Farm City is a breezy and honest account of the trials of becoming an urban farmer in a depressed and densely populated part of this city. In it Novella describes how she raises poultry (her turkey was slaughtered by the junkyard dog that lives next door), grows vegetables, breeds rabbits, restricts her diet to what she can grow or barter, and raises two enormous hogs that she feeds from the dumpsters of upscale organic restaurants. These she later turns into salami, *coppa* and prosciutto. I wander round the garden as Novella talks to her neighbour, a Yemeni shopkeeper with a hennaed goatee, who is going to help her slaughter one of her goats. As they talk, I nibble on the odd pea shoot and marvel at the fertility of her soil, the beauty of this higgledy-piggledy garden and the power of nature to transform even the most unlikely of sites into a place you want to linger. At the end of her plot (which she has just bought after squatting for eight years) is a wooden house painted pink. Novella rents the upstairs with her boyfriend, a mechanic. So far what I've seen isn't a million miles from what I do on my allotment (though I have to admit that Novella is a far more efficient gardener). I like to think it's because her garden is right next to her house (mine suffers from being a mile or two away down a busy road) and she has a degree in biology, but as comparisons are always odious, I'll stop there.

Novella raises everything for personal consumption. She doesn't shy away from the business of killing; almost our first conversation is about the necessity of buying a killing cone (a plastic cone that you put ducks in upside-down, so that you can lop their heads off with a large pair of pruning shears).

We wander next door to her back yard, where she keeps ducks, chickens and a trio of dwarf Ethiopian goats. As we come round the corner one of the small, endearingly pot-bellied goats scampers up the wooden stairs that lead to her back door and stares down at us. It really is very sweet-looking and I am glad it's not me that has to slaughter it. I offer assistance and chuck a bit of sawdust at the ducks' part of the yard. Although I've worked my own fairly large plot for more than ten years, there is something about this level of engagement with self-sufficiency that makes me feel like a part-timer. This really is just a back yard, and not a very big one at that, but it is also very much a farmyard – it smells like one and feels like one; you trample on straw and muck, and animals come at you. Just the other side of the fence a muscular junkyard dog lollops over; he seems bored and lonely rather than vicious, and serves to remind me that this really is an urban farm. Upstairs on a balcony there are rabbits (six does and one buck). Last year there were two enormous pigs in this tiny yard. I am dumbstruck by Novella's capabilities, but I am also quite pleased that I am not her neighbour.

I am reminded of this again when reading Fernand Braudel's *The Structures of Everyday Life*. Braudel quotes a German treatise from 1722 that scolds artisans for behaving like peasants and filling the streets with dung and livestock. It urges the banning of farms in towns. I have a feeling this kind of farming wouldn't really catch on in our far more densely populated European cities. I might long for a goat of my own (think of all that soft, creamy goats' cheese), but for now I will have to content myself with bees.

The next day I visit another kind of urban farm and one very much in the heart of San Francisco. The Hayes Valley Farm is a community garden built on top of an old freeway up-ramp in central San Francisco. The ramp is all that's left of the freeway system that the city once planned; this 1955 scheme would have seen San Francisco sliced up by ten elevated roads, ripping out its heart in the process. This road and another were partly built before the citizens rose up in revolt. Not having learnt its lesson, the city tried the same thing again in the early Sixties, when plans were drafted to build a freeway through Golden Gate Park and across the neighbouring Panhandle. Once again a public outcry stopped the road-builders. It is testament to the energy and spirit of the local communities that these plans failed on both occasions. Fifty years later the community spirit that drove those protests is much in evidence among the young volunteers shovelling woodchip and manure on an impossibly blue-skied sunny afternoon in late January.

For the last year or so the 2¼ acres have been slowly transformed from a barren strip of concrete to a fertile plot of land. Beneath tall eucalyptus trees rows of broad beans are interplanted with broccoli, marigolds, mustards and kale. On Thursdays and Sundays anyone can walk in and volunteer. This is just what I did. A hand-painted sign announces on arrival 'THE HAYES VALLEY FARM – IT WILL GROW ON YOU'. We scribble our signatures down on some kind of indemnity form and write our names in felt-tip onto a piece of blue masking tape that we stick to our chests. There are two work groups; one is shuffling dusty, partially composted woodchip and compost into mini-terraces. They are trying to make water-collecting contours with flat tops, called 'swirls'. This is a permaculture garden; the plants are chosen to do well in the microclimate peculiar to the Hayes Valley (a small, shady valley of sea breezes and mists). When I ask if they grow tomatoes, a volunteer named Brett replies, 'If you want tomatoes, try the Castro' (the next district over the hill).

The design and planting aim at more than just providing food for the local community. The garden must thrive without impacting on the environment. The plants – especially perennial plants – grow in glorious, straggling diversity up sloping beds designed to maximise the rainfall and do away with the need for watering. Unlike the city, which needs the watchful eyes of its citizens, this garden is designed to look after itself. What it lacks in aesthetics, it makes up for in self-sufficiency. It is also very productive. We harvested a tableload of crunchy, tight broccoli heads and great sheaves of cavolo nero (called dino kale here). It's an extremely urban setting, and whilst I struggled to pull apart two plastic paint buckets to collect up the harvest, the driver of a pickup truck who was stuck in traffic leant out of his window and called out some advice. His suggestion didn't work, but by then the flow of traffic had moved him on.

The volunteers I worked amongst were mostly in their mid-twenties to early thirties, and their competency as gardeners varied wildly, but they were all happy to be there and worked unselfconsciously alongside each other. We piled up our harvest on a table at the front gate and were allowed to take home what we wanted. I took a little for my landlady. Before I left I suggested that they grew some sorrel, a perennial plant well suited to this cool, shady spot. It was my small contribution to the fertile beauty of this inner-city haven.

It may be the climate, the abundance and quality of San Francisco's vegetables or the fruitful mixing of many cultures, but I have never eaten so well and as variously as I did in the week I spent exploring the cafés, taco trucks, market stalls and restaurants of this lovely city. At a minute, no-frills Japanese restaurant called Eiji in the Castro district I ate silken tofu, curdled moments before with *nigari*. The tofu was served in a pottery dish, with another small plate with a series of circular indentations containing different toppings: thin shavings of pickled ginger, sliced spring onions and radish, the nettle-like perilla (*shiso*) and flakes of *bonito* (dried fish). The special of the day was aubergine cooked in a way I had never previously come across, but was happy to replicate once I got home.

Aubergine with Walnut Miso

Serves 2

> *2 slim aubergines (as smooth and fresh as you can find)*
> *a little olive oil*
> *sea salt*
> *2 tbsp walnuts, chopped and lightly toasted*
> *2–3 tbsp miso paste*

Preheat the oven to 180°C/gas mark 4.

Slice the aubergine tops and bottoms off and then cut the body into very thick pieces horizontally (not through the stem). You will probably end up with two or three cross-section pieces per aubergine, depending on how big they are. Rub the top of each piece with olive oil and sprinkle with sea salt. Roast in the oven for about 30 minutes.

Meanwhile, combine the walnuts with the miso paste and loosen with a little olive oil if the mixture is very thick.

Take the almost-tender aubergine out of the oven and spread a thick layer of paste on top of each piece. Put back into the oven for another 10 minutes, or until the top is browning and hot. Eat with a salad as a light lunch or supper.

Lutfun's garden

If you want to see a vegetable garden with a unique selection of crops, head to the Spitalfields City Farm, just behind Brick Lane in East London. There you'll find a sprawling mass of sheds, animal enclosures and poly-tunnels. It's home to Shetland ponies, donkeys, sheep, pigs and chickens, but it's also where you will find a gardener of great skill and inspiration, Lutfun Hussain.

Step inside the polytunnels in high summer and you will find yourself lost amongst shield-sized gourd leaves, giant green pumpkins and searingly hot chillies. Amidst all this fertile bounty you will find the modest, smiling figure of Lutfun, perfectly at ease amongst her plants, with a relaxed but purposeful air about her. Lutfun is from Bangladesh, where there is a long tradition of female gardener cooks. Twelve years ago she started a women's gardening group, the Coriander Club, at the farm. Her aim was to provide the women in her community with an activity outside the home. As well as providing a link to a more rural life, they also produce masses of the fresh vegetables that are most often used in Bangladeshi cookery. It seems Lutfun can get almost anything to grow (although she did admit to a failure with henna). As well as *kudo* (bottle gourd), the Coriander Club grows *mooli* and mustards, snake gourds and naga chillies (the hottest in the world), aubergines, amaranth, *chichinga*, ribbed gourds, garlic and okra.

Lutfun's garden produces food in every season. It is a place of beauty throughout the year, with tulips and cyclamens in spring and abundant marigolds in summer. Lutfun's enthusiasm was equal to my own and we happily swapped lists of our favourite vegetables, fruits and flowers. I gratefully took away her recommendations for plants I can raise on my allotment and promised to return with some globe-artichoke seedlings for her in the spring. I also learnt a good tip from her on how to grow coriander that won't run to seed too quickly. If you plant the seed in autumn, so that the plant over-winters, it will be stronger and better-established when the growing season begins again the following spring. The Coriander Club has published its own cookbook (available at the farm); it has lots of tips on how to grow Indian vegetables such as the long white radish, *mooli*, which is so good sliced up raw in a salad.

Pumpkin Chutney

Inspired by Lutfun's garden, I came up with this recipe for pumpkin chutney; rich and spicy, it goes well with Indian food, but is also delicious in a sandwich with a good hard cheese.

Makes about 5 jars

> 2 tsp cumin seeds
>
> 1 scant tsp fenugreek seeds
>
> 1 tsp fennel seeds
>
> 1 tsp coriander seeds
>
> 2 whole dried red chillies
>
> 2 heaped tsp black mustard seeds
>
> 1 tsp ground turmeric
>
> 8 fresh curry leaves (optional)
>
> 1 x 5cm square of tamarind pulp, soaked in about 100ml of kettle-hot water
>
> 6 tbsp vegetable oil (mustard oil would be perfect, if you can get hold of it),
>   plus a little extra to seal the jars
>
> 1 butternut squash or a few slices of pumpkin (approx. 750g), peeled and diced
>
> 6 garlic cloves, peeled and finely chopped
>
> 3 long red fresh chillies, seeded and finely chopped
>
> 5cm thumb of fresh root ginger, peeled and finely chopped
>
> 400ml distilled malt vinegar
>
> 150g dark brown sugar
>
> 2 tsp sea salt

Toast the cumin, fenugreek, fennel and coriander in a dry pan until aromatic, then tip out and, when cool, grind to a fine powder. Place in a bowl along with the dried chillies, mustard seeds and turmeric, and the curry leaves if using.

Using a wooden spoon, rub the tamarind through a sieve into another little bowl. Scrape the pulp off the bottom of the sieve. You should have a good 2–3 tablespoons of it. You are now ready to start making the chutney.

Heat the oil in a large stainless steel saucepan. When it's hot, add the butternut squash or pumpkin and fry until soft and a little coloured. Add the garlic, fresh chillies and ginger and fry for another 5 minutes before adding your spice mixture. Fry for another 2 minutes, then add the vinegar, sieved tamarind, sugar and salt.

Cook the mixture over a medium heat until you have a thick jam-like consistency (roughly 30 minutes). Stir frequently. Taste the chutney. Don't worry if it's very vinegary, for this will calm down as it ages. Add a little more salt if you think it needs it.

Spoon your chutney into sterilised jars (see page 115). Pour a little oil over the top to seal the jars, then screw on the lids. Leave for 1 month to allow the flavours to develop.

GROWING YOUR OWN URBAN SALAD PLOT

Anyone can sow a summer's worth of salad, but could you keep yourself and your family in tasty leafy greens from January to December? The concept is far from novel. In 1622 the diarist and gardener John Evelyn published a meticulously planned salad calendar, listing thirty-five different types of edible leaf, designed to keep your salad bowl full throughout all four seasons. Its extraordinary variety is something we should all strive for.

Growing leafy greens year-round requires a little forethought and some planning, but it is highly recommended; not just in terms of taste, but as one of the ways to really connect with the seasons and the changing levels of light and heat. You do have to think ahead, as you will need to sow seed for leeks, cabbage and winter salad from mid- to late summer onwards.

One of the easiest ways to keep yourself in home-grown greens is to make a late-summer sowing of chicory. Chicory is a great vegetable for anyone who goes away a lot over the summer, as you can delay your planting until the end of August or even September. You can also easily grow chicory in pots, so the space required is not prohibitive. Even if you only have a balcony you could still keep yourself in crunchy bitter leaves throughout the winter. As well as being frost-hardy, chicories are also very attractive and there are scores of different kinds. One of my current favourites is the dark-red hearting chicory, 'Rosso di Treviso'. It's a beautiful plant with leaves that gradually turn from green to red as the summer heat leaves the ground. The catalogue from Edwin Tucker Seeds records that it is a very ancient variety dating back to the sixteenth century. Once you've tasted it, you will see why it's been popular for centuries. I like it mixed with other leaves, or on its own dressed with sherry vinegar alongside a sweetish dish such as pumpkin risotto, for a highly flavoured, deeply colourful autumn lunch or supper. Like witloof, it can be lifted in autumn and forced indoors to create paler, more tender shoots.

Even more unusual-looking is 'Grumolo' chicory, from Piedmont in the far north of Italy. It forms tight rosettes of dark red and also jade-green, which grow very close to the ground. Both varieties produce heads so attractive that you could almost wear them as a buttonhole. This chicory is extremely hardy and good at surviving tough winter weather. Cut it in the spring and a second crop of leaves will grow (although not with such symmetry). According to Joy Larkcom in her indispensable book *The Organic Salad Garden*, this chicory also tolerates 'poor soil, weedy conditions and low temperatures'.

Among the catalogna chicories is the very beautiful and tasty, pale lemon-green and red-flecked 'Castelfranco'. Also worth growing is the dande-lion-like *puntarelle*, sometimes known as 'asparagus chicory'. It is tall with long, narrow, serrated leaves. It comes from the south of Italy, so is less frost-tolerant. Use its pale-white bulb in an early spring salad combined with blood-oranges (pared of pith), thinly sliced and dressed with a fruity olive oil (see recipe on page 145).

Once you have a taste for the bitter chicory family you can indulge yourself with many different varieties. Franchi Seeds (an Italian company) have almost forty on their list, exquisite in their range of shape, colour and taste. It's enough to make you give up growing flowers.

Puntarelle and Blood-orange Salad

The bitter, almost liquorice taste of the white-and-green chicory bulb performs a light-footed tango with the sweet and tart taste of the blood-oranges and the earthy pepper of the oil in this dish, which tastes as exquisite as it looks.

Serves 2

> *1 puntarelle (chicory) bulb*
> *4 blood-oranges*
> *1 tbsp olive oil*
> *sea salt and black pepper*

Prepare the *puntarelle* by pulling off the outer leaves. Don't discard them, as you can add them to a bowl of mixed salad leaves or braise them. Slice the *puntarelle* bulb finely, then drop the slices into a bowl of iced water whilst you prepare the oranges.

Using a sharp knife, cut off the top and bottom of the oranges, then remove the rest of the peel and pith as carefully as you can. Slice the oranges into thin discs and remove the pips.

Arrange on a serving dish (or individual plates) with the *puntarelle* and zigzag over the oil. Season and serve.

REARED

Butchery – And and not *But*

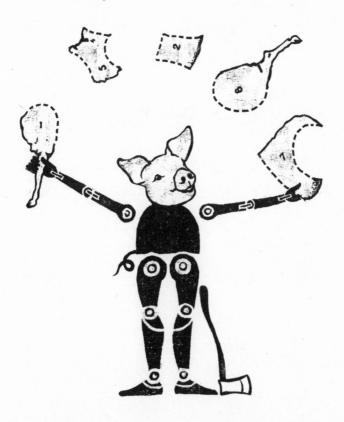

*Murder and sudden death seem as unnatural there as
they should be anywhere else. They can't, they can
never become acceptable facts. Food is far too pleasant
to combine with horror. All the same, facts, even
distasteful facts, must be accepted and we shall see
how, before any story of cooking begins, crime is
inevitable. That is why cooking is not an entirely
agreeable past time.*

The Alice B. Toklas Cookbook

If you want to eat meat, you must accept that killing comes before cooking.
As Alice B. Toklas says, 'crime is inevitable'. But most of the time we don't
consider this fact; we get our meat from butchers and we get someone
else to do our killing. I love bacon, but I certainly don't want to cut a pig's
throat. Does that make me a hypocrite? Probably. But it doesn't make me
unusual. Most of us (Woody Allen aside) don't really want to think about
death of any kind, at any time. Plenty of us don't even want to be confronted
by bits of animal (hooves, ears, tails) that remind us that this was once a
living, feeling thing.

The depth of antipathy to the way our food is procured can be seen in
the way that the word 'butcher' has entered the language outside cookery.
Serial killers and war criminals earn the tag 'butcher'; making a mess of
carving or cutting is 'to butcher' the meat. It carries with it the added sense
of frenzied hacking, a sense that is far removed from the skilled job of
reducing a carcass to a series of cuts, which actual butchery requires. For the

customer, butchery is usually a distasteful act, or at the very least a frightening one. I stand before the gleaming glass cabinet in our local butcher's, happy to buy any cut of meat there, pleased to be the recipient of their labours. But if the butcher is at his block, with his cleaver smashing down through flesh and bone, I shudder and clutch my small daughter close to me. In this, as in so many of our attitudes towards the way our food is delivered, we are hopelessly conflicted and, faced with such a confusion of emotions, most of us prefer not to think about it too deeply. We comfort ourselves by buying meat from farms where animals have led decent lives, and we block out the squealing in the abattoir.

Perhaps we should give vegetarians more respect for facing life's realities head-on, rather than sweeping them under the dining-room carpet like the rest of us. I am, like so many others, a mostly unthinking meat-eater, but it does give me pause for thought that those with souls as large as Gandhi and Tolstoy were vegetarian. We accept that death is part of the pact we make when we crave bacon, but we are too cowardly to spend much time considering the death of the pig. Chefs aside, very few of us will ever witness a slaughter or watch an animal being reduced from a carcass to a series of cuts. When you read John Berger's *Pig Earth*, his visceral description of a cow's slaughter hits you like a hammer:

> *The son severs and twists off the four hooves and throws them into a wheelbarrow. The mother removes the udder. Then, through the cut hide, the son axes the breast bone. This is similar to the last axing of a tree before it falls, for from that moment onwards, the cow, no longer an animal, is transformed into meat, just as the tree is transformed into timber.*

Ordinary households no longer raise and slaughter their own animals. What was a commonplace event has become an aberration. The connection we once had with the meat that we eat has gone. On the rare occasion when we have to kill a live animal (usually a fish or crustacean) we do it but, if we are honest, most of don't want to. There is an instinctive revulsion against the taking of another life that is part of what makes us human. In the *Alice B. Toklas Cookbook*, Alice describes how she buys and kills a live carp. It is her first kill:

> *Horror of horrors. The carp was dead, killed, assassinated, murdered in the first, second and third degree. Limp, I fell into a chair, with my hands still unwashed reached for a cigarette, lighted it, and waited for the police to come and take me into custody.*

Toklas takes butchery out of the cookbook and into the detective story. Those unwashed hands reaching for a cigarette are straight out of Raymond Chandler, yet underneath her flippant *noir*ish tone there is an acceptance that the fish's death is important. Respect is the key here. I realise that is similar to the tone that Novella Carpenter uses when discussing the slaughter of the animals that she raises on her urban farm in Oakland, California, in her book *Farm City*.

It makes me realise that if we take a little time to think about what happens to the animal that becomes the meat on our table, then we are stripping the insulation away. We may not want to give up eating meat, but we can make sure that when we do buy meat we know where it has come from and how it was raised. The untimely death of a beast on our behalf is something that we should all take time to think about now and again. We may not have to see it, but we should not forget it.

Our modern condition is hopelessly muddled, but the bond between animal and keeper was once simpler and more honest; it permitted the duality that now causes us so much confusion. I have never reared anything for meat, but I have committed premeditated chicken-murder. I spent hours, not months, in the company of an animal that I knew would die for my convenience, and even then it was an uncomfortable experience. But if you haven't eaten fresh meat for months, your feelings about what you would and wouldn't do to put that meat on the table change. In my case I had spent eight months living in a concrete-walled, tin-roofed shack in a very rural part of Zimbabwe as part of a gap-year teaching project. I had eaten mango after mango, and dish after dish of the local leafy green – this tough spinach beet chopped up with onions and tomatoes and the occasional egg was my everyday fare. I also ate the bland, stodgy local maize porridge, *sadza*.

I was very tired of all of it, but choice was limited, with no refrigeration, kitchen, running water or electricity. The nearest small town was about ten miles away and the bus service was infrequent. There was a bottle shop nearby selling beer, fizzy drinks and canned food. I cooked my meals on a rudimentary stove, which was little more than a tin can with wicks welded to a hollow drum filled with kerosene. Despite these limitations, I was determined to cook a decent goodbye supper for the two VSO teachers who also taught at the school. Between them, Miss Smout and Mr Smears had helped me become less of an embarrassment as a teacher. I was very grateful for their tolerance and patient kindness.

That is how I came to spend an afternoon watching a white-feathered chicken, its legs tied together, scrabbling in a circular motion on the concrete outside my room. It was brought to the hut that I shared with four other teachers at around lunchtime, and by mid-afternoon it seemed to have been awaiting its death for years. Once it broke free and flapped across the floor in panic and dismay. There was no doubt in my mind that it knew it was going to die. I had to grab it and tie its legs back together, all the time feeling like an executioner.

If you ignore the odd crab, this is the only time I have bought a live creature, killed, prepared and eaten it. In the end it was not me who dealt the killer blow, although I did hold the chicken down. I got my neighbour, Mrs Jasi, to kill it. She was a strong woman, broad in the body, and brought the hatchet down decisively. The chicken's head came off in one blow, but the headless body ran around for a bit, in what seemed like hopeless cliché, and then fell over sideways. I boiled a saucepan full of water and scalded the bird's skin by pouring it over the carcass. I then sat down to pluck it, letting the feathers blow away into the scrubby wasteland beyond our house. It was satisfying rather than revolting. I cooked it in a saucepan with some thick, sticky brown sherry (Don Juan) from the local bottle shop. The chicken stuck to the bottom of the pan and my fellow teachers and I picked the caramelised skin and flesh off it with relish, whilst drinking the remaining sherry from yoghurt pots. I can still taste that dish; it was by far the most delicious thing I had eaten in all my months of *sadza* and greens. That chicken died for me, but if appreciation is an apt measurement of worth, then its death was not in vain.

PIG FEAST

The pig has intelligent eyes, and his fear was now intelligent. Suddenly, lunging and kicking, he fought like a man, a man fighting off robbers.
John Berger, *Pig Earth*

In Spain the pig-killing and the *matanza* (feast) that follows it take place when winter bites deep and the weather is cold enough to stop the meat from spoiling. So it seems right that my own high-tech version of this event takes place on a night when the cold seeps up from the pavement through the soles of my shoes and the wind seeks out the chinks in my coat.

I hurry inside the glass doors. The noise is very loud. Rapid beats quicken the pulse, squeals (animal and electronic) of feedback assault the ear; the bass travels up through my feet. This is a live performance of 'One Pig', an electronic composition that celebrates the life, death and consumption of a Large White pig. We are in an experimental music venue, Café Oto in Dalston, East London. At the front of the room are five men in white coats: the composer and four band members. They could be butchers, doctors or technicians. They certainly aren't farmers.

The band is standing in front of about eighty people who are seated at tables laid for dinner. There are hay bales, a drum machine, a keyboard synthesiser and a man bobbing and plucking at the red cables that form a cage around him. This is the 'musical pig sty', or 'Sty Harp'. By pulling on the cables wired up to stacks of electronic devices, this band member triggers pig-sounds. The percussionist plays a pigskin drum (made from the hide of the animal we are listening to). It's something between a hoedown, a harvest supper and a rave, and I love it.

Composer Matthew Herbert has taken the clang and thump of electronic music and used the audio life of a pig – every oink, grunt and skittering hoof. The album progresses month-by-month, and the happy squeals of a piglet give way to the sounds of a far larger animal moving about. There is a mounting sense of menace; the movements of the animal sound nervous as it gets into a van and is driven away. It was illegal for the actual killing to be recorded, but Herbert manipulates the sounds so that we are in no doubt what is about to happen. As we progress through the year the musician playing the Sty Harp, changes coats. He takes off his white coat to reveal a deep-red jacket underneath. The sounds build, reverberating up to crisis point. Then comes the ringing plink of blood dripping into a bowl. The pig's life is over and the next stage, his transformation from carcass to cuts of meat, has begun.

A man steps up to the microphone and drags a hacksaw against a bone. It's an uncomfortable sound. This is music mixed with the reality of animal husbandry and slaughter. While others may disagree, I find it very far from grim. Instead it links us back to what we have lost: the connection between raising an animal and then slaughtering it. With a wall of noise Herbert gives this back to us; his crashing waves of sound are stripping away the insulation, bringing us closer to the reality of life and death. It is something the smallholder faces daily, for if you raise your own livestock or poultry this is something you must consider every time you reach down to scratch your pig's appreciative back with a stick or to throw grain down to your birds.

Tonight the emphasis on celebration means that this pig's life is honoured – in this case, by the skill of the chef and the care with which the meat is cooked. The chef is Rosie Sykes; she was there at every stage of the pig's life, from birth to weaning through fattening and then slaughter. Rosie was involved in his butchering and arranged the feast that saw him parcelled up into different cuts and sent off to be cooked by various chefs. Jason Atherton braised the head with five-spice and borage; the pig's shoulder was cooked in cherry beer and served in spelt and crackling buns; he was also made into bacon, salami, a pork pie and lardy-cake ice cream. Fergus Henderson (from the nose-to-tail-eating restaurant St John) fried his tail.

Tonight the audience aren't eating the pig that was slaughtered for the record. That all happened a year ago; the sounds of cooking and eating had to be recorded and then used for this show. This is a different pig, but its meat is just as honoured by the skill of its preparation.

Tail- and ear-frying are next onstage. Rosie puts on a white coat and steps up to the front. She has a large greyish-green-looking pig's ear on a plate, some thick pieces of breaded tail and a bowl of wiggly pig tail-ends dipped in flour. She heats up a big pan of fat and the sound of bubbling oil and smell of sizzling pigskin fills the air. As they listen the audience nibbles on tiny bread rolls and squares of pork crackling. Soon they will eat rillettes, followed by pork braised with celery and prunes, and belly chops served with lentils and roasted pumpkin, before ending with apple crumble and clotted cream.

Later, in the kitchen, we wait for the performance to end, before dishing up the mounds of rillettes, gherkins and slices of sourdough. These go out and we wait; as the time nears for the main courses to go out, the atmosphere in the kitchen heats up a bit. As a non-professional, I am given the task of removing the yellow leaves from a large box of watercress. Rosie and the two other cooks, Laura and Tom, slice the pork loin off the bone and get the gravy ready. At the same time as the meat main courses, we send out long oval platters of freckled chicory and watercress.

No sooner have they gone out than the waiters come back with immediate requests for more salad. It is obvious that not all the avant-garde music lovers feel that comfortable about listening to an animal's death and then eating its flesh. Young children, befuddled by anthropo-morphic cartoons, struggle with this daily. It's hard to watch *Babe* and then eat up your sausages. Modern meat-eaters are a very confused bunch. How to balance our affection and reverence for animals with our desire to eat meat is something that is hard to relearn. It's something that past meat-eaters did much better. John Berger talks about this in his book *About Looking*:

Animals . . . were subjected and worshipped, bred and sacrificed.

Today the vestiges of this dualism remain among those who live intimately with, and depend upon, animals. A peasant becomes fond of his pig and is glad to salt away his pork. What is significant, and is so difficult for the urban stranger to understand, is that the two statements in that sentence are connected by and and not but.

The noise has been cacophonous, the fact of the pig's death unavoidable. The crashing sounds brought back the excitement and energy of the illegal raves that I went to as a teenager, but this time fuelled by wine and sumptuous food, not Ecstasy. It's like nothing I've ever been to before and I think it's a fairly unbeatable combination, but not everyone is happy. PETA, the animal-rights group, has strongly criticised Matthew Herbert for what they see as his exploitation of an animal's death. But I think they've got it the wrong way round: Herbert respectfully illuminates the journey of the animal that becomes the meat on our table. That said, it's strong stuff and I am sure one or two people have undergone a vegetarian conversion tonight.

I take home a small pot of rillettes and the long back and rib bones left over from the roast, to make stock for a rich carrot-and-potato soup. This ear-splitting celebration is as close as I am going to get to a modern-day *matanza.* We may not have scraped the pig's skin free of bristles and turned every last piece of intestine into something edible, but it has been a collective experience and one that ended with a full belly and a good feeling.

Rillettes – Potted Pork

Belly pork, salted, cooked slowly in fat and then shredded and flavoured with spices and seasoning, makes a lovely coarse meat paste. Sealed with a thick layer of lard, it keeps for months. The fat prevents the air (and microorganisms) reaching the meat and causing spoilage. Slow-cooking the meat also gets rid of the moisture necessary for bacteria to flourish. Rillettes make a good simple lunch or supper, eaten with chutney, some cornichons and crusty, chewy toast. Double the amount and you have enough to feed a roomful of people – it's simple and beats flaccid vol-au-vents any day of the week.

Serves 4

> *1kg pork belly (rind removed) and shoulder, diced into 1cm pieces*
> *2 or 3 cloves*
> *½ tsp ground allspice*
> *1 tsp freshly chopped thyme leaves*
> *1 tbsp orange zest*
> *sea salt and black pepper*
> *2 tbsps goose or duck fat or lard*
> *a bouquet garni made with parsley, thyme and bay*
> *1 tsp sherry vinegar*

Preheat the oven to 140°C/gas mark 1.

Combine the meats with the spices, chopped thyme, orange zest and seasoning.

Pile the mixture into a small casserole with a heavy lid and add either a little goose or duck fat or lard. Push the bouquet garni down into the middle. Season with a little more pepper, but don't add any more salt at this stage. Put on the lid.

Place in the oven (or over a low heat on the hob) for 5–6 hours. When the meat is very tender (it should collapse when pressed with a wooden spoon), take it out and drain it through a sieve, collecting the fat in a bowl. There will be both clear and cloudy fat, and some juices. Pour off the clear fat at the top and reserve both clear and cloudy fats separately. Separate the meat juices and use for something else (see below).

Put a clean bowl underneath the meat and press it down so that any extra fat drips through the sieve. Then, fistful by fistful, squeeze the meat – doing this by hand, rather than machine, means that you can squeeze out any bones. If you prefer, you can pound the meat using a pestle and mortar. The mixture should still be stringy not pulverised.

Tip the meat onto a board and, using two forks, pull it apart into thin shreds. Season it with salt and pepper. Return the meat to a large pan and add the cloudy fat and the sherry vinegar. Stir well and heat until all is well mixed (about 15 minutes). Pot the rillettes into small sterilised jars (see page 115); but you don't need to sterilise them if you are going to be eating it all within a week.

Pour over the clear fat to a depth of about 1 cm and reserve the rest. Wait for the fat to solidify, then refrigerate the jars. The next day, melt the remaining clear fat again and top up the rillettes so that there is a thick layer of fat on top. Sealed in this way, they will keep for two months in a refrigerator or cold larder. Do allow the rillettes to come up to room temperature before serving, and eat them within a week once you have broken the seal of fat.

THE MEAT JUICES

If you had also added the meat juices to your pork, you would have achieved a different result: meat encased in a jelly, as in brawn. You can keep these rich meat juices in the fridge, or freeze them to add to a quick soup of tinned white beans or to enrich a gravy.

Offal

Being a modern peasant means eating up your offal. Eating only the prime cuts of an animal is wasteful, and expensive too. As demand drives industry, it may also lead us into a nightmarish food future. In Margaret Atwood's apocalyptic novel *Oryx and Crake* all food is produced in laboratories. A creature has been designed that will grow twenty chicken breasts in two weeks. This gross, headless tube with its accelerated growth is like a 'chicken hookworm', an 'animal protein tuber':

> [It] *was a large bulblike object that seemed to be covered with stippled whitish-yellow skin. Out of it came twenty thick fleshy tubes, and at the end of each tube another bulb was growing.*

Eventually, after cataclysmic events occur, the narrator is left as a kind of dystopian Robinson Crusoe, trying to survive in a wilderness where 'ChickieNobs' run wild. This may be science fiction, but we should all be aware of the effect that our food choices make.

Eating offal is a habit we have fallen out of love with, but one that every modern peasant would do well to rediscover. The trouble is that most of us are squeamish. For the modern meat-eater brought up on cubes of lean meat, the sight of an animal's internal organs offends. We just aren't used to chopping up brains, lungs, spleens or even kidneys. I am no different, but, having forced myself to eat more offal, I now love it – not every day, but now and then. I am far from brave, so I have sought recipes that don't exactly conceal the fact that I am eating offal, but neither are they in-your-face.

Gayettes **or Faggots**

Gayettes (in Provence) or faggots (in Wiltshire) are the perfect choice for the offal-phobic cook to start with. They were often made on the day of the pig killing.

Traditionally, various non-beauty-prize-winning parts of the pig (kidneys, heart, lungs, spleen, liver) are minced together with flesh and fat, then mixed with spices and blanched greens. This mixture is shaped into balls which are then wrapped in caul fat (the lacy membrane that covers an animal's internal organs) and baked. The result is rich, rough pâté-like balls that can be eaten hot with mash, or cold with mustard and pickles. They are offal, but in a highly palatable form. I bought my first *gayettes* from a charcuterie in a Provençal town close to the Italian border and they were every bit as good as they looked. I was instantly converted.

Don't be put off by the need for caul fat. If you can't find it, then you can wrap the *gayettes* in blanched cabbage leaves and pack them close together in a well-buttered gratin dish. Unless you are butchering your own pig, you may find it hard to source lungs or spleen, in which case stick to what you can get: pig or chicken livers (veal liver is expensive) and/or kidneys. However, most butchers will get caul for you if you ask for it in advance. Fat is usually discarded, so you may even get it for free. You can use a combination of 50:50 minced shoulder and belly pork.

Serves 4

> *1 bunch of spinach leaves*
> *1 bunch of chard leaves*
> *a little olive oil*
> *500g pork mince*
> *200g pork fat, minced*
> *100g pig's liver, finely chopped*
> *100g chicken liver, finely chopped*

1 or 2 kidneys, diced (optional)
1 shallot, finely chopped
2 garlic cloves, finely chopped
1 tbsp brandy
a small bunch of freshly chopped sorrel (10–15 leaves)
a pinch each of ground nutmeg, cinnamon and cloves
a few sprigs of freshly chopped thyme leaves
a good pinch of sea salt and several grindings of black pepper

Wrapping
150g or 2 sheets of caul fat, or 16–18 cabbage leaves, separated, blanched in
*   boiling salted water and then refreshed in cold water*
splash of white-wine vinegar

Preheat the oven to 180°C/gas mark 4.

Wash the spinach and chard. Blanch the chard briefly in boiling salted water and drain well. Place in a saucepan with the washed spinach and some olive oil. Heat until wilted, then drain and leave to cool, before squeezing out the water and chopping finely.

Mix all the other ingredients (except the wrapping) together until well blended. Shape the mixture into balls about the size of tangerines.

Soak the caul fat (if using) in a bowl of water with a splash of vinegar – this makes it easier to unwrap. Spread the lacy membrane out and cut into squares about 8 x 8cm. Put a dollop of the faggot mixture in the centre of each membrane square and pull the edges in to form a nice little bundle, à la Dick Whittington. Alternatively, put the paste into the centre of a cabbage leaf and draw the edges together, folding them around. Put your parcels, seam down, into a well-buttered or larded gratin dish and dot with butter.

Bake for up to 1½ hours or until well browned. Baste three or four times, starting after about 20 minutes or when the juices begin to run. Put a sheet of baking parchment over the *gayettes* if they start to brown too much. Either leave them to cool and eat cold with mustard or chutney, or serve hot with mashed potato and vegetables. I find the richness of the forcemeat goes well with sauerkraut (see page 119).

Brains

Good fresh brains are firm-looking, the form cleanly and symmetrically
defined, the surface moistly glistening in aspect; they are white with a
pearl cast, only the filigree network of thread-like veins in the surface
membrane showing red.

Richard Olney, *Simple French Food*

Have you ever wanted to eat brains? Most people wince at the thought of it. If I am honest, I did too. Even so, one recent summer morning I found myself in the kitchen of chef and food writer Simon Hopkinson, about to prepare a pair of calves' brains. The air was heavy, threatening sudden storms. Wind tossed the tops of the trees in the gardens opposite. The flat was simultaneously exquisitely tidy and cluttered. I smelled cigarette smoke, coffee and something crisping in a pan. Two elegant Burmese cats, one light and one dark, twined themselves around Simon's legs. It felt grown-up. I wanted to move in.

How did I come to be here? Simon has never made any secret of his admiration for Richard Olney; they share a love of 'purity of effect'. Not only had Olney eaten several times at Simon's South Kensington restaurant, Hilaire, but Simon had also stayed with Olney at his Provençal home. So to take one step closer to a writer who has long fascinated me, I asked Simon if I could come to his house and cook brains, and he said yes.

Richard Olney was a rarity among great food writers – a cook whose food was as highly polished as his prose. The precise, revelatory nature of his writing was matched in life by an extraordinary level of technical skill in the kitchen, a level that very few professional chefs attain. There are other great prose stylists in the world of food, just as there are highly skilled chefs who write books, but in no one else were these two qualities so perfectly balanced. The writer M. F. K. Fisher may muse beautifully and lyrically, but no one can convince me that she could really cook; and while Elizabeth David's prose is peerless, her instincts as a cook err on the side of simplicity (no bad thing) rather than highly wrought technique. Olney's ability to excel in two distinct areas of expertise was rare and exerted a strong fascination.

If you have loved food for years, have regularly and willing immersed yourself in the ritual of reading about it, preparing it and then eating it, there will be writers whom you trust above all others; whose books, once opened, always increase the sum of your culinary knowledge; whose recipes never fail you. Even in the pages of those trusted books – books whose dust jackets are curling, frayed and spotted with grease – there will be pages that you skip over. The brains page of *Simple French Food*, Richard Olney's 1974 classic, was one such. Whether due to conditioning or squeamishness, I had never wanted to cook brains, but one day curiosity got the better of me. I was amazed by what I learnt.

Olney has a painter's eye. He describes what he sees, not what he expects to see. His description of brains takes that ingredient away from the slaughterhouse and the contents of a split and bloody skull and onto the jeweller's bench. He is right to use words such as 'pearl', 'filigree' and 'rosy', for some parts of an animal are so alien to our narrow modern palates that they must be reimagined before we can even think of stomaching them. There was something in his description of these brains that made me long to have a go at peeling back the blood-streaked membrane to discover the 'subtlety and nuance' of brains poached in a vinegar court bouillon. It was also a test of Olney and myself. Could I enjoy something that my instinct told me to abhor, just because he told me to? Or would I fail to live up to his exacting standards?

The brains, far from being repulsive, were curiously beautiful, kinked in fat bubble-letter Ms and Ws. The membrane was thin and translucent, and peeled back beautifully, something Olney said would only happen with the freshest of brains. These brains had come in little rectangular plastic boxes. I don't know why, but the fact that they had been pressed into a rectangle disappointed me. Once released from the box, however, they soon plumped out and took on the reassuringly familiar shape (admittedly from cartoons) of a brain.

Brains don't feature much on today's restaurant menus, but if you do find them, they will most likely be served fried with a sauce of brown butter and capers. In London they currently appear this way at both the Knightsbridge bistro Racine (whose chef Henry Harris once worked for Simon Hopkinson) and at Bibendum, the South Kensington restaurant that Simon once cooked at and still has a hand in. This classic combination is, according to Olney, the 'purest way to appreciate brains'. I asked Simon when he had last eaten brains and he replied that it was two weeks ago, at Bibendum, 'with brown butter and capers!' Today, however, we were trying something else: *Cervelles de Veau Froides à la Crème*, a dish of chilled brains covered in a dressing of double cream whisked together with lemon juice and mustard and garnished with chives and chopped celery. It sounded rich, but turned out to be a good dish for a sultry summer day.

Some people cannot tolerate imperfection. Olney was one of them. Simon, in his own gentle way, is another, and in this case the ideal choice of cooking companion. We slid the membranes off standing side-by-side at the counter, each at our own bowl. I couldn't help but notice that, even taking great care, my clumsy fingers were ripping the surface of the brain. I tactfully deferred to Simon and was set to chopping a carrot for the court-bouillon (see page 165). How do you chop a carrot for a world-class chef? I did it with great care. I cut thin discs with the reassuringly uncheffy plastic-handled knife that Simon passed me.

We filled a large oval Le Creuset dish with water and home-made tarragon vinegar from a bottle densely packed with tarragon leaves, and put the whole lot on to boil with the aromatics and the carrot. When the liquid had infused, we slid the brains in too and gently poached them for twenty minutes or so, lid ajar. Meanwhile we made the cream dressing. For this recipe to work the brains would have to be chilled and we only had a couple of hours, so when they were firm (something Simon checked by pressing his fingers down on top of the brains) we placed them on a plate in front of the open window. They were dull now and slightly discoloured, with a brownish tinge, but this wouldn't matter, said Simon, as the dressing would cover them. Once the brains had cooled, Simon cut them vertically into half-centimetre slices; inside they were shiny, very subtly marbled and quite appetising-looking.

Simon spread them out on two plates, pointing out the brainstem to me as he did so. Then he poured over the dressing, finishing them by sprinkling over the chives and celery – the cream and green colours were pretty on the plate. We sat down at the table and ate them. The brains were, as Olney had promised, 'wonderfully creamy' with 'a firm yet melting' texture. They were rich – not something you would want to eat every day – and somewhere between a mousse and the yielding-but-firm texture of rare liver. Whilst we ate the thunder boomed, lightning flashed and the rain fell in sheets outside the window.

Calf's Brains with a Cream Dressing, Chives and Celery

Serves 2

1 fresh calf's brain
2 celery sticks, peeled and finely diced
a small bunch of chives, snipped into small pieces

Court-bouillon
1 litre water
2 tbsp tarragon vinegar
1 carrot, 1 onion and the green parts of a head of celery, all peeled and thinly
*   sliced*
a bouquet garni made with parsley, thyme and bay
sea salt
1 tsp black peppercorns

Sauce
1 tsp Dijon mustard
juice of ½ lemon
sea salt and black pepper
200ml double cream (the pourable kind)

Tip the brains out of their packaging and into a bowl of cold water to soak whilst you prepare the court-bouillon.

Assemble all the court-bouillon ingredients in a heavy-based pan and simmer for 30 minutes, with the lid on, to infuse.

Whilst the aromatics are simmering, peel the membrane off the brains. Do this very carefully and try not to rip the surface. Slip the brains into the court-bouillon and simmer very slowly for 20–30 minutes, with the lid half on.

Lift the brains out gently with a slotted spoon and place them on a plate to cool. (Olney recommends laying a cloth moistened with the court-bouillon over them, to prevent discolouring, and putting them in the fridge to cool. We let ours cool on a plate in front of the window with no ill effects.)

To make the sauce, whisk together the mustard, lemon juice and salt and pepper. Taste and adjust the seasoning, adding more lemon if need be. Whisk in the cream.

Slice the brains thinly (about ½ cm thick) and lay them on a plate. Pour over the sauce and then sprinkle over the celery and chives. Serve with steamed new potatoes, scrupulously peeled and dressed with very good olive oil, salt and black pepper.

Sausage

For food writer Jane Grigson, France was the country for fresh sausage. Writing in 1967 she noted that the sausage was still 'an honourable form of nourishment and pleasure'. If she were alive today she might be happy to observe that some English sausages now fit that description too. French sausage has, in her words, 'ebullient variety', being freshly made in all regions in many forms with 100 per cent meat (aside from the seasoning). The same could very well be said of German sausage. 'Wurst and philosophy, these are the German masterpieces,' said the gourmet aesthete Elizabeth Robins Pennell in her *Guide for the Greedy by a Greedy Woman*, first published in 1896. So perhaps it should come as no surprise to find a German behind one of the best current examples of the craft of sausage-making. The proprietor of the Franconian Sausage Company is a chef named Jean-Paul Habermann, who may sound French, but is actually from northern Bavaria. Large in spirit and in body, Jean-Paul takes enormous pride in every aspect of his business. The British banger can sometimes be the repository of minced meat trash (that is, left-over bits of meat recovered from the carcass by high-pressure hoses at the abattoir). Jean-Paul is quick to set his sausages on a higher plane.

'I am not a butcher,' he says, laughing and chuckling at this preposterous thought, 'I am a chef, I don't use lips, ears and arseholes. I,' he says thumping his broad chest, 'have a heart.'

Habermann worked as a chef for sixteen years, but got tired of the long hours and lack of weekends. He decided to start making sausages and, with a loan from his wife Donna's family, was able to get going. As with almost every other artisan enterprise I've visited, the Franconian Sausage Company occupies a railway arch. The relatively low rents that Network Rail charge have acted as a start-up loan for all kinds of food-related companies – companies that might otherwise struggle to get off the ground. Setting up in butchery means more than just finding a workshop. It's a costly business: you have to build sterile workrooms with hygienic floors and expensive, highly specialised machinery. Once you've done that, you have to build a reputation. Donna and Jean-Paul are no longer married, but they still run the business together.

By concentrating on one type of production – the mincing and spicing of meat – they have become successful, with a reputation as the experts to go to for bespoke products. This fact is borne out by their client list, which includes many famous London restaurants. The Franconian provides a unique service: the manufacture of high-quality sausages of every kind at very short notice (for some customers the cut-off time is 5 p.m. the night before).

Focus has also honed Jean-Paul's ability to combine spices, and this skill is now instinctive. That doesn't mean he has become blasé – far from it. His attention to detail is intense. This becomes apparent when we visit the spice room. On shelves lining a cubbyhole behind the office are rows of plastic ice-cream boxes. In them are many of the spices that you associate with pork, such as nutmeg, mace, pepper and paprika, along with some less obvious ones like cardamom.

This last spice was used in a bespoke sausage that the Franconian made for the Corbin & King restaurant, the Delaunay in Aldwych. This was a dense tube of pigs' liver and cardamom. The relative intensity of spices such as nutmeg and mace has fallen off in recent years, says Jean-Paul. This affects the amount he must use; it also affects the price, for not only are the spices less potent and must be used in greater quantities, but they are also more expensive. He thinks he may spend from £6,000–10,000 a year on spices alone.

Sausage-making in Europe dates back to Roman times. Grigson points out that the words 'sausage', *saucisse* and *saucisson* all derive from the Latin word *salsus* ('salted'). The first sausages were created so that the small parts of the pig could be preserved in salt to eat in winter. They were not fresh, but dried and smoked. While Habermann already smokes many of his sausages (Toulouse sausages, frankfurters and small cocktail sausages) he is eager to start making air-dried salami on a larger scale. To do so he will have to create a 'weather station', a room in which the humidity and temperature can be rigorously controlled. His desire is to produce a new kind of British charcuterie that does not ape Europe, but reflects the environment in which it is made.

Jean-Paul is bolstered by the success of British artisan cheeses, which use traditional methods to create products as idiosyncratic as their makers. He wants to use British meats and flavours to make original products. He claims to be the only person to produce a smoked black pudding, and already makes a *torizo* (a beef chorizo), as well as venison salami made with locally produced Jensen's gin. Jean-Paul wants to make mutton and wild-boar salami as well. He wants to cater for those barred on religious grounds from eating pork, and has already experimented with veal bacon made from calf's belly.

The next place we see is the meat storeroom, where two large crates hold plastic-wrapped beef, pork and salt-marsh lamb. Habermann gets several pallet loads of meat delivered to his sausage workshop each week. I don't want to call this craft business a 'factory', but with more than four tons of product coming out each week, I suppose you could. The beef is Welsh, the pork Irish. Habermann uses Irish pork because, while the British may pride themselves on animal welfare, he is uneasy about what the slaughtering process in Britain does to meat. He doesn't even contemplate Spanish pork, which he says always arrives bruised. The stress of an animal at slaughter can be assessed by testing the pH levels in the meat. According to Jean-Paul, if an animal was stressed at death, the meat goes off quickly, so he doesn't use it.

In this arch there is an admin office, a warren of rooms containing dried goods and spices and a larger room housing the machinery. Habermann is loyal to the technology of his native land; every single machine in here is German. The most terrifying is a bowl with a star-shaped blade with curved, upward-thrusting knives which rotate at 5,000 turns a minute. 'Look at that,' says Habermann, chortling, 'if Sweeney Todd had had that, they would never have caught him – anything goes in there, it comes out as mousse.'

The insides of a hot dog must be made from meat processed into a very smooth emulsion. The only problem is that if the mixture gets too hot, it can split. To combat that the Franconian make their hot dogs with 20 per cent iced water. The result is recognisably hot doggy, but denser and meatier – they definitely fill you up. 'Cheap hot dogs are just fat and water,' says Jean-Paul. 'You can pop them like smarties, until they kill you.'

I shudder and walk on to a ceiling-high metal box, a multi-functional machine that is smoker, steamer and cooker. 'Ah, this machine,' says Habermann, 'I love this machine so much it's sad.' He also seems to love his staff, who, despite the monotony of stuffing meat into sausages day after day in a freezing, windowless box, appear cheerful.

Habermann has lived and worked in England for many years, but the influence of his Bavarian childhood and his accent remain strong. He grew up on a farm and recalls the making of fresh black pudding on pig-killing day. The blood was poured into a basin by his grandmother and cooked immediately, to form an enormous caseless black pudding. His eyes gleam as he recalls how it fluffed up. 'You couldn't stop eating it!' he says. 'With mashed potato and red cabbage, it was just the best.'

When I ask him if he had an ideal sausage in mind when he began, he looks at me almost pityingly. 'Of course,' he says. 'The Nürnberger.' This bratwurst sausage is the pride of his native Franconia, and for Jean-Paul it sets a high standard.

Habermann can make you any kind of sausage. The day I went, I watched link after link of game sausages emerge, to be followed by *koftes*, which are squirted out as balls of spiced minced lamb or game and then pressed by hand onto a thin wooden stick. He warns against sausages that are too uniform. 'People complain if they find gristle,' he says, 'but if you never find gristle, it's a shit product.'

TOP TIPS FOR THE HOME BUTCHER

- Mix the meat for your sausages with the paddle attachment of a food-processor, before you start adding any spice. This lets the meat 'open up', and then you can season it with herbs and spices to greater effect.
- Jean-Paul's ratio of salt and spices to meat is 1kg of meat to 15g salt to 2.1g pepper to 0.1g cinnamon or nutmeg or 0.2g less-potent herbs and spices.
- Use meat and rind in your sausages. The rind (around 10 per cent) gives elasticity, but Jean-Paul warns against using too much. A black pudding that he commissioned from a German sausage-maker had so much rind in it that, after a couple of weeks, it was as bouncy as a rubber ball.
- One of Jean-Paul's favourite sausages is the one he makes for Mark Hix's restaurants: a 50:50 mix of veal and pork, seasoned with cognac and bay leaf. The cognac apparently makes all the difference.

Home-made Sausages

If you want the taste of home-made sausages without the hassle of buying casings and funnels, mix and season your own sausage meat and then shape it into cylinders by hand, or wrap it in pastry or cabbage leaves. Skins are not compulsory. If it is sausage-shaped, it is a sausage.

I first came across the skinless sausage when working on a feature film in Glasgow. The local fried breakfast included a Lorne sausage: a flat square of bright pink sausage meat that is very alarming on first acquaintance, but grows on you (sort of). As I live in East London, I thought I would include a recipe for a now-extinct traditional British sausage, the Epping, which is also skinless and, according to *The Oxford Companion to Food*, once consisted of pork mixed with beef suet, bacon, sage and spices. A less complicated encased version of it is still available at Church's Butchers (established 1888) on Epping High Street. They use a made-to-order seasoning mix of dried sage, salt and pepper. I have used fresh sage and onion tops from the allotment.

Makes approx. 6–8 sausages

> 500g pork shoulder or leg, minced
> 500g belly pork, skin off, minced
> 2 tbsp freshly chopped sage leaves
> 1 tbsp finely chopped green onion tops
> 15g salt
> ½ tsp freshly ground black pepper

Mix the meat in a food-processor with a dough hook. Let it combine for 1–2 minutes, then add the sage, onion tops and seasoning. If you wish, you can keep mixing it for another 1–2 minutes in the processor, but you will get a better bind if you knead it by hand at this stage.

Take the meat out and spread it on a sanitary work surface (glass, marble or steel), or use a plastic chopping board. Knead the meat by smearing it across the counter until the mixture coheres and has become slightly lighter in colour. Cover and refrigerate until you need to use it.

Apart from frying it, you can use the sausage meat crumbled on top of pizzas, as part of a tomato sauce for pasta or to stuff a cabbage. Freeze whatever you don't need.

FORAGED

Fungi

Peasant life is rooted to a particular place. Foraging for ingredients gives you a practical understanding of times past, when culinary choices were shaped by the seasons. If you can also grow your own food, then the first-hand experience of that labour will give you common ground with other producers. By linking ourselves to the seasons – even if it's only via a veg box or a field mushroom picked on a country walk – we can share in the small producer's delight as he gathers a basket of mushrooms, collects spring honey that tastes of elderflower blossom, cuts slender green spikes of asparagus or wraps up sides of home-cured bacon.

The names of things are very important. Knowing the names makes them real; it helps them stand out. Names have power; they illuminate. If you can name trees, flowers, plants and birds you are adding breadth and colour to the world around you. When you can differentiate, you can remember, and fixing things in your memory slows time. In the case of fungi, you are also acquiring knowledge with life-or-death significance.

'I love a broad margin to my life,' said Henry Thoreau. And while he was writing about taking a whole day to simply sit and think outdoors, I like to think that a deeper knowledge of the natural world adds another kind of margin to our lives. In the late 1930s my grandmother was bringing up two small boys. She taught herself the names of the common wild flowers they passed on their daily walks down the high-hedged Devon lanes. So began an interest that sustained her until her death in her nineties. By which time she had become a notable botanist with the names of hundreds of rare ferns, orchids and flowers rattling around her brain. As well as slowing time by teaching yourself to look for and name what is around you, you also get the satisfaction that comes from scraping away the surface, going down into that which is both deeply real and eternal.

For those who love to seek out and eat wild foods, mushroom-hunting, which usually takes the form of a gentle ramble through the woods, would seem a fairly innocuous habit; it must rate quite low in terms of risk of serious injury when compared with shooting or even fishing. If you use bullet or hook rather than basket and knife you take all the risk up front, while for the fungi-obsessed death waits at the table. I had heard enough stories of accidental poisoning to make me extremely nervous of gathering anything other than a field mushroom. Ignorance is definitely not bliss when it comes to mushrooms.

'The best place to study fungi is in your own particular environment,' says Patience Gray, whose love of fungi and deep knowledge and skill at identifying and then cooking them are revealed in her iconic food memoir, *Honey from a Weed*. Gray's interest in wild mushrooms was first stimulated by wartime necessity. She was living with her young son and daughter at her grandmother's house on the edge of a pine forest in Sussex. The nearest village was a mile away and she didn't drive. Food was scarce (this was something of a consistent theme throughout her life) and so she was forced to look around her for whatever was growing wild. She began sensibly enough with the help of an expert, a biologist from the Ministry of Agriculture. At weekends they gathered everything they could find, edible or not and then identified them. They whittled their specimens down from 200 to a list of thirty delicious wild mushrooms. Sixty years later her daughter Miranda can still remember the most delicious of all: the orange milk cap (*Lactarius deliciosus*), which Gray (by then living in the extreme south of Italy) describes in her usual succinct, hunger-inducing prose as being at its best when 'oiled, dressed with garlic, salt and parsley and cooked on an oiled plaque in the oven'.

A GENTLEMAN OF THE WOODS

I had no biologists from the Ministry of Agriculture to hand, but what I did have was a very dedicated mushroom-forayer. Martin Ellory is a cook, writer and lover of fungi; a friend of a friend, famed as someone who knows a lot about mushrooms and where to find them.

Unlike that of Patience, with her easy access to Salentine pine forests, my particular environment happens to be London parkland, characterised by turf that has been trampled by football boots, scorched by canine urine, packed down by off-road buggies and mountain bikes and broken up by tarmac paths. As an ideal environment for finding fungi it's a far cry from the prolific beech glades of the New Forest. Fool that I am, I mistakenly assume that a fine day is the perfect one for a foray (confusingly you forage for wild foods in general, but foray for mushrooms). I call Martin up and arrange to meet him outside the overground station on Hampstead Heath.

Heat shimmers in the road as my shirt gradually unsticks from my back while I wait for Martin – it had been a fierce and stifling bike ride across town. After about ten minutes he appears. He is tall, dark-haired and, unlike most other foragers I have met, fairly clean-looking. He is also proud of his skill. Martin's worry that we won't find anything manifests itself in him instantly pushing a carrier bag towards me; inside are several ziplock bags containing five different kinds of fungi that he has found and dried. They are his insurance: small, dusty grey-and-black curled circles called Jew's ears (the fungus *Hirneola auricula-Judae*), so called because they grow from the bark of elder trees (the tree that Judas hanged himself from); hornlike trompettes; fairy-ring champignons; and the seaweed-like whorls of the yellow cauliflower fungus. But my greedy cook's eyes widen most at the stuffed bag full of sliced porcini mushrooms.

The day we meet is a spectacular and unseasonal scorcher. The temperature on this late September day is breaking all kinds of records. Heat rises from the Heath, and this dry heat means that moisture-loving mushrooms are scarce, while the bright light means that what is there is hard to see. We start in an area where each summer fairs and circuses park their caravans and trailers. The ground is hard and dry. We are looking for fairy-ring champignons (*Marasmius oreades*), the latter part of whose Latin name (*oreades*) means 'mountain nymph'. The fungus reveals itself by lighter rings of grass, and on wetter days after rainfall in a thick crop of small pale-brown mushrooms with a little nipple-like rise on the cap.

We stand on the edge of a pale ring that I would never have seen unless it was pointed out to me. By Martin's calculation, this particular colony is thirty years old. The growth is about 20cm a year and our circle is about 6 metres in diameter. Thirty years of stamping fairground feet have not extinguished these particular inhabitants of the Heath, but few people eat them now, although once this mushroom was a staple of peasant life. Common and abundant, it was added to meat pies to give bulk, texture and flavour, in the same way as oysters were.

Though these mushrooms are common and tasty (gaining in flavour when dried), care should be taken not to confuse them with the toxic *Clitocybe rivulosa*, or 'false champignon', which often grows alongside. This very poisonous mushroom is greyish-white and has a cup-shaped cap with a depression in the centre. Confusion arises from the fact that, when it is wet, the 'false champignon' looks brown. A quick look at the gills of the toxic mushroom reveals them to be thin, crowded and running down to a short stem, in contrast to the edible fairy-ring mushroom, which is longer-stemmed and has more thickly spaced gills.

It is illegal to pick mushrooms on Hampstead Heath unless you are part of an organised foray, but there is nothing to stop you looking around and trying to identify what you find. We walk steadily around the Heath for about two hours. We find plenty of *Russula* (charcoal-burners), but their wide spectrum of colours and easy confusion with toxic mushrooms make them best avoided by beginners. Along the way we also find (or rather Martin points out to my blind, untrained eye) birch boletes, bay boletes and chestnut boletes (*Gyroporous castaneus*). None of them are in any condition to eat, so we are not tempted to break the law. We find rotted specimens of St George's mushroom (*Calocybe gambosa*), but no sign of the ceps (*Boletus edulis*) that Martin tells me sometimes grow thickly beneath some trees close to a main road. The habit of fungi propagating under stress means that you often find them near roads or paths. The tarmac stops them from spreading any further, so instead they propagate.

As we walk I learn a little more about the sensibility of this particular forayer. Martin has his own code of the woods. Of all the mushroom books that his interest has prompted him to read, his favourite of all is a simple pamphlet held together by staples and produced by the Mycological Association of the Pyrenees. The book is written (in French) by the president of that association, a self-proclaimed peasant and gentleman *du bois*. His code is as follows: mushrooms grow wild, and as a free food they should not be sold for profit; nor should you collect more than you can eat yourself. This last point is a particularly hard one to hold fast to. Martin recently found himself faced with a forest clearing blanketed with ceps and took more than he could possibly eat. On the way home the basket broke as he was going over a stile and his precious hoard was scattered. He felt he had been judged, especially when the bag that he then used turned out to have plastic woven into the cloth; this made the mushrooms decompose and go slimy. He still seemed genuinely upset by the experience.

Martin also believes that you should leave the wood and the fungi as you find them. If you pick up a mushroom and then decide not to take it, you should replace it as it was. If you do gather more than you can use, you should pass the surplus on to a friend. You must not stamp on and destroy poisonous mushrooms, although this is what children – with their horror of and fascination with deadly mushrooms – always want to do.

Martin has his own strong views on what mushrooms should and should not be used for. Mushroom soup is an abomination, as are recipes that generically call for 'wild mushrooms'. This sweeping generalisation fails, according to Martin, to take into account the wide range of different flavours and textures of fungi.

Here are three recipes that I hope he will approve of:

Fairy Pie (or Chicken-and-Mushroom Pie, for the less whimsically inclined)

This method of first poaching a chicken, and then using the stock and meat to construct a chicken pie, is Simon Hopkinson's. It is reliably good and thoroughly heartening, though it does take a bit of time. I have adapted it to include dried fairy-ring champignons. Soaking them first in the stock adds to the richness of the pie's liquor.

Serves 4

> *Flaky pastry*
> *200g plain flour*
> *100g butter*
> *½ tsp sea salt*
> *squeeze of lemon juice*
> *100–150ml ice-cold water*

Sift the flour into a bowl, then drop in the butter, turning it to coat it in the flour and, as you do so, cut it into small cubes. Add the salt, cover and refrigerate for ten minutes or so.

When the flour and butter are nice and cold, take the bowl out of the fridge. Add a squeeze of lemon to the ice-cold water. Use a table knife to mix and chop the flour and butter together, adding the water little by little until everything begins to cohere. Gather the pastry up in a piece of cling film (it will still look quite stringy). Knead the pastry briefly through the cling film, then refrigerate for at least 1 hour.

Half an hour before you need to use the pastry, roll it out, fold it in half and then into quarters, give it another brief roll and then refrigerate it again.

Pie filling
1 free-range chicken (approx. 1.5kg)
2 cloves
2 celery sticks
1 carrot
1 shallot
a few parsley stalks
1 small fennel bulb, outer leaves removed and sliced into slender ½cm strips
2 leeks, washed and sliced into rings, green parts reserved
300ml water
a handful of dried fairy-ring champignons (approx. 50)

Sauce
40g butter
50g plain flour
325ml milk

Egg wash
1 egg
1 tbsp milk

Put the chicken, breast down, in a large saucepan or flameproof casserole dish with the cloves, celery, carrot, shallot, parsley stalks, fennel strips and the green parts of the leeks. Pour in the water and bring to the boil. Cover and simmer for 20 minutes, then turn over the chicken and simmer for another 15–25 minutes. Take the chicken out, tipping out any juices from inside it, and allow to cool. Strain the stock through a sieve.

Immerse the dried mushrooms in a cup of kettle-hot water and leave to soak for half an hour.

Make a white sauce by melting the butter in a pan and adding the flour. Stir and cook briefly to form a roux. Heat the milk gently in a separate pan and then whisk into the roux gradually, beating all the time. Cook over a very low heat (use a heat diffusion mat if possible), whisking occasionally, until smooth and thick, then set aside.

When the chicken is cool, remove the skin and cut the meat up into mouthfuls.

Slice the fennel bulb. Put the drained mushrooms and stock into a pan and add the sliced leeks and fennel. Simmer the vegetables until they're just cooked but not soft, then remove and put in a bowl with the chicken. Reduce the stock by half, then whisk it into the white sauce. Simmer until very smooth. Pour over the chicken and vegetable mixture and allow to cool.

Preheat the oven to 180°C/gas mark 4.

Put the chicken mixture into a pie dish and butter around the lip. Roll out the pastry to about 5mm thick. Cut a strip and fit it around the lip of the pie dish, then press it down firmly. Cut a larger piece to fit over the entire pie, then press the pastry edges together (dip your fingers into some flour if it's all getting a bit sticky). Trim off any excess and go round again, pressing the pastry down with the tines of a fork. Brush the surface of the pie with egg wash and decorate. Cut out small pastry shapes (I like flowers and small, very simplified birds). Make a couple of slits to release the steam.

Bake for about 1 hour – the pastry should be golden and a rich smell of pie should fill the kitchen. Let the pie sit for 10 minutes before serving it with mashed potato.

Chanterelles on Toast

In Sweden the link between the countryside and the city is still strong, with ingredients brought in daily for roadside sales. My friend Frank arrived from Stockholm with a carrier bag of chanterelles that he had bought from a street vendor for a relative song. Blanched and then fried, they made three plates of exquisite mushrooms on toast, washed down with special-offer Prosecco from the local off-licence.

Serves 4

> *1kg chanterelles, foraged or bought*
> *50g butter*
> *2 garlic cloves, peeled and crushed with the flat of a heavy knife*
> *sea salt and black pepper*
> *3 slices of sourdough bread, toasted*

Wipe the chanterelles with a clean tea towel and cut off any woody parts of the stems. Place a medium-sized heavy-based pan on the stove and half-fill it with salted water. When the water comes to the boil, plunge the mushrooms in and cook for 2 minutes. Lift them out with tongs or a slotted spoon. Boil the liquid down to reduce it by half to a flavoursome brown sauce. Once this is done you can fry the mushrooms.

In a heavy-based frying pan heat the butter and garlic and, when the butter has melted, add the mushrooms and stir well. Fry for 1–2 minutes before adding the sauce from the pan. Stir well and season, before spooning onto the sourdough toast on individual plates.

Potato and Porcini Gratin

Serves 4

> 600g waxy yellow potatoes (Charlotte are good), washed but not peeled
> 200ml single cream
> 100ml milk
> 50g dried porcini mushrooms, soaked in a cup of kettle-hot water for 30
>   minutes
> 1 garlic clove, peeled and lightly crushed
> 1 tbsp butter (approx. 15g), plus a little for greasing
> sea salt and black pepper
> 3 tbsp finely grated Parmesan

Preheat the oven to 180°C/gas mark 4.

Slice the potatoes very thinly (using a mandolin is quickest). Put them in a colander and rinse under the cold tap, stirring them around with your hand. Toss the slices, wrapped up in a clean tea towel, until dry.

Whisk the cream and the milk together in a bowl. Drain the mushrooms and pat dry on kitchen paper.

Rub the garlic over the inside of a gratin dish (a deep ovenproof ceramic dish), making sure you don't leave any lumps of garlic behind (just the juice). Butter the dish. Put a single layer of potato slices over the bottom. Season lightly. Add a few slices of the reconstituted porcini. Repeat the layers until you have used up all your potato slices and mushrooms. Dot the top of the gratin with small pieces of butter and pour over the creamy mixture.

Sprinkle the top with grated Parmesan. Cover the dish with foil and bake for 45 minutes, then take the foil off and bake the gratin for another 15 minutes, bringing the total cooking time up to 1 hour. Test the middle with the point of a knife to make sure all the potato is cooked through; give it another 10 minutes if you need to.

GYPSY FORAGERS

The one herbal reference book I could not be without was written by a remarkable woman. Juliette de Baïracli Levy (1911–2009) was a pioneer of herbal medicine. She was born and educated in Manchester and began training as a vet, but gave up her studies after two years in revulsion at the common practice of vivisection. Instead, she followed an alternative path and dedicated her life to recording the herbal knowledge of Gypsies, farriers and peasants. She is most famous for her two books of herbal medicine, *The Illustrated Herbal Handbook* and *The Herbal Handbook for Farm and Stable*, but wrote many books of memoir and travelogue recording her life travelling with Gypsies all over the world and bringing up her two children in Spain, the New Forest, Galilee and Greece.

Whether she is describing eating foraged strawberries and drinking fresh goats' milk with the Gypsies of Granada, keeping bees in the New Forest or picking wild roses to sell with Gypsies from the West of England, de Baïracli Levy writes with all her senses and her books are full of light and colour. She also offers a respectful insight into the knowledge and ways of a much-maligned group of people. Everywhere she travels she is treated with kindness and welcomed by the Gypsies, once her genuine interest in them has been established.

De Baïracli Levy describes many instances of foods and medicines foraged with Gypsies, including the practice of collecting wild honey and storing crab apples in straw so that they are red and crisp for Christmas. Foraging for herbs to treat dogs and horses has always been a part of Gypsy life and still goes on in this country. Mary Bromiley, an old friend and expert in equine physiotherapy, has told me of the annual talks she has regarding medicinal herbs, with Gypsies whom she meets during the centuries-old horse fair at Bampton in North Devon. They tell her that the use of pesticides on verges makes collecting herbs increasingly difficult. In the city it is always best to pick on land that you are sure has not been sprayed. I have picked bunches of wild rocket growing high up on brick walls beside the canal and harvested bag loads of nettles in a silty ditch beside my allotment.

LIME-FLOWER TEA

In late June and early July the London parks are full of the scent of honey. The common lime (*Tilia x europaea*) is in bloom. A cross between two native species, it may not be as lovely as our native wild varieties, but its presence is still very welcome. Its tasselled blooms can be picked and dried to make a tisane with the scent and taste of honey. Stand next to a lime tree in July and you will hear the roar of hundreds of bees at work.

Take a basket and fill it with lime flowers. At home spread them out on a tray (out of direct sunlight), and after a day or two pack the dried blossoms into a clean jar or tin. When you need a restorative cup, put a dessertspoon of dried flowers into a teapot and fill with boiling water. The tea has calming, mildly sedative qualities, making it a good drink for bedtime or any time of the day when your nerves are feeling frayed. It is also good for soothing aching heads and griping stomachs. Clover flowers, nettles and lemon verbena can also be picked and dried for tisanes.

Nettles and Dandelions

Nettles offer iron-rich leaves at a time of year when home-grown greens are in short supply. They are as tasty and nutritious as the most carefully reared spinach, yet they grow wild all around us, for the most part ignored, if not abhorred. It's not really surprising, for a nettle bites the hand that brushes it; it is one of the most notorious of our indigenous wild plants. Its leaf, once grasped, is never forgotten. Even those blind to every other form of nature can point out a nettle.

The leaves of a nettle contain a burning fluid (formic acid) that blisters human skin but, just like the bee, its sting is sweetened by powerful benefits, and it is both friend and foe. Bees give us honey (not to mention beeswax and the vital work they do as pollinators). Nettles provide greens that are a rich source of minerals and vitamins just when they are most needed, at winter's end.

'Woodland is the natural home of the Nettle,' says Geoffrey Grigson in his *Englishman's Flora,* 'but it travels round with man, grows out of his rubbish, gets a hold where he has disturbed the ground, clings to the site of his dwellings, long after the dwellings themselves have disappeared.'

He goes on to say that this habit of nettles to grow where man has been led to the traditional belief that nettles grew from the bodies of dead men, or in Denmark that clumps of nettles grew where innocent blood had been shed. Richard Mabey lifts the veil on this superstitious belief by explaining in his *Flora Britannica* that nettles will grow naturally in 'fertile, muddy, disturbed' ground, in the silt-rich soil of river valleys and in woodland glades enriched by animal droppings. This is because it needs soil rich in phosphates, which is why we find nettles where men and animals have been. He records how thick patches of dense nettles still grow on the remains of Romano-British villages on Grovely Ridge near Salisbury, which have not been inhabited for 1,600 years. I now know why the silty banks of the gully at the back of my allotment are thick with nettles in springtime.

Aside from childish accidents with clumps of nettles, my knowledge of the other uses of nettles came first from a fairy tale. In the story of the wild swans, a sister must weave eleven nettle-cloth shirts for her brothers, princes who have been turned into swans. She toils each night in secret, working in a graveyard thick with nettles, and in doing so is mistakenly identified as a witch. When she refuses to reveal her purpose in the graveyard she is sentenced to death by burning. As she is taken by cart towards the pyre, through crowds of jeering onlookers, the swans – her brothers – alight on the sides of the tumbrel and, beating their wings, form a shield between her and the mob. The nettle shirts have been completed, except for one arm, and are flung over the swans. Eleven princes now stand beside their sister, one still bearing a wing, which had not been covered by the nettle cloth. This fairy tale is alarming and thrilling in equal measure, combining horror at the thought of having to grasp and weave the ferocious nettle with excitement at the dramatic reversal of fortune, worthy of a blockbuster movie.

Though it might be the last thing you would feel like weaving, nettle cloth was apparently rather a fine thing. Geoffrey Grigson records that the Scottish poet Thomas Campbell (1777–1844) wrote of sleeping in nettle sheets in Scotland and of dining off nettle tablecloths. In more recent times Germany used nettles to make military clothing when it ran short in the First World War. But before you rush out to harvest nettles and start spinning, you might want to know that it took 40kg to make a single shirt.

I doubt anyone will actually want to make nettle cloth, but eating nettles is far less work. It is reassuring to discover from Juliette de Baïracli Levy in her *Illustrated Herbal Handbook* that, aside from tasting good, the 'whole plant is powerfully medicinal from the roots to the seeds'. Nettle roots can be used to treat lymphatic ailments and to expel kidney stones, while the leaves – when eaten as greens and mixed with oats and butter – 'tone up the whole system' and are a cure for anaemia, rheumatism, sciatica, arthritis and infertility. She also records the Gypsy cure for rheumatism, which was to bind together bunches of nettles and then flog the afflicted joints. The stinging and tingling that were produced allegedly rid the joint of pain and restored circulation. Modern medicine has borne out this remedy by using bee venom to soothe inflamed joints. De Baïracli Levy also recommended making nettle tea get rid of catarrh, and using it as a hair wash to improve the hair's colour and texture and to get rid of dandruff.

Nettles appear in the place names of villages such as Nettleton, not far from where I grew up in Wiltshire, and in many different forms as dialect names. Its colloquial names in Britain reflect its magical associations and include 'devil's sheet', 'devil's plaything', 'heg-beg', 'hidgy pidgy' and 'hokey pokey'. I will give Beatrix Potter's impudent Squirrel Nutkin the last word:

> Old Mr B! Riddle-me-ree!
> Hitty Pitty within the wall,
> Hitty Pitty without the wall;
> If you touch Hitty Pitty,
> Hitty Pitty will bite you!

I use nettles in the garden and in the kitchen. On the allotment I cut down nettles and then steep them in a barrel. After a week or two the plants rot down to make a foul-smelling green manure that can be used as a liquid feed in the same way that people use comfrey. Here are a few more palatable uses.

Nettle Frittata

Serves 4 alongside other dishes, or 2 with a salad

1 carrier bag of nettle tops
a little butter for frying
a little olive oil
a pinch of cayenne pepper
a little grated nutmeg
sea salt and black pepper
4 free-range eggs
2 tbsp milk
1 tbsp freshly grated Parmesan

Fill your sink with water and then, wearing rubber gloves, wash the nettles. Use kitchen scissors to snip off the tops, discarding any rough-looking stems or manky-looking leaves. Drain the nettle tops in a sieve or colander.

In a large heavy skillet or frying pan heat a knob of butter and a little oil and add the nettles. Cook over a medium heat, adding the spices and seasoning. Stir continuously until the nettles have wilted, then put them in a sieve to drain. Use tongs to squeeze out any excess moisture. Wipe out the frying pan.

In a bowl beat the eggs (not too vigorously) and add the milk and Parmesan.

Heat a little more butter in the pan and, when the pan is hot (but before the butter browns), add the egg mixture. Swirl it around the pan and, when it begins to coalesce, add the nettles. Continue to swirl the egg mixture around the pan, loosening the edges of the frittata with a knife and tipping the liquid egg into any gaps. When the egg mixture is set, but before the bottom is too brown (around 5 minutes), loosen the bottom of the frittata with a spatula.

Place a plate slightly smaller than the diameter of the pan on top of the frittata and, using oven gloves, tip the pan upside-down, then slide the frittata off the plate back into the pan and cook for a few more minutes. This dish is best served warm, rather than hot from the pan.

Nettle Porridge

In his diary for February 1661 Pepys records eating this dish. His lunch may have been frugal, but he had lobster for supper.

> *25th. Sir Wm. Pen and I to my Lord Sandwich's by coach in the morning to see him, but he takes physic to-day and so we could not see him. So he went away, and I with Luellin to Mr Mount's chamber at the Cockpit, where he did lie of old, and there we drank, and from thence to W. Symons where we found him abroad, but she, like a good lady, within, and there we did eat some nettle porrige, which was made on purpose to-day for some of their coming, and was very good.*

Here is my version, a savoury porridge that makes a sustaining, nutritious and very economical lunch. More to the point, it is far tastier than you might imagine, with hints of spinach and mint. Go on – try it!

Serves 2

> a bunch of tender nettle tops
> 100g porridge oats
> approx. 125ml each of milk and water
> a good pinch of sea salt (probably more than you would put in your breakfast
>   porridge)

Wearing rubber gloves, take the handful of nettle tops and snip off the tender leaves. Fill a pan with salted water and bring to the boil. Plunge the nettles into the water and push them down. Allow the water to come back up to the boil and then drain.

Squeeze the blanched nettles in a clean tea towel to remove all excess water, then chop finely.

Pour the porridge oats into a medium-sized heavy-based pan. Add enough liquid to just cover (half milk, half water). Add the chopped nettles to the pan, then a pinch of salt and cook slowly, stirring as the mixture thickens. If it thickens too much, add a little more milk and water, beating well to break up the nettles. The end result should be a creamy bowlful flecked with green.

Nettle and Walnut Pesto

Blanching the nettles removes the 'sting', so you only need to wear rubber gloves when they are uncooked. This recipe makes a small pot of pesto.

Serves 4 (with pasta)

1 carrier bag of nettle tops
1–2 garlic cloves, peeled and crushed
1 tsp sea salt
30g freshly shelled walnuts, roughly chopped
30g Parmesan, grated
black pepper
100ml extra-virgin olive oil

Wearing rubber gloves, rinse the nettles in plenty of cold water. Then snip off the tender tips and leaves and discard the stalks. Weigh out 100g of the leaves.

Bring a pan of salted water to the boil and plunge the nettles in. Let the water come back up to the boil, then remove the nettles and refresh in cold water. Drain well.

With a pestle, pound the garlic and sea salt together. Add the nuts, cheese and pepper and keep mashing, adding the nettle leaves a few at a time. Add a little of the oil and keep mashing: it takes time, but the smell will keep you going. You can cheat and use a food-processor, but it won't taste as good. Add the rest of the olive oil in a thin dribble, stirring all the time until you have a thick, unctuous paste.

Place in a small bowl or jar and cover with a thin layer of olive oil. Your pesto will keep well in the fridge like this for a week or even two. Use as normal pesto, with pasta or stirred into thick vegetable and pasta soups.

DANDELIONS AND SORREL

Dandelions and sorrel are some of the first green leaves to appear in early spring (in fact sorrel will usually grow all through the winter in the city). The timing of each is good, but together they also make a great combination. There is bitterness and crunch from the dandelion, acid lemon from the sorrel. Their vibrant green makes a perfect foil for the opaque orange flesh of smoked salmon or gravadlax.

You can easily blanch dandelion leaves by putting a flowerpot, with a tile or brick on top, over the whole plant. Once plunged into darkness, the leaves will grow paler, longer and sweeter. In about a week you should have a tangled mass of pale lemon-and-white spiked leaves.

Pick only the smallest and most tender sorrel leaves and combine them in equal proportions with the blanched dandelion. Dress lightly with a few drops each of lemon and olive oil, sea salt and pepper. Eat alongside slithers of Hansen & Lydersen smoked salmon or gravadlax (see page 229) dressed in nothing but black pepper, and with some fresh sourdough bread.

A FORAGED SUPPER FOR A FRIEND

A local, seasonal approach to cooking is fine in spring and summer, but when February manifests itself with a chill, biting wind and winter seems reluctant to release its grip, then cooking locally grown ingredients seems an absurd fantasy. But if you look for them, the first signs of spring are already appearing in the vegetable garden and beyond.

I wanted to cook a special meal for a friend – a friend who is a serious cook herself. Deciding what to make for someone whose own cooking you admire can be hard. If you can offer them something they cannot get elsewhere, then you begin at a slight advantage and must hope that skill, not nerves, wins out and your meal is a success.

I began by going down to the allotment; seeing things growing always lights up my culinary imagination. Weeds are a hundred times more vital than ordinary garden plants and always show themselves above ground first. I was on the lookout for dandelions and nettles and was hoping rather optimistically for some early rhubarb. It was a cloudy and unpromising morning. I pedalled down to the allotment with Matilda, aged three, on the back of my bike and the sun came out. When we got there I dug a hole and found Matilda some worms to play with, and whilst she was happily occupied I scrambled down the side of the ditch that brings a shallow stream past the far end of my plot. It is a silty, mineral-rich bank, the perfect site for growing lush green nettles, and I found plenty. I wore thick gardening gloves and snipped the tops off with scissors, straight into a plastic bag. I went searching for dandelions next and, whilst doing so, found a self-seeded bed of *mâche* (corn salad) growing up through my cockleshell path. I picked a few young leaves of sorrel, some green onion tops, a handful of chervil and some dark-red thumb-sized leaves of 'Rosso di Treviso' chicory. We then did some digging for an hour or two and created a soft, dark mound of earth, in which to pop Charlotte potatoes at the weekend. Matilda lay back against it and the sun came out. It was the first time her small body had stretched out against the soil in a long while. She breathed out gratefully and smiled. It felt good to be outdoors again. Before we left we checked the nest of ladybirds that we had found clustered together in a corner of the shed and took one out to play with.

When I got home I decided to make the following recipe:

Dandelion and Bacon Salad with a Hot Vinegar Dressing

This dish takes its inspiration from recipes by Edouard de Pomiane and Richard Olney. Early in the year you are unlikely to find large, intact edible dandelion heads of leaves. You will find that the outer leaves are a bit tough but just cut these off retaining the tender inner leaves. Later in the season you can use the entire head, cut like a head of whole lettuce.

Serves 2, or 4 as a side dish

> 3 or 4 rashers (approx. 90g) good-quality streaky bacon, cut into thin strips
> 2 big handfuls of dandelion leaves, cut at the join with the root, washed care-
> fully and dried well in a tea towel or salad spinner
> 1 tbsp red-wine vinegar

Fry the bacon, starting in a cold pan, over a low heat until the fat starts to run. Turn up the heat and continue frying until the bacon is crisp on all sides.

Warm a ceramic salad bowl by filling it with hot water and then drying it, or by popping it in a low oven for a few minutes.

Put the dandelions in the warmed salad bowl and tip the contents of your pan (bacon and fat) over the leaves. Quickly swirl the vinegar round the pan, to pick up any remaining fat, and turn the heat up high. When the vinegar boils pour it over the salad too and serve immediately (so that the bacon fat doesn't harden) with plenty of good crusty bread.

Spring Soup of Jerusalem Artichokes, Lentils and Dandelions

March is a lean time in vegetable gardens, but at about the time you dig up your Jerusalem artichoke patch (or find them in your local market) you may well see the first vigorous growth of dandelions in your garden (or someone else's). Eating spring weeds is a centuries-old tradition and a great way of adding minerals and iron to your diet.

Serves 2

1 tbsp olive oil, for frying, plus a little to serve
1 garlic clove, peeled and lightly crushed
1 shallot, peeled and finely chopped
6 Jerusalem artichokes, peeled to about the size of an egg, then chopped into
 roughly 1cm pieces
2 medium potatoes, peeled and chopped into roughly 1cm cubes
2 tbsp Puy lentils
a handful of tender dandelion leaves, roughly chopped
sea salt and black pepper

Heat most of the olive oil in a pan and allow the garlic to colour a little, before adding the shallot. Fry over a medium heat, stirring from time to time to prevent them from catching and becoming bitter.

When the shallot starts to soften, add the artichokes, potatoes and lentils. Cover (but only just) with boiling water from the kettle and simmer for about 20 minutes.

Just before serving, throw in the chopped dandelion leaves and cook for 1–2 minutes. Add the remaining olive oil in a thin stream and season. Serve at once.

PICKLED, PRESERVED, SALTED & SMOKED

Chutneys, Ketchup and Pickles

'Thrift' is another word that, like 'peasant', requires reassessment. Thrift usually goes hand-in-hand with a sense of hardship and penny-pinching, of not having money for luxuries. But its positive sense is making the most of what is to hand. The wastefulness of our current food system is something we should all be more mindful of. What does thrift mean in practical terms for the modern peasant? The first thing is cooking with the produce that is in season. And what you don't eat fresh you can preserve using vinegar, sugar, salt or smoke, with a variety of techniques that have been used for hundreds of years to extend the shelf life of perishable ingredients.

Having a larder well stocked with pickles and jams is one way of storing up summer plenty (when fruit is cheap) for lean times. The following recipes will help you rediscover ancient methods of food preservation in which waste is kept to a minimum and foods are preserved at their peak. The frugal habits of the peasant kitchen mean boiling bones for stock, cherishing offal as an ingredient, fermenting milk and salting meat and, most accessibly of all, pickling excess vegetables and turning excess fruit into jams and jellies.

Fruit and vegetables can be bought, grown or, if you are really radical, gleaned. Many fruit and vegetable markets stack up boxes of waste produce for anyone to take away at the end of the day. If you aren't familiar with gleaning, then French film-maker Agnès Varda's documentary *The Gleaners and I* (2000) provides a thoughtful essay on modern versions of this age-old activity (enshrined in law in France).

More recently, in his book *Waste*, Tristram Stuart describes collecting so many boxes of unwanted mangoes from Spitalfields Market that he was able to produce mango *lassi* for an entire wedding party. Whilst not everyone has the appetite for 'freeganism' (reclaiming waste food), we can still keep personal waste to a minimum by preserving our own excess for future consumption in the form of jams, jellies, chutneys or cordials. None of these confections need more than basic cooking skills. Most importantly of all, they taste infinitely better than shop-bought goods. Cutting down on food waste may be a worthy cause but, most importantly for me, it's also a tasty one.

Basic Chutney Recipe

Before we had freezers we dealt with surplus by pickling and, in particular, by making chutney – our traditional national response to a glut of fruit or vegetables. Chutney-making is far easier than making jam or marmalade as there is no setting point to worry about. This makes it a very encouraging preserve to start off with. Once you have mastered one chutney recipe, you can easily adapt the process. Gluts and offers of spare plums or apples usually come as a surprise, so an adaptable recipe is essential. Chutney is preserved by the vinegar and sugar in the recipe, so it's important to get these proportions correct. The sugar should always be added after the fruits have softened and broken down.

Makes about 5 jam jars (350ml each)

> 1–1.5kg fruit (plums, apricots, peaches, pumpkin, squash, rhubarb, tomatoes,
>   apples), peeled and sliced or diced, as necessary
> 1 tbsp pickling spices (to make your own, put the following spices in a jar and
>   shake well, measure out 1 tbsp of this mixture and store the rest in the
>   cupboard for another day: ½ teaspoon each of cumin, black pepper,
>   mustard and coriander seeds, a few shards of cinnamon bark, 4 cloves, 2
>   small dried chillies, 4 cardamom pods)
> 2 good-sized onions, finely chopped
> 450ml distilled vinegar (clear, not dark brown, for a better colour)
> 450g cooking apples (if you use the larger quantity of fruit, omit the apple,
>   above)
> 250g sultanas, or you can use apricots, figs, dates, prunes, etc.
> 1 tbsp finely grated ginger
> 500g soft light brown sugar
> 1 tsp sea salt

Prepare the fruits. Put the pickling spices into a small piece of cloth and tie it up tightly with string, and set aside.

Put the onions and half the vinegar in a large pan, simmer for 10 minutes, then add the fruits, sultanas and ginger. Simmer until the fruits have broken down. Add the sugar, the rest of the vinegar, the bag of spices and the salt. Stir until the sugar has dissolved and then simmer very gently until the mixture thickens and starts to look jammy. You should be stirring almost continuously at the end, to make sure the mixture does not catch. You will know when it is ready as the liquid on top will disappear and, when you draw your spoon across the bottom of the pan, you will hear a satisfying sizzle.

When you are happy with the consistency, spoon the chutney into hot, sterilised jam jars (see page 115) and screw on the lids. If the lids are metal, put greaseproof paper between the lids and the chutney to prevent corrosion caused by the vinegar content. Leave the chutney in a cupboard for at least 1 month before eating.

VARIATIONS

If you like your chutney spicy add 6 fresh red chilli peppers, seeded and very finely chopped, at the same time as the fruits, sultanas and ginger.

Whole spices can be added along with the sugar, they add flavour but also make the chutney look attractive. Be careful not to add too many as the flavour will strengthen during storing.

Whole spices

1 tbsp mustard seeds (good in tomato chutney)

1 tsp cardamom seeds (good in apricot chutney)

3 or 4 star anise (good in rhubarb chutney)

3 or 4 pieces of cinnamon stick (good in plum or peach chutney)

Fruit Ketchup

Home-made ketchup is a marvellous thing; tangy, tart, fruity, sour and spicy, it raises simple savoury snacks to the gastronomic sublime. It hits so many tastebuds at once that it's enough to make you yodel. It is halfway between chutney and brown sauce. If you love condiments, then you will definitely love this. You can make it with plums or wild berries, but I made mine with rhubarb (thank you, Rosie Sykes, for a brilliant idea). Eat it with a steak pasty, a cooked breakfast or a bacon sandwich.

Makes approx. 1.5 litres

1 tbsp pickling spices (see page 203)
1kg rhubarb, trimmed and chopped into chunks
1 tbsp finely grated fresh ginger
1kg red onions, peeled and diced
800ml distilled malt vinegar
approx. 200g unbleached granulated sugar
sea salt and black pepper
a hearty pinch each of ground nutmeg, ginger, mace and cloves

Place the spices in a small piece of cloth and tie it up tightly with string. Place in a preserving pan or large saucepan (not copper) with the rhubarb, ginger, onions and a quarter of the vinegar and simmer until soft. Take out the spice bag, then push the mixture through a sieve with a wooden spoon, or use a mouli vegetable mill.

Measure the pulp and add 100g sugar and 300ml vinegar for each 600ml of pulp.

Cook the pulp, sugar, vinegar, seasoning and pinches of spices in a pan until a good consistency is reached (about 40 minutes). Skim off any froth that forms and stir frequently. When the mixture has reached a thick, glossy pouring consistency, pour into hot sterilised bottles (see page 115) with clips. It should keep for 6 months.

Quick Pickle

Japanese meals often start with a small serving of lightly pickled vegetables. These are very thinly sliced and have been soaked in a brine of rice vinegar, sugar and salt for up to a week. You can adapt your pickle to the vegetables of the season (carrots, fennel, cabbage, cauliflower, leeks, chillies, etc.), so if you're stuck with a glut or a veg box you don't have a chance to eat, get pickling. Here I have used beetroot and rhubarb, an idea that I pinched from the London noodle restaurant Koya, which offers *otsukemono* (home-made pickles) in endless seasonal variety.

Makes approx. 8 servings of pickles

> *3 or 4 rhubarb stalks*
> *3 small or 2 large beetroot*
>
> *Brine*
> *250ml kettle-hot water*
> *130ml rice wine vinegar*
> *4 tbsp sugar*
> *1 tbsp sea salt*

Trim the rhubarb and slice it in half lengthways, then cut into 4cm chunky batons. Peel the beetroot and, using a mandolin, slice them into very thin circles (if they are too large, cut them into half-moons).

Combine the brine ingredients in a bowl and stir well until the salt and sugar have dissolved. Pour this over the prepared vegetables. If you want to preserve the bright pink of the rhubarb, divide the brine in two and pickle the rhubarb and beetroot separately. Cover and leave for 3–4 days (minimum) or preferably a week. Keep in a covered container in the fridge for up to one month.

Sweet Cherries 'Pickled' in Brandy

This recipe should be made only when good British cherries are in season and plentiful. The pickled cherries are ready in about one month and can then be used as an alternative to a brandy-soaked sugar cube in the bottom of a champagne cocktail, or alongside sweets (custards or fools) or savouries (pâté and cold meat pies of ham and chicken).

Makes 1 jam jar (350ml)

150g cherries
200ml brandy
4 tbsp sugar
2 tbsp water

Mix all the ingredients together in a bowl, then pour into a sterilised jam jar (see page 115). Leave on a shelf for 1 month, shaking it from time to time.

Pickled Onions

Find the hardest, smallest onions you can. In *Food in England* Dorothy Hartley recommends using the 'walking' or Egyptian onion, which bears its bulbs at the top of its stalks. Shallots are rather easier to get hold of.

Makes 2 jam jars (350ml each) or 1 large jar

> *150g sea salt*
> *600ml water*
> *500g shallots or very small onions, peeled*
>
> *Spiced vinegar*
> *300ml white-wine vinegar*
> *300ml distilled malt vinegar*
> *1 tsp coriander seeds*
> *1 tsp black peppercorns*
> *1 or 2 shards of cinnamon bark*
> *2 dried red chillies*
> *3 bay leaves*
> *1 tsp mustard seeds*

Mix the salt with the water. Stir to dissolve the crystals.

Keep the onions whole, and pop them into the brine, then weight them down with a saucer and a clean pebble. Leave for 3–7 days. When you are ready to make the pickle, strain the onions, rinse under running water and pat them dry.

To make the spiced vinegar, pour both vinegars and all the spices into a stainless-steel pan and bring to the boil. Simmer for 5 minutes. Make sure you put on an extractor fan or open a window, as the vinegar fumes will be very powerful. Strain the mixture into a jug and allow the vinegar to cool. Discard the spices.

Pack the onions into sterilised jars (see page 115) and pour over the vinegar. Seal, label and date, and leave in a cupboard for 1 month before using.

Green Gooseberry Chutney

Small, hard green gooseberries make a mouth-puckeringly sour-sweet chutney that seems destined to accompany thick slices of ham and some home-made coleslaw.

Makes about 6 jam jars (350ml each)

1 tbsp pickling spices (see page 203)
300g onion, finely chopped
300ml distilled vinegar (clear, not dark brown, for a better colour)
1 tbsp finely grated fresh ginger
100g raisins or sultanas
350g soft light brown sugar
½ tsp sea salt
1kg hard green gooseberries, topped and tailed

Preheat the oven to 180°C/gas mark 4.

Put the pickling spices into a little bag (see page 203).

Simmer the onion gently in half the vinegar for 10 minutes. Then add the ginger, raisins or sultanas, sugar, the rest of the vinegar, the bag of spices and the salt. Stir until the sugar has dissolved, and then simmer very gently until the mixture thickens and starts to look jammy.

Very gently add the gooseberries. Mix them in gingerly to avoid them breaking up and then simmer for about 10 minutes until they are nicely amalgamated.

Spoon the chutney into hot sterilised jam jars (see page 115). Seal, label and date, then leave in a cupboard for at least 1 month to allow the flavours to develop.

Spiced Plum Chutney with Five-Spice

If you are faced with a glut of plums or are offered some by friends, they will most likely be Victoria plums and there will probably be a lot of them. They are far better for cooking than for eating as they lack the subtle depths of other plums such as gages. They are, however, an excellent ingredient for chutney, especially when enhanced by the numbing prickle of Chinese five-spice. This sour-and-spicy chutney goes very well with cold meats such as turkey. As it will be made in September, when heavily laden plum trees are begging to be picked, it will have matured in plenty of time for Christmas.

Makes about 5 medium jars (350ml each)

> 1–1.5kg plums (you could also use apricots, peaches, pumpkin, squash,
>   rhubarb, tomatoes, apples or a combination)
> 1 tbsp pickling spices (see page 203)
> 2 good-sized onions, finely chopped
> 450ml distilled vinegar (clear, not dark brown, for a better colour)
> 3 red chilli peppers, seeded and finely chopped
> 1 tsp chilli flakes
> 250g sultanas
> 1 tbsp finely grated fresh ginger
> 500g soft light brown sugar
> 3 or 4 pieces of cinnamon bark or ½ cinnamon stick
> 1 tbsp Chinese five-spice (see page 212)
> 1 tsp sea salt

Prepare the plums by slicing them open and pulling out the stones. The fruit will break down during cooking, so you don't have to chop them up any further. Put the pickling spices into a little bag (see page 203).

Put the onions and half the vinegar into a large pan, simmer for 10 minutes. Add the chillies and the chilli flakes, sultanas, ginger and the plums. Simmer until the fruits are soft.

Add the sugar, the rest of the vinegar, the cinnamon, the bag of pickling spices, the five-spice and the salt. Stir until the sugar has dissolved, and then simmer very gently until the mixture thickens and starts to look jammy. Stir well towards the end to stop the mixture sticking to the bottom of the pan and burning. Spoon the chutney into hot, sterilised jam jars (see page 115). Leave in a cupboard for at least 1 month before eating.

Home-made five-spice mixture
4 star anise
2 tsp fennel seeds
2 tsp Sichuan pepper (if unavailable, substitute 1 tsp black peppercorns and 1
*   tsp chilli flakes)*
6–8 cloves
¼ cinnamon stick

Grind all the spices together to a fine powder in a spice grinder. Keep in a jam jar and use as required.

Preserves

I am a fair-weather forager. My foraging usually takes place in July when the lime trees are in blossom, or on sunny days in autumn when there is such a profusion of wild fruit that it seems almost rude to overlook it. More often than not I pick blackberries to make into the apple-and-blackberry compote that I have eaten every autumn since I was a small child. More recently a Wiltshire walk took me alongside an ancient piece of woodland butting onto a chalk escarpment. As we jogged down the steep, closely cropped hillside several plum trees stretched out their branches beseechingly, as if longing to be relieved of the burden of their dark-purple fruit. We converted an old jumper into a bag and brought back a couple of kilos. To these I added some cultivated damsons to make my plum jam.

Wild plums, or bullace, have very dark-purple fruit, and the damson is a cultivated species derived from the bullace. According to Richard Mabey, most plums that you find growing in the wild are seeded from garden or orchard specimens of other varieties that have been grafted (two different varieties spliced at root and trunk and grown together, for better productivity), but have then reverted to their original rootstock. Are the plums I gathered in the wood wilder than the damsons, derived from wild plums, gathered in the garden? I don't know, but I do know that they will make a very deeply flavoured sour-sweet jam that is reminiscent of Iranian and Persian sour jams. This Middle Eastern flavour is no coincidence.

On my trip to Patience Gray's farmhouse, Spigolizzi in Apulia (see pages 4–10), I discovered a bit more about the damson. The damson tree in Patience's southern Italian garden bears small, very dark-blue fruit; with these she made an 'astonishingly delicious and perfumed jam', which she called 'Damascene', as the plant's origin was Damascus. In her book she wondered if Crusaders returning via Otranto and Brindisi from the Holy Land might have carried dried Damascus plums with them, discarding the stones as they travelled on. One of these might have germinated and been the ancestor of Patience's tree. The jam I ate there, made by her son Nick and his wife Maggie, tasted similar to the one I made with wild Wiltshire plums.

Perhaps due to her refusal to install electricity and thus refrigeration, Patience never cooked with butter – only olive oil – and habitually ate a butter-free breakfast of ricotta and plum jam on toast.

Wild Plum Jam

Makes about 6 jam jars (350ml each)

2kg damsons or wild plums
500–750ml water (depending on how ripe the fruit is)
2kg unbleached granulated sugar

Heat the sugar in a cool oven (110°C/gas mark ¼) on a baking tray to aid its dissolving ability.

Pick over the damsons, discarding any that are overripe or blemished. Place the fruit in a colander and pour over some cold water. Drain the fruit, then place in a large preserving pan or heavy-based saucepan over a low heat with the water and bring to the boil very slowly.

Cook the damsons until they are pulpy, stirring now and then to break up the flesh and release the stones. Check that the skins are very soft, as they will not get any softer once the sugar is added. Whilst the fruit is simmering, skim off any stones as they rise to the surface. This is a laborious but meditative task.

Add the sugar, stirring continuously until it has completely dissolved. Bring the jam to the boil again and cook quickly. The quicker the setting point is reached, the better the flavour will be. Start testing the jam after 10 minutes. An easy way to tell if it is ready is to dip a spoon in and hold it above the pan; if a drop of syrup remains suspended, it will set. This is called the flake test. Alternatively, use a jam thermometer: when the jam is ready it should register 105°C. Skim off any scum and pour the jam into hot sterilised jars (see page 115). Cover with discs of waxed paper, then seal, label and date, and keep in a cool, dark place for up to 12–18 months.

Apricot Jam

This is my favourite jam; served on toast with plenty of cold, unsalted butter and washed down with strong, milky coffee, it is the very best way to start the day.

Makes about 9 jars (350 ml each)

3kg apricots (underripe rather than overripe)
2.5kg unbleached granulated sugar

Halve and stone the apricots, reserving about 20 stones. Slice the flesh of the halved apricots into crescents and place in a pan with the sugar. Using a nutcracker, break open the reserved apricot stones and take out the bitter-sweet kernels. Chop them roughly and add them to the pan.

Heat the fruit very gently until it begins to release its juices, stirring frequently. Increase the heat to medium until the mixture comes to a simmer, then cook for about 1 hour until a thick and sticky, jammy consistency has been reached. Using a jam thermometer, or the 'drop' method on page 214, check to see if the setting point has been reached. Skim off any scum and then pot the jam into sterilised jam jars (see page 115). The jam is ready to eat when cool. Seal, label and date, then store for up to 12–18 months.

Dandelion and Burdock Cordial

Traditional dandelion and burdock beer is fermented. However, if you want the bitter, spicy taste of that drink right away, without having to buy specialist beer-making ingredients, you can make a dandelion and burdock cordial instead. You will probably have most of the ingredients already. Use a good wild-flower book and identify the burdock root *and* leaf, so that you don't confuse it with toxic plants such as deadly nightshade. Serve the cordial over ice with soda water; add a shot of rum for a cocktail to celebrate the beginning of spring.

Makes approx. 500ml

2 large burdock roots
4 dandelion roots
500ml water
3cm thumb of ginger, cut into fat coins and smashed a little
2 star anise
300g sugar
2 tbsp black treacle
zest and juice of 1 lemon

Wash and scrub the burdock and dandelion roots well. Cut into sections and boil in the water along with the ginger and star anise for 5 minutes. Line a sieve with clean muslin or a J-cloth and strain the liquid into a bowl.

Return the liquid to a clean pan and, over a gentle heat, dissolve the sugar and black treacle in it. Add the zest of the lemon and the juice. Do not allow the mixture to boil. Taste, and add a little more lemon juice or sugar as necessary.

Decant into bottles, allow to cool and then refrigerate. If you do not think you will drink all the cordial within 1 week, you can put half in a plastic bottle and freeze it.

Salted

The problem of how to preserve food so that it can be eaten at leaner times of the year has been with man since prehistoric times. Food, especially meat, spoils quickly. Salt has been used for centuries as one way to stop that decaying process. It is often combined with drying (and sometimes smoking) to create ingredients that can be eaten safely many months after they have been slaughtered or harvested.

In brief, salt acts as a preservative mainly by drawing water out of the ingredient being preserved (through the process of osmosis). On top of this, salt upsets the activity of the enzymes that are naturally present in food and cause decay. The history of salt, and its cultural importance across the world, is a vast subject and one that I won't be tackling here. All I will say is that it is well worth mastering this most ancient and basic of preserving techniques.

HOME-CURING BACON

Salting meat for a week and then eating it takes a certain amount of nerve. Our modern-day brains are hard-wired to fear spoilage, especially when it comes to meat. The result is that home-curing has fallen almost entirely out of favour. I think it's one kitchen habit that really is worth resurrecting. Don't let fear of the unknown put you off. Trust in this age-old process and you will be very pleased with the results.

When sliced into cream-and-white-striped pink rashers, the very first batch of streaky bacon that I made fried to a delicious crisp. I had rubbed belly pork with an aromatic salt, sugar and spice mixture. The smooth white fat took on the flavours of the fennel, juniper and coriander to create a recognisably bacony taste with something a little bit extra. It tasted great, but I would be a liar if I said it was an anxiety-free exercise. I am not immune to kitchen neurosis. The first time I made this bacon I cooked and ate a rasher or two, then waited two days. I listened nervously to my stomach, attributing every gurgle to the onset of botulism. I almost looked up the symptoms on the Internet, but held off. At the weekend I fed the bacon to my family. Even my husband – a most sceptical modern peasant and bacon snob – loved it.

In 1821 William Cobbett described bacon as an almost universal panacea and promoter of civil and domestic peace:

> *A couple of flitches of bacon are worth fifty thousand Methodist sermons and religious tracts. The sight of them upon the rack tends more to keep a man from poaching and stealing than whole volumes of penal statutes, though assisted by the terrors of the hulks and gibbet. They are great softeners and promoters of domestic harmony.*

It seems nothing much has changed. Bacon is probably still on most people's list of favourite foods. But it took sausage-maker Jean-Paul Habermann's enthusiasm for home-cured bacon to get me salting. Home-made bacon is so good, he assured me, that once you have made it you will never go back to buying it. He advised against using rare-breed pig meat, as the fat-to-meat ratio would be too high. An ideal piece of pork belly would be roughly 70 per cent lean to 30 per cent fat.

All good advice, but I had the offer of a piece of Mary Holbrook's British Lop pig (fed on the whey from her cheese-making). The flavour of her pork is unusual and very fine – somehow creamier than normal pork. I could not resist trying it out as bacon, and in this case the meat (though streaked with fat) was not overwhelmingly lardy and was just within the optimum 70:30 ratio. So go to a good butcher, use your eyes and judge for yourself.

A professional butcher would use sodium nitrate (saltpetre) to preserve the pink colour after cooking and prevent bacteria from spoiling the bacon. Using ordinary sea salt works fine for small batches of bacon that will be used up quickly; the meat tastes better, but has a grey colour when cooked. Fergus Henderson doesn't bother putting saltpetre in his brine recipe, so I too decided not to use it. On a recent trip to France the butcher sold me small whole pieces of salted bacon, rubbed with spices, which had a phenomenal piggy flavour but also turned grey after cooking. But if you like your bacon crispy you probably won't notice this, so don't let the colour put you off.

Home-cured Bacon

It would be possible to cure a whole pork belly and then hang this salted bacon in a cool and airy larder or outbuilding, but this is not something that many city dwellers have. Instead I chose to do a smaller piece (about one-third of the belly), which, after curing for four or five days, I cut into two pieces, storing one in the fridge and the other in the freezer for future use.

Makes 20–25 slices

> *500g sea salt*
> *125g brown sugar*
> *1 tbsp freshly ground black pepper*
> *approx. 1.5–2kg pork belly*
> *a little white wine*

> *Aromatics*
> *1 tbsp juniper berries or cardamom seeds, lightly crushed*
> *5 bay leaves, finely chopped*
> *1 tbsp coriander seeds*
> *1 tsp fennel or ½ tsp powdered cloves*

Make sure your hands are extra clean. In a large bowl mix the salt, sugar, pepper and aromatics together. This is called the dry-cure mixture.

Put the pork belly on a board and rub the dry-cure mixture into the skin and every cranny of the meat. Use a spoon, not your hand, to scoop the mixture out of the bowl – that way any salt mixture left over can be used later on (see page 221) without fear of contamination by the raw pork.

Put the belly in a ceramic dish and cover with cling film, or place in a plastic box (I use a picnic cool box). Leave in a cool place for 24 hours. If you are worried about your house being too warm, pop the dish in the fridge.

The next day pour off the liquid that the meat has exuded and rub the meat with more of the dry-cure mixture, again using a spoon to scoop it out. Turn the belly over. If you are doing a whole belly, cut it into three, and keep moving the top to the bottom as you repeat this process every day.

After turning the meat each day for 5 days, dampen a clean cloth with white wine and use it to rub the salt off the pork belly. Soak what is now bacon in a bowl of water for about 6–8 hours to stop it being excessively salty. Then drain and pat dry with kitchen paper.

To make cutting the bacon easier I always slice off the skin. Take a large kitchen knife and, keeping the blade horizontal, slice between the skin and the flesh, keeping a layer of fat on top. Pulling the skin away from you as you slice makes this easier. If you have very sharp knives you may prefer to keep the rind on. Either way, wrap each slab in cling film and store in the fridge, putting any excess in the freezer. The bacon will keep in the fridge for a couple of weeks, should your appetite allow this.

I like my bacon in a thick sourdough-toast sandwich with mustard and a very hot cup of coffee.

SALT COD

Pain has the ability to stretch time. And I have suffered through some very long days. But, leaving childbirth aside, the day I went cod-fishing in the English Channel was one of the lengthiest and grimmest in my life.

It was supposed to be a fun day out, and for most people it was. I had joined a small group of friends, workers from the Towpath Café (see page 46) and a group of Albanian chefs, to charter a day-boat from Dover. It was an open boat about forty feet long. We headed out into deep water, within sight of France. We were using drop-lines with heavy lead weights. The skipper was a man who had fallen out of love with humanity (women most of all) and treated us with barely concealed disdain. We weren't a very handy bunch. Our clumsy fingers struggled with the unfamiliar equipment; we tangled lines and our weights knocked the side of the boat. If the captain could have thrown us overboard, I think he would have. The one outstanding fisherman amongst us was a woman, an artist from New Zealand. She caught more fish than anyone, then sat down at the end of the day and adeptly gutted the lot on deck. As beautiful as she was skilful, she was a wonderful riposte to the skipper's misogyny.

The fish, mainly cod and mackerel, were easy to catch. After the first half-hour or so I started being sick, and the only way to stop that was to lie flat. After a while I gave up trying to fish and lay down. I wasn't the only one who had gone green. Three of us were similarly affected. All around us people hauled in fish and feasted on delicious picnic food. We three could eat nothing. The hours trickled past. The boat rocked queasily up and down. Finally, eight hours after we set out, we returned to the harbour. The minute my feet touched the shore I felt as right as rain, but I couldn't face eating fish. I was left with a big bag of fresh cod, so I made it into salt cod.

The traditional method of curing cod is to first pack it in salt and then hang it up to dry. If you were setting up home on a fjord for the winter you could take the fish out of the salt, wrap it up in cheesecloth and then let it dry out. But I am not sure the air quality in the inner city is good enough, so I just leave it in the salt until I need it. Pollock used to be cheaper and more sustainable than cod, but some cod is now available from sustainable sources, so I can happily recommend using it. Get the fishmonger to take the pin bones out for you.

Home-made Salt Cod

Serves 3

1 box (250g) coarse sea salt
600–750g cod or pollock, cut into square fillets and pin bones removed

Sterilise a large glass jar (see page 115). Place a good thick layer of salt in the bottom. Add a layer of fish, then cover with salt. Continue layering the fish and salt right up the jar. At the top add an extra-thick layer of salt. Tighten the lid and store in a cool place for about 48 hours.

After a day or two the fish will exude some liquid, so drain it off. The salt cod is ready in 1 week. I ate mine in a sauce of tomato and olives.

Salt Cod with Peppers and Black Olives

Jacob Kennedy's wonderful *Bocca Cookbook* has been an inspiration in many ways, but especially in the form of this recipe. Here is my slightly amended version.

Serves 2

> 2 small shallots, chopped
> 1 red pepper, seeded and sliced into thin strips
> 1 bay leaf
> 1 large garlic clove, peeled and crushed with the flat of a heavy knife
> 1 x 400g tin tomatoes, or 400g small, ripe tomatoes in season, skinned
> 2 tbsp capers
> 8–10 black olives, stones in
> black pepper
> 400g salt cod, soaked for 24 hours (change the water 2 or 3 times)
> a little butter
> 1 tbsp freshly chopped parsley, to garnish

Preheat the oven to 180°C/gas mark 4.

Sweat the shallots in a little olive oil and then add the red pepper, bay leaf and garlic. Cook slowly until soft (about 10 minutes), then add the tomatoes. Cook for a further 20 minutes or until the sauce has broken down and the oil has floated to the top. Add the capers and the olives. Add a few grinds of black pepper.

Drain the fish and pat dry. Cut each piece in half. Feel for any small bones that are left in and pluck them out (tweezers are good for this). Lightly butter a gratin dish and lay the fish in the bottom. Spoon the sauce over the fish.

Bake for about 15 minutes, or until the sauce is bubbling in the middle. Before serving, sprinkle with the chopped parsley. Serve with crusty bread or some steamed new potatoes dressed with olive oil and black pepper.

Smoked

You can get all kinds of smoked food (some more palatable than others), but this method of preservation is most commonly associated with fish and meat and these were probably the first to be made. Just as with salting, it's a process that is many thousands of years old and was probably discovered by chance when a fire was lit to dry meat (or keep flies off). The first smoking would have been done on an open fire, and later on in a chimney or a purpose-built smokehouse (or sometimes a converted upturned hogshead barrel).

Smoking works best when combined with another preservation process (salting or drying). Fuel (wood or peat) is burnt to create smoke, which in turn leaves tarry, resinous deposits; these kill any bacteria and create an impermeable fly-proof coating on the surface of the food. When the flesh is sealed off from the air it is prevented from spoiling. In the past smoked fish would have been an important part of many people's diet, and smokehouses (with beams across the ceiling from which the meat or fish was hung) would have been a common sight. While I would love to tell you how to smoke a salmon in your back garden, in this case not every artisan's process can be reproduced successfully at home. The mechanical ingenuity, engineering skills and space needed to successfully smoke fish are way out of my league (plus it's far too smelly). What remains with me from the day I spent salmon-smoking is the commitment to refining a single product and the desire to carry on an old tradition in a way that is utterly modern and alive.

As I lock up my bike in a mews just off Stoke Newington Church Street I know I am in the right place. The rich, sweet, smoky smell is pervasive. It is a complex aroma, with layers of smell on lots of different levels – unusual but far from unpleasant. It is coming from the back of a light industrial warehouse split up into artists' studios. On the other side of the mews a building is being torn down and the sound is deafening. It is an assault on the senses. Right around the corner is an alleyway painted red. It is piled up with polystyrene fish boxes. At the end of the small courtyard is a plywood door, behind which is a white-tiled room with sinks down one side and, beyond that, a dark cave. This is a working fish-smokery. What was once a defunct boiler room, complete with vast 1950s boiler, is now the headquarters of the salmon-smoking business Hansen & Lydersen, which produces 130kg of smoked-salmon sides each week. Inside the unit the smell intensifies. I pick up a book off the shelf (*Growth of the Soil* by Norwegian writer Knut Hamsun). It is kippered. The smoke has saturated every page.

The proprietor of this business is a fourth-generation Norwegian salmon-smoker. He is 6 foot 5 inches tall and broad-shouldered, and he likes wearing bright-yellow oilskin dungarees. He smokes his salmon according to a recipe devised by his great-grandfather in 1923. There is nothing unusual about a craft handed down through generations of the same family. That is, until you locate his business, which is not in rural Norway, but in a mews in north-east London.

Ole-Martin Hansen came to London to study sound design six years ago. Necessity forced him to look for a way of making money, and his response was highly original. He looked to his heritage and decided to revive the family salmon-smoking business that had lapsed a generation before. Ole began with the recipe devised by his great-grandfather, Lyder-Nilsen Lydersen. The salmon is cold-salted and then smoked with a mixture of juniper and beech woods, to a recipe that was highly popular in its time.

Great-Grandpa Lydersen was a salmon fisherman who smoked his salmon in Kirkenes, a small town 240 miles north of the Arctic Circle. This business was taken over by Ole's grandfather in 1962. It was this man, an artisan and engineer, who left behind notebooks full of plans for his own simple system of cold-smoking using an electric fan. This superseded the traditional method used before him, of hanging the salmon in a chimney. Using these plans, Ole converted the boiler room, cleverly utilising the existing chimneys as his extraction point.

His product is very fine: dense, deep-orange slivers of lean salmon cut in thick vertical slices and sold wrapped in white greaseproof paper. It needs very little accompaniment. 'No lemon!' says Ole. You cannot believe such a simple system is behind it. It begins with very high-quality farmed salmon.

This comes from the clear Atlantic waters surrounding the Faroe Islands and is produced to exacting standards of sustainability.

Ole began his business on a shoestring; he had just £300 in the bank. When he first started he used public transport to collect the raw salmon. He went down to Billingsgate fish market at 5 a.m. twice a week. The large polystyrene boxes of fish came back with him on a big red London bus. Ole's business is doing well now and so he can afford to get the fish delivered.

Straight after they arrive at the workshop the salmon are gutted, filleted and swiftly salted; they are then left to cure for twelve hours before being cold-smoked. The smoke is produced by burning beech and juniper wood that has been milled to the consistency of flour. 'Sawdust' is too crude a word for it; better to call it 'wood flour' as Ole does. The fire is made with a ratio of 30 per cent juniper and 70 per cent beech wood, which comes from a sustainable source in Denmark. The fire is lit in a basic-looking pot-bellied garden stove (bought by Ole for £20 from Homebase). Whilst I am there he sets fire to some wood flour on a tile using a blowtorch, so that I can smell it. It smells good, though also – weirdly – a bit like marijuana. The smoke produced is sucked up through ten metres of tinfoil tubing to a plywood cupboard. I ask Ole if home-smoking in a little cupboard-sized smokery would be worth doing, but he shakes his friendly Viking head sadly at my question. 'You need about ten metres of tubing to cool the smoke.'

Inside the cupboard the smoke is wafted by a fan across the sides of salmon that are hanging up. The smokery is caked with thick black resin inside. It's a dank and slightly spooky space. Outside, on a long blackboard Ole has chalked up a simple diagram to help visitors better understand his system, with coloured arrows and wiggly lines. Once the fire is lit it smoulders for twelve hours. Ole must wake at midnight to stoke it. The whole process from salting takes about twenty-four hours. It is very much a craft – one that requires instinct and experience.

Beside the smoker is further evidence of Ole's unconventional approach. It is an old upright piano. The long production period of smoking gives him plenty of time to practise his jazz numbers.

A pallet load of premium wood flour that Ole has been desperately waiting for arrives from Denmark just after I get to the smokery. He leaves me, apologising profusely as he does so, to go and oversee delivery, with the words 'You can always play the piano.' Sadly I am not as musically talented as him.

Ole's mother and aunt were instructed in the art of salmon-smoking by their father, but chose not to continue the family business. Despite this, it is partly memories of childhood feasts overseen by his mother that fuelled Ole's desire to bring this top-quality product back to life. 'We used to fish for trout under the midnight sun,' he says. 'My mum would make picnics of slivers of salmon on her own wholemeal sourdough.'

Ole still prefers to eat his salmon simply. For him it is a product that comes directly from nature and should not be messed about with too much. He likes to eat it with a hard-boiled egg or some *smetana* (Polish sour cream) and Norwegian flatbread. Demand for Hansen & Lydersen salmon is at a peak at the moment, with 130kg of salmon being produced each week. As the main labour force, Ole has his hands full, but he has many plans. He wants to design a line of oilskin clothing, and produce pure fermented cod-liver oil to an ancient recipe. This traditional product was once a staple of Norwegian homes; stored in barrels outside, it sustained health.

Just before I left, Ole retrieved a side of salmon from the cold store. He sliced it vertically into long wedges, then carried it over to a home-made table of sorts, a slab of tree trunk on wonky sapling legs. I took a packet home with me and ate it with a sorrel and dandelion salad. Ole had never heard of (or tasted) sorrel, so in return for the packet of salmon I promised to come back with some.

I won't attempt to make my own smokery – it's too smelly and I don't have the space – but Ole's simple combination of a dollop of crème fraîche and a sprig of dill works equally well on a slab of home-made gravadlax.

Gravadlax

Gravadlax is simply salmon cured in spices, herbs and salt rather than being smoked. It should last about seven days in the fridge after you have cured it. I used to chop the cure up by hand, but puréeing makes it much more effective (a great tip pinched from Simon Hopkinson).

Serves 6–8 as a starter

> *600–750g salmon fillet*
> *a large bunch of fresh dill (reserve a few sprigs for garnish)*
> *10g black peppercorns*
> *2 tbsp vodka or gin*
> *80g sea salt*
> *100g caster sugar*
> *crème fraîche, to serve*

Slice the salmon fillet into two halves lengthways and take out the pin bones. You can find these by gently running your hand over the top – you may feel the odd prickle of bone; this is easily removed with tweezers. Wipe the fish clean with damp kitchen towel and pat dry.

Chop the dill roughly and coarsely grind the pepper (you might want to use a spice grinder or pestle for this amount). Mix them together in a food-processor with the vodka or gin, sea salt and sugar to a smooth green purée.

Take a ceramic dish and place one-third of the purée in the bottom. Put one fillet on top of this, silver-side down; spread the next third of purée over it and top with the other piece of fish, silver-side up. Top with the remaining purée and put a piece of cling film over the dish so that it hangs down over the sides. Weight this down with a saucer with something heavy on top. Place in the fridge.

Flip the fish over after 24 hours, then chill for another day. You can eat it in 48 hours or wait a day or two longer. When you are ready, wash the fillet under a tap (leaving the odd speck of dill) then pat dry. Lay your hand flat on the salmon and, with a sharp knife, cut down vertically to get thin slices of fish, leaving the skin behind.

Serve on fresh sourdough bread (or the 66% Rye, see page 38) with a teaspoon of crème fraîche and a sprig of dill on top of each serving.

THE PRACTICAL PEASANT'S YEAR

Peasant Work

In a city the hours spent working a plot of ground and growing food can sometimes feel like affectation. If there is food cheaply and easily available at markets and grocery stores, why do it? The reason is easy to understand once you begin, for the benefits of spending time digging, pruning, weeding and watering go far beyond food production. Everyone feels better in body and mind when they spend time outside in a green space. I am not alone in appreciating this. The think tank the New Economics Foundation recently published a pamphlet entitled 'National Gardening Leave', in which its authors, Andrew Simms and Molly Conisbee, argue with convincing force and plenty of evidence that a four-day week and a massive expansion of growing spaces and allotments would benefit the economy, save the government millions of pounds, strengthen communities and make individuals considerably happier, healthier and more fulfilled.

For myself, I only know that a trip to the allotment is always restorative. The work may be hard, the plot unsightly, the brambles rampant, but I will return home with an image of the blazing sunset that has painted the sky over East London flaming red and orange, or of the frog I have watched hop through my herb patch. After more than a decade of tending it, I now know that I could not survive city life without my small piece of borrowed ground.

WATERING

My first thought on summer mornings is always 'Has it rained?' But often there is only sun, another day of continuous blazing rays. Glorious sunshine may suit you and the bees, but a gardener needs some rain. The sun warms the soil, but if a seed is to have any chance of success then it needs moisture. When rain is scarce, my allotment becomes a dustbowl. The carefully planted seeds blow off the plot in mini tornados. I enjoy the sun, as I bask in our back-yard hammock, my daughter's warm little body curled into mine. We watch the chlorophyll-full leaves of the robinia tree, lime-green against an azure sky, and dream of rain.

To grow something is to become aware of the elements. Earth, air, sun and rain become part of your consciousness. When the sun comes out, the desire (often frustrated) to rush down to my allotment becomes almost unbearable. I am irritable and gruff until I can escape out of the green wooden gate, seeds stashed hopefully in my bag, with my small, wooden-handled folding knife and a plastic bag pushed down into my large back pocket.

I must first cross water before I can water. The sight of the River Lea, wide and stately where the Eastway crosses Hackney Marshes, soothes my thoughts of wilted seedlings and arid seedbeds. The water is high and looks clear and cold early in the morning; thin green river weeds stream back in fluttering ribbons, showing the direction of the current. A single swan hangs immobile centre-stream. The air is opaque, the sunny skies have trapped gases in the atmosphere and there is a smog warning. At this early hour all I am aware of is opacity, for the air – an element usually so transparent as to be forgotten – is suddenly apparent. I cycle on, alive to an extra dimension.

When I get there I grab two plastic watering cans from the shed and plunge them into the water tank, the air rushing in great hiccuping bubbles. This action, raising two full cans at once, always feels like a workout, and my arms get strong at this time of year. It is a good, vital feeling. Watering is not without its stresses, for the tanks fill slowly and some of my fellow plot-holders are unscrupulous about emptying the tank nearest their plot and then turning their attention to mine. I have never worked out why they need so much water, but I sympathise with a West Indian fellow plot-holder who, frowning disdainfully in the direction of a white-haired Turkish grand-father and his smiling wife, says simply, 'Them two, they sha na murrcy.' I look at them through the narrowed eyes of a vegetable grower competing for water, and they take on a rapacious aura as they methodically and relentlessly drain each tank down to an inch of brown water. One way round this is to fix guttering on your sheds and greenhouses and collect water in rain barrels.

If you can't water often, then make sure that what you do counts. Close planting helps to avoid excess evaporation. Soak the ground beneath the plants heavily, rather than sprinkling water on the leaves. Try to water in the early morning or evening. In the hot summer months mulch the ground around your plants with compost, grass cuttings, cut-up hessian coffee sacks or even torn-up newspapers. Water plants more at specific times for maximum effect. For instance, beans and peas need lots of water when they are flowering, and leafy greens should be given a good soaking two weeks before they are to be harvested – tomatoes twice-weekly. If that's all too hard to remember, then you can't really go wrong if you keep seedbeds well watered and give your established plants a thorough soaking once a week.

SCYTHING

I am afraid of blades. That may be an odd thing for a cook to admit, but it's a fact. Funny then that I should have been so drawn to the blunt-looking, wooden-handled sickle on sale at our trading shed one Sunday morning. The grass grows high on my plot's paths and my only attempt to borrow a petrol strimmer from the shed (or get my husband to do it) practically ended in divorce (the machine was a little cranky and hard to start, and it was a hot day). The sickle seemed like a good alternative. Ever since I read Leo Tolstoy's description of Levin scything a meadow alongside the peasants on his estate, I have wanted to do it myself. But I had no trusty old peasant to observe when I first started mowing. This may be why I almost cut my thumb off. I brought down the blade too hastily and it met the flesh of my thumb just below the knuckle, leaving an angry red mouth. I am squeamish at the best of times, but somehow being alone at the allotment made it ten times worse. I am not proud to say that my legs turned to jelly as I clutched the thumb and blood welled out between my fingers. I panicked and, unable to look at the wound, phoned home, then sat down in a heap on the floor.

About twenty minutes later a concerned-looking rescue party arrived: my husband carrying our youngest child, followed by two worried-looking older daughters bringing plasters and water. The wound healed in a couple of weeks and I had learnt an important lesson. Now I tuck my left hand behind my back and swing forward; my action is not graceful, but the grass falls back in thick, satisfying swathes and the paths get mown.

I am not the first to think scything a skill worth learning. William Cobbett recorded his own pleasure at seeing a boy 'just turned six' helping his father reap a Sussex meadow. Before you wonder at the complacency of nineteenth-century parents, Cobbett himself remarked upon the fact that 'it was no small thing to see a boy fit to be trusted with so dangerous a thing as a reap hook'; despite this he was not convinced that 'teaching children to read tends so much to their happiness, their independence of spirit, their manliness of character, as teaching them to reap'.

These jobs, like hand-weeding or carting manure, are not the ones (like harvesting) that you look forward to, but they are often the most satisfying. The time I spend on my allotment (not to mention the money spent on seeds or compost) is not the most logical or effective use of my time. If you add up the parking tickets I get whilst unloading compost, and the time spent pulling up armloads of bindweed for a small handful of strawberries at the end, the equation doesn't work. Why hand-weed rows of carrots when I can buy a perfectly good bunch at the farmers' market? Because losing oneself in the reverie of work feels good in a way that sitting at a desk never does. There is a deep calm, a concentrated peace that comes from the monotony of tasks performed outside. Tolstoy put it much better in *Anna Karenina*:

The longer Levin went on mowing, the oftener he experienced those moments of oblivion when his arms no longer seemed to swing the scythe, but the scythe itself his whole body, so conscious and full of life; and as if by magic, regularly and definitely without a thought being given to it, the work accomplished itself of its own accord. These were blessed moments.

I too have had these blessed moments, even as my back aches from digging, or my fingers tingle from the unwanted embrace of a nettle or ache from the puncture of a thorn. Need is much more than a simple economic equation. Yet, just like Levin, I too must struggle with the fact that sometimes my laborious production of vegetables or home-made bread or marmalade feels put on. What am I trying to prove? Am I just being self-indulgent? Am I playing at something that for others in the world, locked into an endless cycle of subsistence farming, is far from romantic?

I could never be completely self-sufficient; there are too many things I need that can only be bought. How could you do without essentials such as coffee and tea, spices, sugar and salt, not to mention washing powder, toilet paper and toothpaste? Yet at times I nearly am and, even in this small way, it feels good. One lunchtime a few years after I got my allotment I looked at my plate and had a revelation. I had eaten a lunch of bread that I had baked, salad I had grown, sauerkraut and yoghurt I had fermented and squashy strawberries picked from my own plot. Without even thinking about it, I had provided myself with all that I needed, and it felt good.

GROWING

In a city one season can feel much like another. Re-establishing a connection to the earth is one way of breaking the year up into recognisable seasons. If you can get access to a small patch of ground or even just a pot to plant something in, then you can liberate yourself from that feeling of monotony, of time rushing past unmarked. In my allotment each new growing season begins with the same feeling of optimism – the earth is rich and dark and full of promise. The ground is cleared of weeds, dug, fed, raked and watered. Seeds are sown in trays and nurtured on windowsills, neat rows of plants are planted out in late May.

However, by the beginning of September the ground is often rock-hard and dusty, there are thistles and plantains with long, deep roots, and my plants are shrivelled and unproductive. There is a momentary depression – a feeling that so much hard work has been in vain, that the hours put in have not paid off. Vegetables have a habit of hiding themselves behind mottled, mildewed leaves at this time of year. A little patient searching of my allotment usually yields a row of forgotten potatoes, a bunch of self-seeded rocket, a handful of freckled borlotti beans or some pale-green courgettes planted late in the day and only just beginning to fruit. There are raspberries, wine-dark dahlias and lemon-yellow sunflowers. This is enough to keep me going and to encourage me to heave the seed-heavy weed plants up out of the ground; to rake the dusty ground and water it; to start the cycle again by planting onions, garlic and chicories for winter growing.

Making a hole in the earth and dropping a seed in is always a moment filled with hope; it starts a new chain of production. If you have failed earlier in the year, now is your chance to try again. In some years you just have to be philosophical – if too much rain, or too little, has spelled disaster, sometimes all you can do is shrug and feel relieved that this is not your only source of food. What you mustn't do is give up. The tenacity that comes with trying to produce a crop is important; if you can carry on even when your garden threatens to slip into weed- and pest-filled chaos, there is a strength there that can be gained and is almost as worthwhile as the produce you take home.

COOKING ON FIRES

The roaster reappeared with a new, shorter spear, thinner, and a great lump of raw hog-fat spitted on it. This he thrust into the red fire. It sizzled and it smoked and spit fat, and I wondered. He told me he wanted it to catch fire. It refused. He groped in the hearth for the bits of twigs with which the fire had been started. These twig-stumps he stuck in the fat, like an orange stuck with cloves, then he held it in the fire again. Now at last it caught, and it was a flaming torch running downwards with a thin shower of flaming fat. And now he was satisfied. He held the fat-torch with its yellow flares all over the browning kid, which he turned horizontal for the occasion. All over the roast fell the flaming drops, till the meat was all shining and browny. He put it to the fire again, holding the diminishing fat, still burning bluish, over it all the time in the upper air. At last the old roaster decided the kid was done.

He lifted it from the fire and scrutinised it thoroughly, holding the candle to it, as if it were some wonderful epistle from the flames. To be sure it looked marvellous, and smelled so good: brown, and crisp, and hot, and savoury, not burnt in any place whatever.

D. H. Lawrence, *Sea and Sardinia*

Cooking on a fire can be sublime. Not only is it an extremely versatile source of heat, but it also offers warmth, illumination, reverie, delight and magic. In his 1921 travel book *Sea and Sardinia*, D. H. Lawrence describes how he and Frieda arrive in a Sardinian village to find that the only inn is a filthy, inhospitable hole. Their gloom is briefly lifted by the discovery of a 'gorgeous' fire in a large, dark, dungeon-like room, a fire that Lawrence likens first to 'a rushing bouquet of new flames', like fresh flowers, and then to a waterfall that flows upwards. He and Frieda bathe in 'flame-light', letting it ripple over their faces as if they are plunging into some 'gorgeous stream'. They hungrily watch an old man expertly roast a kid that has been skilfully flattened out and impaled on a long blade, the meat splayed out like a fan.

Lawrence describes the old man doing the roasting as sitting like 'time and eternity', with 'flame-flushed' face, 'fire abstract' eyes and a sacred intensity. It looks as if Frieda and Lawrence will at least get something good to eat. But alas, no – the roasting is the high point of the evening, which ends with them being served a bony portion of the now-tepid kid in a dirty dining room. If you were ever in any doubt of the transformative effect of cooking on a fire, of its elemental effect on the spirit, then Lawrence nails it down. It is a startling passage. It leaves you in no doubt that cooking on a fire is uplifting, but is also a form of culinary time travel; a way of connecting down through hundreds of years with all those who have used flame to heat and cook food before.

'Man can live without food, but he can't live without fire,' says Lawrence, quoting an Italian proverb, and I have to agree with him. In Britain we most often cook on a fire outdoors. French and Italian kitchens sometimes have hearths placed at cooking height (Richard Olney's *French Menu Cookbook* comes with instructions for building one), but it is not common in Britain – more is the pity. My own experience with cooking on a fire comes from the few days I spend each summer camping on a friend's farm on Exmoor and cooking every meal outdoors. It isn't always easy; we have suffered floods and cloud-bursts that have almost washed us away. But it has given me a great love of preparing and cooking food on a fire. It's a subject worthy of a whole book, and in fact a rather wonderful one has already been written. *The Magic of Fire: Hearth Cooking* by William Rubel has 100 recipes and exhaustive instructions for transforming your domestic hearth into a kitchen. It's out of print, but you can read it via Google Books. Rubel's recipes and descriptions of just how good food cooked in ashes, over embers, grilled, roasted or boiled is, are enough to tempt even the most sceptical cook and have inspired me to try out his recipes for ash-baked fish and onions.

After vegetables (fennel, courgettes, asparagus, leeks,) the food I most frequently cook outside is probably steak. One of our favourite family meals is T-bone steak grilled over vine-wood. I get my vine-wood when I prune the vine on my allotment each winter and dry it off ready for summer barbecues. If you are lucky you might be able to find neighbours or public gardens that are throwing out their trimmings, even if you don't have any growing space of your own.

Make a fire of good charcoal and, when it is glowing, throw the vine-wood onto it. When it has flared up and died down, cook the steak for a few minutes on each side, depending on how rare you like it. Serve with boiled new potatoes, or oven potatoes with rosemary, or simply grilled bread and salad and plenty of horseradish.

Another dish that is often cooked outside and over vine-trimmings is the Spanish rice dish paella. Whether I make it with seafood or chicken and chorizo, it's a dish that I've come to love as party food. It looks beautiful, is something your guests probably won't have cooked at home, and the unwrapping of the paella at the table is an event in itself. Plus all the cooking is done in one pan, which means that you won't spend all night washing up. Paellas can be made with seafood, snails and rabbit, although these may not find favour with all your guests; the recipe opposite is tasty, but less gastronomically challenging.

Chicken and Chorizo Paella

Serves 4 (scale it up as you wish; 8-person paella pans are easy to buy)

*2 dried nora peppers, soaked for 30 minutes in a teacup of kettle-hot water, or
use 1 tbsp pimentón paprika*
750ml boiling chicken stock
1 large free-range chicken (approx. 1.5–2kg)
1–2 tbsp olive oil
2 red onions or shallots, peeled and chopped
1 fennel bulb, cored and thinly sliced
2 garlic cloves, peeled and crushed
*4 medium or 2 large tomatoes, skinned (see page 242) and roughly chopped,
or 1 x 400g tin of tomatoes, drained*
3 long narrow red Romano peppers, skinned (see page 242) and cut into strips
2 cooking chorizo (approx. 200g), sliced into fat coins
a small bunch of fresh marjoram or oregano
2 or 3 saffron strands
300g paella rice (Bomba or Calasparra)
1 small glass white wine or sherry
100g peas, podded (or frozen and defrosted)
a bunch of asparagus, trimmed
2 tbsp freshly chopped parsley

Scrape the flesh out of the softened nora peppers and set aside; sieve the soaking liquid and add it to the chicken stock.

Joint the chicken into legs, thighs, wings and breasts; cut each breast into four long pieces.

Heat 1 tablespoon of olive oil in the paella pan and brown the chicken, then remove and set aside. Add a little more oil and make a *sofrito* by cooking the onions and fennel until soft, then add the garlic, tomatoes and red peppers along with the nora pulp. Cook until jammy.

Add the chicken joints (but not the breast meat), the chorizo and marjoram or oregano and stir. Cook briefly. Then add the saffron to the boiling chicken stock and stir it. Pour the rice into the pan and stir until it is well coated. Add the wine or sherry and let it evaporate a little, before adding 600ml of the chicken stock. Stir well.

Now leave the paella alone for 15 minutes on a very low heat (you can move the pan around on top of the barbecue or hob to make sure it cooks evenly). After the 15 minutes push the chicken-breast pieces down into the rice. If the pan looks as though it's drying out, add a little more stock. Scatter over the peas and add the asparagus (spears facing outwards like the spokes of a wheel).

Test the rice and, when it is cooked through but with a little bite to it, take the paella off the heat and scatter the parsley over. Cover with a tea towel or some foil and let it rest for 10 minutes. This ensures that any slightly nuttier rice on top is cooked through. Serve with lemon wedges, sourdough bread and a salad of mixed leaves.

TO SKIN PEPPERS

Place the peppers directly onto the shelf in a hot oven (200°C/gas mask 6) until they blister and blacken a little. Transfer them to a bowl and cover it with cling film. When they have sweated and cooled down, peel off the skin and remove the seeds and stems, reserving any juices along with the flesh. You can do this the day beforehand if you like, and keep them in the fridge under a layer of olive oil.

TO SKIN TOMATOES

Lightly score a cross in the bottom of a ripe tomato. Place in a bowl and pour over boiling water from a kettle. Leave for one minute then drain. Stick a fork in the unscored, stalk end of the tomato and, using a knife or your fingers, peel off the skin.

Back-yard Paella with Sorrel, Squid and Hot Green Peppers

An unexpected ingredient (whether bought or foraged) is often the starting point for a memorable meal. When my neighbour on the allotment, Hatifa, walked over to my plot with a cupped handful of shiny, pale green peppers fresh from her garden, I felt I had to put them to good use. This paella was cooked that night on a small barbecue in our back garden. Dusk fell as we waited, so that our faces glowed with anticipation (and the light from the fire) as we peered closely at the bubbling pan.

Serves 4

3 or 4 long green or red chilli peppers, skinned (see page 242) and cut into
   strips
2 tbsp olive oil
1 onion, peeled and finely chopped
2 garlic cloves, peeled and lightly crushed
5 or 6 fresh tomatoes, skinned (see page 242) and roughly chopped
1 fennel bulb, finely chopped
2 cooking chorizo (about 200g), sliced
1 small squid, cleaned and cut into rings
300g paella rice (Bomba or Calasparra)
sea salt and black pepper
1 tbsp freshly chopped marjoram
750ml boiling chicken stock
10–15 sorrel or chard leaves, stems removed
a big handful of mussels or clams
8 large prawns
a handful of asparagus or chard stems
2 tbsp freshly chopped flat-leaf parsley
1 lemon, cut into quarters, to serve

If you want to cook the paella outside rather than indoors, build a small fire in a barbecue or fire pit and allow it to burn down to a good bed of coals with some flames (but not too low, as you need a good 45 minutes' cooking time). Whilst the fire is still quite hot, take a paella pan (roughly 30cm in diameter) and heat the oil, then fry the onion, garlic, tomatoes and fennel, stirring frequently. When the *sofrito* is soft, but not coloured, add the peppers and chorizo. When the fat has been released from the sausage, tip the pan and take out one or two spoonfuls, leaving a little to coat the rice.

Add the squid and cook briefly. Once it starts to stiffen and lose its elasticity, add the rice. Season with salt and add the marjoram. Add 600ml of the boiling stock and cook the mixture for 15 minutes on a low heat without stirring. Add a little more of the stock (kept simmering) if it looks as if the paella is drying out too quickly.

Layer the sorrel or chard leaves flat over the rice. Push in the mussels or clams, pointy side down, then arrange the prawns and the asparagus or chard stems. Allow your decorative instincts free rein to make an attractive pattern.

Cover the paella with a clean tea towel or tin foil and leave to steam for another 15 minutes. The dish should be dryish, with a good crust of rice on the bottom of the pan. Serve with parsley scattered over the top, and with plenty of lemon wedges.

LIVING OUTSIDE

To speak truly, few adult persons can see nature. Most persons do not see the sun. At least they have a very superficial seeing. The sun illuminates only the eye of the man, but shines into the eye and the heart of the child. The lover of nature is he whose inward and outward senses are still truly adjusted to each other; who has retained the spirit of infancy even into the era of manhood. His intercourse with heaven and earth, becomes part of his daily food. In the presence of nature, a wild delight runs through the man, in spite of real sorrows.

Ralph Waldo Emerson, 'Nature'

Being out of doors is the best medicine I know of. Whether I have spent the day sleeping in a hammock at the back of my garden, working on my allotment or lying on a blanket under a tree on Hampstead Heath, I know that afterwards I will sleep better, feel happier and be kinder to those around me. I am convinced that being inside too much is bad for us.

To get myself through the grey days at the start of the year when bad weather keeps me indoors, I dream of summer (past and future). Every August I camp on a friend's farm just below Dunkery Beacon, the highest point on Exmoor. We pitch our tents in a wide, open field with the moor stretching up and away behind us.

The first thing we do is dig out a large rectangle of turf for our fire, making sure to stack the sods neatly so that we can replace them when we go and leave the field as we found it. We dig a fire pit (with help from the line drawings in Dorothy Hartley's *Food in England*) and line and edge the pit with flat stones. Then we balance an old barbecue grille on top. Saucepans and frying pans go on top of this; potatoes in large packets of foil go straight into the coals, as do apples stuffed with butter, cinnamon and raisins and wrapped up in foil. The coals can be raked to provide more or less heat. Whilst we wait for the fire to burn down to cooking height we put our tents up.

Sometimes I cook a flattened chicken that I marinate before we leave home. Saffron and chopped red onion are combined with the more usual lemon-and-oil mixture (see 246) to add a Persian feel to an English summer evening. Once, as we ate our meal, a huge harvest moon, opaque and orange, swam out from behind the trees at the edge of the field and glided upwards. When I get home I find I am reluctant to be inside. I just can't seem to say goodbye to the sky. I find myself lingering by the back door, gazing up at the trees and planning the next trip.

Grilled Chicken with Saffron and Lemon

Serves 4

1 free-range chicken (approx. 1.5–2kg)

Marinade
1 red onion, finely chopped
a pinch of saffron threads, crushed and steeped in 1 tbsp boiling water
3 tbsp olive oil
juice of 1 lemon
sea salt and black pepper

Cut the chicken along its breastbone and lay it on a chopping board. Using your fist, break the joints and flatten the chicken out.

In a large plastic bowl or box combine all the marinade ingredients. Then add the chicken, mix well, cover and refrigerate until you are ready to use it. (For campers, a cool box should be fine.)

Light your barbecue. When the coals are glowing nicely, put a grille over the fire and allow any residue of previous meals to burn off it. Place the chicken on it skin-side down, and cook for a good 10–15 minutes on each side.

You can cook a pot of rice alongside the chicken and some long green peppers. We sliced the chicken and peppers and ate them in great oval flat-breads from our local Turkish bakery in Hackney.

The Year in Changing Ingredients

Peasant cookery is about anticipation. It celebrates the rhythms of the year by eating foods as they come into season. Whether it is the arrival of green garlic, asparagus, cherries, oysters or spring lamb, ingredients should be savoured and used as the centrepiece of feasts to punctuate the year. The following recipes celebrate that fact and are one way of alleviating the monotony of day-to-day cooking. They also use undervalued ingredients that are cheaply and easily prepared and are in keeping with the produce available at specific times of year.

SPRING

Chargrilled Squid and Dandelion Salad with a Lemon Dressing

The classic bistro take on dandelions is to serve a bowl of greens with some fatty lardons of bacon fried to a crisp. If pork is not your thing, then the astringent taste of dandelion also makes a great partner for chewy, sweet squid.

Serves 2

> *juice of ½ lemon*
> *3–4 tbsp olive oil*
> *sea salt and black pepper*
> *2 big handfuls of dandelions, cut where the leaves join the root*
> *1 small squid or cuttlefish (approx. 500g), cleaned and cut into largish strips*

In a teacup mix 1 tablespoon of lemon juice with most of the olive oil. Taste and adjust the dressing for your own palate – I like it quite lemony. Season with salt and pepper.

Wash and dry the dandelion leaves carefully. Place in a large salad bowl.

Heat a ridged griddle pan. Rub a very little oil over the surface of the pan. When it is very hot, sear the squid pieces – they need about 1 minute on each side. They should be pliant and have crisp golden ridge-marks on them.

Toss the squid quickly with the dandelion leaves in the salad bowl, pour over the dressing and serve immediately. If you have the inclination, rub some bread with a little garlic and olive oil and plenty of salt and sear it on the griddle to go with the dish.

Chorizo and Pea Soup
with Braised Artichoke Hearts

This soup is fresh-tasting, but still warming – perfect spring food. Green garlic and onions are the earliest green vegetables and give an advance taste of all the delights to come. The sweet taste of the young alliums helps this sloppy soup of freezer peas and chorizo, topped with poached eggs, to stand out. The original recipe came from The Eagle pub in Farringdon Road, Clerkenwell, but I've used fresh, new-season alliums instead of dried onions for a more powerfully 'green' tasting soup. This early in spring you will probably be using the violet-tipped artichokes imported from Spain or Italy rather than your own. If none are available, substitute artichokes preserved in oil, or omit them.

Serves 2

> *juice and flesh of ½ lemon*
> *3 or 4 small globe artichokes*
> *a little butter, for frying*
> *1 tbsp olive oil*
> *2 small onions (preferably freshly pulled) with their greens*
> *1 head of green (also called 'wet') garlic, thinly sliced (or 2 dried garlic cloves,*
> > *peeled and roughly crushed)*
> *100g chorizo, cut into thick coins*
> *400g peas (frozen are fine)*
> *750ml fresh chicken stock (or water), boiling*
> *2 eggs (optional)*

Squeeze the juice of the lemon into a bowl of cold water. Prepare the artichokes by peeling off the tough outer leaves, stopping when you reach leaves of a creamy-yellow hue. Lay the artichokes on their sides and cut through the middle of the leaves so that you are left with a stubby rose. Place each rose on its side, cut it in half vertically, down through the stem, and, if a choke has formed, remove the soft thistly centre with a teaspoon. As you work, rub the cut edges of the artichoke with the flesh of the lemon to prevent discoloration. As you finish trimming each artichoke, drop it into the bowl of cold water and lemon juice.

Heat a medium-sized heavy-based pan and add the butter and olive oil. Fry the onions and garlic over a medium heat, stewing them gently until they are just translucent. Drain the artichokes, add them to the pan and fry for 2–3 minutes.

Whilst the onion is softening, dry-fry the chorizo until the fat melts and the sausage crisps up. Drain off the fat and put the chorizo into the pan with the onion mixture and then add the peas and the hot stock (or water). Cook for 10 minutes, then remove a cupful of the peas, purée them and return to the pan to thicken the soup.

To make this meal more substantial you can poach two eggs and serve them in the middle of each bowl of peas and artichokes. Eat with rough bread that has been rubbed with olive oil and garlic and seared on a griddle.

SUMMER

Sorrel and *Matjes* Herring Smørrebrød

Scandinavians, and especially the Danes, love their *smørrebrød* (open sandwiches), which are usually made with dark rye breads and an infinite number of toppings. Some of my favourites include *skagen* (tiny shrimps with dill, crème fraîche and salmon eggs), gravadlax with horseradish, and *matjes* herring (herring preserved in a sweet, spicy brine). *Matjes* herring are eaten in midsummer with sour cream, chives and potatoes. They are Dutch in origin, but are very commonly eaten throughout Sweden. This sandwich takes the traditional combination and adds the lemony bite of sorrel. You will find that the slightly curried taste of the herring is surprisingly addictive.

Serves 1

> 1 tbsp sour cream or crème fraîche
> 1 large slice of sourdough rye bread, buttered
> 1 waxy potato, boiled and thinly sliced
> a few leaves of young sorrel, washed, dried and cut into ribbons
> 1 x 210g tin of matjes herring (available from Scandinavian speciality stores
>   and Ikea), drained
> 1 hard-boiled egg, chopped
> a few rings of shallots or red onion, finely chopped, or 1 tbsp freshly chopped
>   chives

Spread the sour cream or crème fraîche over the buttered bread. Layer the sliced potato on top, followed by the sorrel, herring, egg and finally the shallots, onion or chives. This kind of sandwich is best eaten with a knife and fork (and a cold beer).

Octopus, Pea and Red Pepper Paella

Part of being a modern peasant is mastering ingredients that don't naturally appeal. Octopus is one of them. Some foods will never go mass-market, they are just too revolting-looking for the average shopper. Octopus probably isn't top of your weekly menu. It is ugly and takes time to cook, but it is also native, plentiful and cheap. We should all eat more octopus. If you can, get your fishmonger to clean it for you; if not, cut out the beak and eyes, then cut off the head and turn it inside-out so that you can wash out the gunk inside. Cut the arms off and rinse well.

You can tenderise the octopus by dipping it into a large pan of boiling water. Count to five slowly and take it out. Let the octopus cool down and the water come back up to the boil, then plunge the octopus back in. Do this three times. If you have time, you can then freeze the octopus instead as freezing tenderises the flesh. Defrost before use.

Serves 4

1 Cornish octopus (approx. 1kg), prepared as above
1 tbsp olive oil
2 red onions or shallots, peeled
2 garlic cloves, peeled and crushed
4 medium or 2 large tomatoes, skinned (see page 242) and roughly chopped,
    or 1 x 400g tin of tomatoes, drained
3 long tapering red Romano peppers, skinned (see page 242) and cut into
    strips
a small bunch of fresh marjoram or oregano, chopped
2 or 3 saffron strands
750ml boiling chicken stock
300g paella rice (Bomba or Calasparra)
1 small glass white wine

150g fresh peas, podded, or frozen peas
2 tbsp freshly chopped parsley

Bring a fresh pot of water to the boil and cook the octopus very slowly until it is tender (about 45 minutes to 1½ hours). Cut a bit off and chew it to ensure it is properly tender. Reserve a slice or two to make the Octopus and Potato *Pincho* recipe (see page 254) or put all the octopus in the paella. Drain the octopus and cut into pieces about 4–5 cm long. Cut the head into strips, or discard; the head is not as tasty as the arms.

Make what the Spanish call a *sofrito* by heating the olive oil in a large pan and cooking the onions in it until soft. Add the garlic and tomatoes, and the peppers cut into strips. Cook until jammy. You could do this part ahead of time if you wish.

Add the octopus and the marjoram or oregano and stir. Then add the saffron to the boiling stock and stir.

Pour the rice into the pan and stir until it is well coated. Add the wine and let it evaporate a little, before adding 600ml of the chicken stock. Stir well. Now leave the paella alone whilst the rice cooks (about 18–20 minutes).

About 5 minutes before the end, scatter over the peas. Add a little more stock now, if it looks as if the paella is drying out too much. Take the paella off the heat and scatter over the parsley. Cover with a tea towel and let it rest for 10 minutes. Serve with lemon wedges, sourdough bread and a salad of mixed leaves.

Octopus and Potato *Pincho*
with Piparras Peppers

In the Noe Valley district of San Francisco there is a Spanish restaurant called Contigo; it's inspired by Barcelona's best tapas bars, but supplied by the Bay Area's finest producers. It's a heady combination. Whilst standing in line for our table we drank manzanilla sherry and ate little cocktail-stick snacks, such as this winning combination of tender octopus, waxy potato and medium-hot pickled peppers. The small and slender piparras pepper is a speciality of the Basque region, but you could probably pick up something similar in a Turkish or Lebanese supermarket.

Makes tapas for 4

> 8–10 *small waxy new potatoes*
> 2 *octopus tentacles, cooked (see page 253) and cut into 2cm slices*
> 1 *jar of piparras (or similar) peppers*
> *a pinch of* pimentón *(paprika)*

Steam the potatoes and peel off the skins.

Skewer a piece of octopus onto a cocktail stick, followed by a potato (or half a potato, depending on how big they are) and then a pepper. Sprinkle with a little sweet *pimentón* and serve with plenty of sherry.

SUMMER PUDDINGS

Strawberries and Cream in the Style of Dorothy Hartley

Dorothy Hartley, author of *Food in England*, ends the recipe that she gives for strawberries and cream with an exhortation to 'Crust it over with dredged white sugar and serve forth in June, on a green lawn, under shady trees by a river.' Which is another way of saying: don't bother making this in December with a packet of rock-hard strawberries that have been air-freighted halfway around the world.

Serves 4

> *500ml double cream*
> *500g strawberries, hulled (the larger ones cut up)*
> *caster sugar, for dredging*

Whip the cream to give it a little body, but do not make it stiff. Drop the strawberries in, mashing them as you go, until the cream will no longer accept another strawberry. Let the mixture stand for 1 hour. What you have will be smooth pink cream. Serve with a bowl of caster sugar so that guests can help themselves.

Hartley suggests using this scrumptious mixture to fill sponge cakes.

Gooseberry Fool-and-jelly Pudding

Gooseberries appear to ripen all at once and overwhelm you. My picking always seems to happen in a mad rush (I usually end up with ugly red scratches all over my arm) rather than the therapeutic ideal of slowly zinging the gooseberries into a bowl or basket one by one. In this recipe, gooseberry jelly goes underneath a thick gooseberry fool of yoghurt and double cream, which makes for a lighter variation on the traditional fool. You need to start making it at least four hours ahead of lunch or dinner.

Making gooseberry jelly is especially satisfying as it uses up the juice that would otherwise be wasted or might make the fool a bit sloppy. It's not a new idea. Jane Grigson quotes *Kettner's Book of the Table* (1877): 'the water must not be thrown away, being rich with the finest part of the fruit, that if left to stand it will turn to jelly'. Perhaps, but I helped mine along a bit with some gelatine.

Serves 6

> *500g gooseberries*
> *100g granulated sugar*
> *1 tbsp elderflower cordial (or use a couple of elderflower crowns cooked with*
>   *the fruit, if they are in bloom at the time)*
> *3 gelatine leaves*
> *175ml double cream*
> *100ml thick Greek-style yoghurt*

Top and tail the gooseberries (I use a thin serrated knife or a pair of kitchen scissors), then place them in a pan with a little water (just covering the bottom of the fruit) and the sugar and the elderflower crowns (if using) but not the cordial. Simmer gently until the fruits burst apart and are soft. Mash them a little with a fork, then strain through a sieve, reserving the liquid. Remove the pulp and leave to cool. While it does so, make the jelly.

Soak the gelatine leaves in a bowl of cold water. It only takes a few minutes for them to soften, then squeeze the leaves, which will be gluey and plastic, and drop them into the bowl of gooseberry syrup, which should still be hot (if you don't do this bit straight away, you will have to warm up your syrup on the stove; that's fine – just make sure you don't let it boil). Stir well until the gelatine has dissolved, then add the elderflower cordial (if using) at this point. Pour the syrup into individual glasses (I find the small, unsmashable French ones work well for picnics). Cover and refrigerate.

When the jelly has set (the next day, or a few hours later), whip the cream and swirl it into the gooseberry mash with the yoghurt. Spoon the fool on top of the jelly. Serve with a sweet, home-made biscuit if possible (ginger for real perfection).

AT LAST THERE IS A TART . . .

The restorative powers of a truly memorable meal are without debate, but finding such a meal at journey's end often proves unfeasible. We had such a meal this summer at a small inn, in a village high amidst volcanic hills in a deeply green and rural part of France. Getting there took time. The forests surrounding it were fairy-tale thick. Trees stretched out to infinity on either side. Toadstools gleamed luminously in the shadows. The road wound cruelly serpentine, ever upwards. At last we arrived, but we were extremely tired and weary when evening came. Our flagging spirits soon soared, however, as we ate our way through a no-choice five-course dinner that hit many highs; none more so than this greengage tart. It is a dessert that really makes the most of the fleeting season of the gage.

It was the end of a perfectly balanced, truly astounding meal – a meal that really showed me the truth of Richard Olney's words that 'one can only eat marvellously by respecting the seasons'. I can think of many worse ambitions than eating marvellously. The taste of this tart made such an impression on my eldest daughter that I have named my version in her honour.

Beatrice's Plum and Almond Tart

Serves 6–8

Pastry
75g cold unsalted butter, cut into 2cm cubes
150g plain flour
1 tbsp icing sugar
a pinch of sea salt
a cup of very cold water with a splash of vodka in it

Stewed fruit
100g sugar
100ml water
about 15–20 ripe plums (preferably greengages), stoned and halved
1 tbsp apricot or plum jam (optional)

Almond cream
50g butter
50g caster sugar
1 egg, beaten
50g ground almonds

To make the pastry ensure the butter has come straight from the fridge and is very cold. Place the flour, icing sugar, butter and salt in the bowl of a food-processor and blend until the mixture resembles fine breadcrumbs. Add the water mixed with vodka (to make the pastry flakier) a little at a time, until the pastry just starts to come together. Wrap it in cling film, knead the sticky dough briefly through the cling film and place in the fridge for at least 30 minutes.

Roll out the pastry thinly (2–3mm) and press into a well-buttered loose-bottomed 20cm tart tin. Cover loosely with cling film and refrigerate for about 30 minutes.

Preheat the oven to 190°C/gas mark 5. Place a pizza stone or baking sheet in the oven to heat up. Prick the chilled pastry case with a fork, but not too vigorously. Line it with baking parchment, then weigh it down with baking beans or dried pulses. Bake for 15 minutes. Remove the beans and parchment and bake again for 5 minutes. The pastry should be golden and crisp. Turn down the oven to 180°C/gas mark 4.

To stew the fruit, heat the sugar and water together in a saucepan to make a syrup. Let it come to the boil and reduce slightly, then add the plums and cook gently for about 5 minutes. Using a slotted spoon, remove the plums from the syrup and allow to cool. Reserve the juices in the pan for the glaze.

To make the almond cream, beat the butter and sugar together until fluffy, then add the beaten egg a bit at a time. Add the ground almonds and fold in. Spread the mixture evenly inside the pastry case, then arrange the plums in rings. I prefer the cut side up (less soggy), but you may decide for yourself.

Bake at 180°C/gas mark 4 until the almond cream is cooked. When the tart has cooled you can glaze the top if you like as follows. Add the apricot or plum jam to the reserved juices in the pan and simmer gently until you have a thick, glossy syrup. Spread thinly over the top of tart (using a pastry brush or the back of a spoon).

Serve the tart warm or at room temperature with a dollop of thick cream.

AUTUMN

Apple Day Salad with Roquefort and Cobnuts

I love Apple Day (October 21st). It's a chance to celebrate our many great home-grown apple varieties and remind people that there's more to life than Braeburns and Granny Smiths. It was started by the environmental organisation Common Ground and is a date worth marking on your calendar.

Use a tangy Roquefort and a sharp flavoursome apple such as Blenheim Orange or James Grieves in this dish. I include some sprigs of chervil, and the aniseed-like note makes a great partnership with the blue cheese. Speed is of the essence with this salad, as you do not want your apple slices to brown. Work quickly and you should be fine.

Serves 2

50g Kentish cobnuts
2 large handfuls of peppery salad leaves
1 thick slice of Roquefort (about 100g), crumbled
1 large crisp heritage apple (I leave the variety up to you), thinly sliced into
   crescents

Dressing
1 tbsp red-wine vinegar
4 tbsp walnut oil
sea salt and black pepper

Heat a heavy frying pan and lightly toast the cobnuts until they start to smell nutty. Watch them carefully to ensure they do not burn. Remove from the pan and set aside.

Place the salad leaves in a bowl and scatter over the cobnuts, the cheese and the apple crescents.

Whisk together all the ingredients for the dressing. Dress the salad, but don't overdo it (you may not need all the dressing). Mix well and serve immediately.

Ricotta, Dill and Chard Filo Pie

You can make this pie with just chard or with a mixture of leafy greens. I usually pick whatever looks luscious and juicy on my allotment, and end up with a varied bunch of sorrel, beet tops and chard.

Serves 4 as a main course, or 6–8 as part of a mezze lunch

butter, for greasing
a big bunch of chard (approx. 500g) (stalks and leaves)
400g ricotta
2 eggs
1 tbsp finely grated Parmesan
zest of 1 lemon
leaves from a small bunch of dill, finely chopped
a few good scrapings of nutmeg
black pepper
1 tsp sea salt
1–2 tbsp olive oil
1 small red onion or shallot, finely chopped
2 garlic cloves, peeled and crushed with the flat of a heavy kitchen knife
1 small dried red chilli pepper, crumbled
1 packet of filo pastry

Lightly butter a gratin dish (approx. 15cm diameter x 2cm deep). Preheat the oven to 180°C/gas mark 4.

Wash the chard well and drain it in a colander. Strip the leaves from the stalks and put them to one side. Dice the stalks finely. Roll the leaves up into a fat cigar and cut into very thin ribbons (a chiffonade).

In a bowl mix the ricotta with the eggs, Parmesan, lemon zest, dill, nutmeg, a few turns of the pepper mill and 1 teaspoon of salt. Mix well and set aside.

Heat 1 tablespoon of olive oil in a heavy, wide frying pan. When the oil is hot, add the onion and sweat over a medium heat until transparent. Add the chard (stalks and leaves), garlic and chilli pepper. Cook until the chard is tender (about 7–8 minutes), stirring constantly. Remove from the heat and when cool, add to the egg mixture. Mix well.

Remove the filo from its packet and gently unwrap it – don't worry if it rips a bit; this pie is very forgiving. Place a sheet of filo on the worktop and brush lightly with olive oil (it's more traditional to use melted butter, but easier and just as tasty with olive oil). If you don't have a pastry brush, you can always zigzag the oil over the pastry and spread it out with your hand – no one is watching. Place another sheet of filo on top of this piece and brush on a little more oil. Gently lift the pastry up and place in the bottom of the gratin dish; allow up to 5cm to hang over the edge, but trim it if it's too long. Repeat until you have 6 sheets of pastry in the bottom of the dish.

Spoon the chard and cheese mixture into the pie dish. Level it off and top the pie with six more layers of pastry brushed with oil. You can trim this to fit the top of the pie exactly or let it hang over, as you wish. When the pie is assembled, take a sharp knife and score the top diagonally to make a diamond pattern, taking care not to pierce right through the pastry.

Cook for about 20–25 minutes or until the top of the pie is golden and the sides a deep crunchy brown. Allow to cool and serve with a salad of mixed leaves, preferably freshly picked.

THE ETERNAL COMPOTE

The everlasting porridge pot may be the stuff of fairy tales, but in a similar (if less magical) way, my fridge is never without a bowl of some kind of compote. The year begins with a deep-red mixture of redcurrant berries (frozen the previous summer) popped straight from the freezer into a pan of sliced pears and apples from the farmers' market. Later on comes rhubarb, and then a glorious summer-long cavalcade of berries and stone fruits, until autumn brings the next crop of russets, pears and gages.

My compote is most often eaten on porridge for breakfast, or in yoghurt as an excellent instant pudding – the baby of the house is addicted to the red or pink juice of redcurrant or rhubarb compote swirled over her own morning porridge. Any scraps of pastry left over from making a quiche are pressed into my small heart-shaped tins and filled with compote for pretty fruit tarts whose tastiness entirely outstrips the speed of their preparation.

The recipe below can be adapted to suit any fruit – just watch the pan carefully when using soft fruits and berries that cook quickly. When cooking with berries it is unlikely that you will need to add water, but with drier fruit you should use your own judgement. Your ideal is a compote with a rich syrupy juice, not a watery one.

Apple, Pear and Redcurrant Compote

Serves 6–8

3 dessert apples, peeled and cut into slices
3 pears, peeled and cut into slices
100g redcurrants, destalked (frozen are fine)
2–3 tbsp granulated sugar

Place the sliced apples and pears and the redcurrants in a pan and scatter over the sugar. Put the lid on the pan and simmer on a medium to gentle heat. After 5 minutes have a look. The berries will burst a little and the apples and pears should be soft, but not disintegrating. Taste and add a little more sugar or some water if you think the mixture is not sweet enough or too dry. Serve warm or cold.

WINTER

Ham Hock and Cannellini Beans

Ham hocks are a great cheap cut of meat, giving lots of hammy, piggy flavour for very few pence. This extremely nourishing dish is an excellent way to feed quite a lot of people for very little money, and with very little effort. All it takes is time. Puréeing the cooked onion and the garlic is a Spanish peasant-cooked technique that gives the beans a lovely creamy texture. You can cook this dish either in the oven or in a pan on the hob.

Serves 6

> 200g dried cannellini beans
> 1 smoked ham hock
> 1 small onion or 2 small shallots, unpeeled
> 1 head of garlic, unpeeled
> sea salt and black pepper
> a little olive oil
> a handful of flat-leaf parsley, freshly chopped

Soak the beans in cold water overnight (or pop them in a bowl at breakfast time). At the same time soak the ham hock (this makes it less salty) in a separate bowl or pan. When you are ready to start cooking, drain the beans and the ham hock.

Preheat the oven to 150°C/gas mark 2 if you are going to use it.

Put the beans into an ovenproof casserole or pan with a well-fitting lid. Add the onion, garlic and ham hock to the pan and cover (just) with water. Bring to the boil and simmer for 2 hours, either on the hob or in the oven.

Remove the ham hock and set aside to cool slightly before you take off the meat. Remove the onion and garlic from the pan and use a wide chopping knife to squeeze out the soft purée-like centres from the skins. Grind the pulp in a pestle to a smooth paste, then add a little liquid from the pan and stir well to form a soft, creamy sauce for the beans. Return the paste to the beans in the pan.

Cut the skin off the hock and then remove the meat. Cut off any fat or gristle. If the meat is well cooked, it should now pull apart beautifully into long pink shreds – you can do this with a fork.

Return the meat to the pan and mix it in. Your ideal is a pan of creamy beans flecked with tender pink ham, so if you think your ham-to-bean ratio is too high, keep a little of the meat back for a delicious ham-hock hash or ham tortilla. Taste the bean and ham mixture and season. Zigzag over some olive oil and scatter over the chopped parsley.

Serve with a green salad dressed with sherry vinegar and olive oil to cut through the richness of the beans.

Roast Chicken with Chorizo

The chicken in this recipe is stuffed with chorizo, and as the chicken roasts, the meaty orange drips form the perfect basting liquid.

Serves 4

1 free-range chicken (approx. 2–2.5kg)
2 tbsp dry sherry
sea salt and black pepper
small bunch of herbs (rosemary, thyme, bay and parsley)
1 cooking chorizo (75–100g), sliced
500g waxy potatoes, cut into chunks

Preheat the oven to 180°C/gas mark 4.

Rub the chicken with the sherry inside and out and season with salt and pepper. Place the bundle of herbs inside the chicken along with the chorizo.

Place the chicken in a roasting tray surrounded by the diced potatoes. Roast for 2 hours, basting frequently with the red juices from the chorizo. When you remove the chicken to baste it, turn the potatoes so that they crisp up well.

Serve with wilted greens.

Beet Leaves, Walnuts and Raisins

Winter vegetable dishes have a tendency to taste the same, but not this one. Catalan in origin and medieval in style, it uses sweet things (raisins) in a savoury dish. In Spain it is made with pine nuts and spinach, but as walnuts are more readily available in Britain I have used them and substituted beet leaves for spinach. If you find yourself with a nice healthy-looking bunch of beetroot don't throw the leaves away, just select the most tender-looking ones and use them like chard or spinach. Some beetroot varieties, such as 'Bull's Blood', can be grown solely for their leaves.

Serves 2

> *a large bunch of beetroot greens*
> *sea salt*
> *2 tbsp olive oil*
> *a large handful of raisins*
> *a handful of shelled walnuts, roughly chopped*

Wash the greens thoroughly and, shaking them dry only briefly, put them in a large pan, with no water, and season them lightly with sea salt. Cook them, lid on, over a medium heat, moving them around now and again. When they are thoroughly wilted and exuding liquid, drain and set aside.

Heat the oil in a heavy frying pan, throw in the raisins and toss them in the oil. They will swell and retain a swollen, grape-like appearance. Add the nuts and the greens and cook, stirring constantly, for another 5 minutes. Serve immediately.

You can eat this as a tapas dish with charcuterie and olives, or on its own with some crusty bread for lunch.

Apple and Date Crumble

You can use this recipe as a basic formula for crumbles ranging from rhubarb in the early part of the year to sour plum and peach in late summer.

Serves 4

8 dates
100ml kettle-hot water
3 cooking apples, peeled, cored and sliced
4 tbsp sugar
1 tsp ground cinnamon (optional)
2 strips of lemon zest, thinly pared

Crumble topping
100g butter, cut into cubes
200g plain flour
75g unrefined granulated sugar

Preheat the oven to 180°C/gas mark 4.

To make the crumble topping, work the butter into the dry ingredients until the mixture resembles coarse sand, using a food-processor or your fingertips. Cover and refrigerate.

Put the dates to soak in a bowl with the hot water for about 10 minutes. When they have softened drain the dates, reserving the water. Stone them and roughly chop the flesh. Place the apples in a medium-sized pan with the sugar and cinnamon (if using). Add the dates and their soaking water. Simmer until the fruit is just breaking up, then pour into an ovenproof pie dish.

Arrange the lemon zest in the centre. Scatter the crumble mixture over the top, smooth it out with a knife, but don't pack it down. Bake for 30–40 minutes until the juice is bubbling and breaking through the crumble. Serve with thick yellow cream or yoghurt.

Spring Festivals: Fat & Lean

Peasant lives follow patterns of feasting and fasting. Part of modern peasant cookery is about celebrating surplus, but also about having to make do with less at certain times of the year. There is a great pleasure to be had in planning feasts and celebrations, but there is another kind of beauty to be found in living a simpler, more pared-down existence – one in which you make do with the resources available and learn how to cook effectively within an economy of means.

Spring is a season of contrast: traditional religious festivals celebrate both abstinence and excess, with seasons of fasting and feasts such as Fat Tuesday that book-end those fasts.

CHIBOLLING LIKE THE CATALANS

Central heating, electric lights and air-freighted fruit and vegetables tend to lessen the impact of the seasons, but by celebrating with culinary feasts we can try and reconnect with what the changing year once meant in the kitchen. In the past the coming of spring meant a longed-for release from the privations of winter: an end to cold, to dark, short days and to the isolation imposed by bad weather. But greatest of all these joys was the arrival of better and more various foods. Spring brought richer, sweeter milk from livestock newly turned out to pasture, and baskets of tightly furled artichokes, peas, asparagus and broad beans after months of root vegetables. Now that seasonality is a choice, not a prescription, the giddy excitement of spring food is hard to grasp, but that doesn't mean we shouldn't try.

In the Valls region of Catalonia near the city of Tarragona the end of winter and the beginning of spring are heralded with the Calçotada – the feast of the onion shoots. This usually takes place out in the open under the blossoming almond trees. Or that's how book collector Irving Davis describes it in his *Catalan Cookery Book*. I have never been, so I can't vouch for the almond blossom.

Almond blossom aside, for a Calçotada you must have *calçots* (onion shoots). To grow *calçots* you must first 'chibol' your onions (it's not hard – you just have to think six months ahead). In Catalonia the onions are lifted in June or July and allowed to dry in bunches 'in the shade of a fig tree', according to Patience Gray. They are stored in a dark and dry place until September when they begin to sprout. This is the cue to put them back in the earth, planted deep in a trench, with the soil pulled up around them.

Several shoots (six to eight) appear and, as they appear, they are earthed up, which blanches the stem (as with leeks, celery and fennel). Davis usefully explains that '*calçots* comes from *calçar* (*chausser*), to put on one's shoes, boots, stockings' and refers to this special way of growing onions.

I have chibolled onions myself with mild success at my allotment. In Spain *calçots* are grown to the size of a large leek before they are dug up and trimmed of their roots. Mine weren't that big, but they had a lot of flavour. Once pulled and washed, the greens are also cut so that each onion is the same size. These super-sized spring onions are then spread out on enormous bed-sized grills and roasted over coals in town squares. They are thoroughly charred on the outside but that doesn't matter, for only the tender inside is eaten. Standing up, you hold up the *calçots* and strip off the outside, then dip the tender inner part into a sauce made of pounded hazelnuts or almonds.

A London-based Calçotada took place last spring beside the Regent's canal in Hackney. It was a feast organised by the Towpath Café (see page 46). The *calçots* came back from Spain with Jason in two large, pungent suitcases. The Hackney Calçotada was a noisy and exuberant event. There was music, wine, a blazing-hot grill and smears of sauce and ash on happy faces. At one point an excited group of young Catalans passed by. They were amazed to find a Calçotada in full swing. Their shrieks of excitement were almost as good as the sauce, but not quite.

Irving Davis called his sauce a *romesco*, Patience Gray identified it as *salvitxada* (if you want to get picky, a true *salvitxada* should really contain pulverised toast that has been rubbed with garlic). Either way, it is virtually the same appealingly piquant and nutty sauce, which goes well with grilled meats and fish too.

Like many of Gray's recipes, hers for *salvitxada* starts with an exhortation that, while unachievable in most modern homes, still somehow manages to entrance and not forbid. So by all means do as Gray suggests and 'grill a whole head of garlic in the ashes of a wood fire'. Alternatively, you can roast it in a medium oven for half an hour, then use two cloves from it in the following recipe.

Salvitxada with *Calçots*

Makes enough for 4 with *calçots*

> *a little olive oil*
> *60g almonds*
> *1 tomato (a nice, jammy juicy one), skinned (see page 242) and cored*
> *2 roasted garlic cloves (see above)*
> *1 not-roasted garlic clove, peeled*
> *a pinch of paprika*
> *a little freshly chopped parsley and mint*
> *sea salt*
> *1 tbsp vinegar*
> *3–4 calçots per person (if you don't happen to be in Catalonia, you could*
> *substitute large spring onions, but not leeks)*

Preheat the oven to 140°C/gas mark 1.

Rub 1 teaspoon of oil onto a baking tray and add the almonds. Toast them in the oven until they take on a rich golden colour and smell biscuity. Remove and allow to cool.

Light a barbecue and, for true authenticity, throw dried vine trimmings on. (I cut back the vigorous ancient grapevine at my allotment in January and store the resinous, swift-burning stems for use as barbecue fuel in the summer. Do the same and you will find steaks grilled over vine-wood are a very fine thing. It's something done frequently in places where vines are more commonly grown commercially.)

Place the tomato flesh in a bowl. Add the toasted almonds and gradually pound all the remaining ingredients (except the *calçots*) together in a pestle, finally lubricating them with olive oil. The sauce should pour and not be a paste.

When the coals are glowing nicely, char your *calçots* on the barbecue. Take them off and wrap them in newspaper. Let them 'steam' for about 5 minutes. Then strip off the paper and the charred outer layers and dip them into the sauce.

FAT TUESDAY, OR HOW TO MAKE PERFECT PANCAKES

Like millions of other people I eat pancakes with my children on Pancake Day and most Saturday mornings too. Behind that simple statement is a catalogue of disappointments, for a decent pancake recipe is hard to find. Making a light, delicate crêpe that is just strong enough to hold its form when you turn it in the pan isn't easy. For a long time I searched in vain, until I came across Richard Olney's formula for crêpe batter. Made with a high-egg and very low-flour ratio, the pancake it made was thin and almost translucent, its edges a frilly lace of crisp brown, its golden surface mottled with lunar tracings. It tasted just as a pancake should: of eggs and butter, not flour. When it had been sprinkled with sugar and lemon it was perfect.

It is rare that a single recipe can assure you of a writer's worth, but this crêpe batter convinced me that Richard Olney was someone worth listening to. It was recipe love at first sight. He explained not just the proportions, but the how and the why too. He made sure you realised (and no one else had ever told me this) that to avoid lumps you must whisk from the centre outwards, gradually forcing a very thin layer (almost a dusting) of flour into the egg mixture. The recipe included much practical common sense – instead of insisting that the mixture should be rested for 10 minutes, it allowed for the fact that pancakes are often made in a hurry when no other pudding is at hand. Reading between the lines, you felt that whoever had written it had made thousands of crêpes, quickly and joyfully, when unexpected guests had suddenly appeared for an impromptu lunch. The faint whiff of solipsism that hangs over some chef's instructions was entirely absent – this was food that had been shared and enjoyed. There was, above all, the unmistakeable ring of truth behind all his instructions – truth polished through countless repetitions and acute observation.

It was a simple recipe for batter, but it sealed a contract between us. From that day I trusted Richard Olney with my culinary life. Contrary to every other pancake recipe you will read, Richard Olney's takes a mere 30g of flour and is all the better for it. Once you've made one, you'll never make pancakes any other way.

Under Olney's instruction (the recipe is in the *French Menu Cookbook*) last Pancake Day we spread our crêpes with jam. He calls it a 'jellyroll'. We used strawberry jam as a concession to childish tastes. I would have preferred the sour plum jam that Olney suggests. Then we rolled the pancakes up and put them in a buttered ovenproof dish; they were sprinkled with sugar and dotted with butter and baked until the sugar melted and formed a glaze. You can probably imagine how good they tasted.

Perfect Crêpes

This recipe fills the crêpes with Roasted Rhubarb and Blood-orange Compote (see page 278) and makes for a rather more grown-up pudding.

The proportions have been slightly tweaked to add a little more flour than Richard Olney suggests, as I suspect the eggs I use are bigger.

Makes about 12 pancakes

> *50g plain flour*
> *a pinch of sea salt*
> *3 eggs*
> *240ml milk*
> *3 tbsp butter, plus a little extra for frying*
> *1 tbsp brandy*

Put the flour in a medium-sized mixing bowl. Add the salt. Make a small depression in the flour, then crack the eggs in one by one. Using a fork, push the egg out slowly towards the edge of the bowl. A film of flour will adhere to the viscous egg as you slowly beat outwards. Once the egg-and-flour mixture is smooth, add the milk, butter and brandy.

Heat a heavy-based (preferably cast iron) frying pan and rub with a little butter – you don't need very much. Pour in just enough batter to coat the pan when you tip it in all directions (I use a small measuring cup with a lip – 50ml). If you have too much batter, tip the excess back into the cup or you will end up with a stodgy pancake. You will know when the pan is hot enough because the batter should sizzle and form bubbles when it hits the pan.

Watch the crêpe carefully. When it is ready to turn, small beads of liquid should form on the surface and the edges will pull in slightly. I use an ordinary table knife to lift the edge towards the centre, then I flip it over with my bare hands, but you can use a spatula if you like. The pan will get hotter as you continue to make crêpes, so turn the heat down to medium-low as you go.

Fill the crêpes with the following Roasted Rhubarb and Blood-orange Compote, or with whatever takes your fancy.

Roasted Rhubarb and Blood-orange Compote

Serves 4

6–8 rhubarb stalks (depending on thickness)
1 blood-orange
granulated sugar to taste (about 3–4 tbsp)

Preheat the oven to 140°C/gas mark 1.

Wash, trim and cut the rhubarb into 4cm chunks. Put in the bottom of an ovenproof dish (an oval Le Creuset is perfect) or an enamel roasting tray. Zest the orange straight into the dish, then halve it and squeeze over the juice. Mix it all together well, then scatter over a few tablespoons of the sugar, depending on how sweet the oranges are.

Cover the dish with foil and bake in the preheated oven for 50 minutes. Eat on its own with yoghurt or cream, or stuffed inside a crêpe.

LEAN

There are lots of talented chefs in London, but most of them don't make food you would want to eat every day. That is a more singular ability – and one that David Cook has.

If you've had wonderful meals at the London restaurants Moro or Bocca di Lupo or, more recently, at the Towpath, Leila's or 40 Maltby Street, then you may have been lucky enough to eat food cooked by this superlative and ever-smiling Australian chef, a man brimming with enthusiasm and goodwill. His food is skilful, but somehow it remains earthy and essentially wholesome in a way most restaurant food isn't. To sit outside on a cold day beside the canal and eat a plate of his sausage ragù and gnocchi is a transcendent experience. He's almost too good to be true.

Davo's Taramasalata

At Maltby Street I ate this deliciously silky taramasalata, which was served with some crisp, golden toast fried in duck fat. Whoever designated tara- masalata a food allowed during periods of fasting (Advent and Lent) never ate a plate prepared by Davo.

Serves 2–4, as part of a mezze lunch

> *100g smoked cod's roe (tarama)*
> *1 small garlic clove, peeled and crushed in a mortar with a little salt*
> *1 tbsp lemon juice*
> *2 tbsp water*
> *½ piece pitta bread, soaked in water to soften and then squeezed*
> *100ml vegetable oil*
> *100ml olive oil, and a little extra to serve*
> *sea salt and black pepper*
> *½ tsp, or a good pinch,* pul biber *(Turkish red-pepper flakes, sometimes called*
> *Aleppo pepper)*

Scrape the eggs out of the skin and place in a food-processor with the garlic, lemon juice, water and squeezed bread. You can use a pestle and mortar if you want to be more traditional. Whiz or pound until smooth, then add the oils slowly, as for mayonnaise – a dribble at a time with the motor running. When it is thick and unctuous, adjust the seasoning to taste.

To serve, place the taramasalata on a plate and make an indentation in the top; pool on a teaspoon of extra olive oil and sprinkle with Turkish *pul biber* flakes. Serve with radishes, cucumber and Little Gem lettuce and some toast.

Herb Soup

Recipes don't come much leaner than this ancient soup of boiled herbs and water, which seems to date from the dawn of time and can be enjoyed at any point in the year, but especially when there is little else growing. It might be just an archetypal peasant dish, but 'archetypal' is a dangerous word to use when writing recipes. The ingredients required for dishes that have achieved national or regional significance frequently provoke bitter debate. There are, however, some very basic recipes whose paucity of means reveals their true antiquity and undeniable authenticity. These simple, ancient dishes are the archetypes that inspire cooks in the same way that myths and fairy tales are fertile ground for writers.

Just as myths contain clearly delineated stock characters, so some ancient cookery relies on simple, almost crude combinations. The most basic of these is a primitive soup made from salted water combined with aromatics, especially thyme. Beloved of shepherds, who walked over the hillsides where the wild herbs grew, this simple, almost magical infusion is traditionally drunk in Provençal homes as a pick-me-up or a cure for a hangover. It is also a traditional remedy to boost the health of a frail child. I had a pale and waxy girl at home from school one day, so I made this soup for her (I made sure she didn't see the raw egg being mixed in). It had a strengthening effect.

Serves 1

> *2 garlic cloves, peeled*
> *2 sprigs of sage*
> *1 tbsp olive oil*
> *1 egg*

Bring a small pan of slightly salted water to the boil and add the garlic, sage and oil. After 15 minutes of simmering take it off the heat.

Crack an egg and separate it. Place the yolk in a bowl. Slowly pour the hot aromatic water through a sieve over the egg yolk. Stir to thicken and serve at once.

Thyme and Bread Soup

Here is a similar soup made with thyme.

Serves 2

> *800ml water*
> *a small bunch of dried thyme*
> *2 slices of dried bread*
> *1 tsp sea salt*
> *1 tbsp olive oil*
> *2 eggs*

Bring the water to the boil and add the dried thyme. Simmer for 10–15 minutes. Place a slice of dried bread in the bottom of each soup bowl. Sprinkle over a little sea salt and then pour over the oil. When the thyme has infused pour the hot water over the bread. Break an egg on top of the bread (before pouring over the oil) if you wish to make it a bit more substantial.

THE ARCHETYPAL
MODERN PEASANT

Recipes from Patience's Kitchen

I began this book stumbling about on a rocky hillside, my flip-flops wet and slippery with dawn dew. So it seems right to return to that arid Salentine landscape and finish with the recipes that I cooked during my few days at Spigolizzi. The example of Norman and Patience's hard working life and the magic of their hilltop farmhouse have stayed with me, even amidst the clatter and roar of city life. I think of the threshing circle, the bleached sky, the wild chicory and the stone figure gazing east, each time I stoop to cut dandelions on my damp and drizzly allotment.

Polipetti, Moscardini, Seppiole (Little Cuttlefish)

Patience describes these delicacies as 'rather like bleached sea anemones'. The very tiniest of cuttlefish might be hard to find, but more commonly available cuttlefish cut into strips can be substituted.

Serves 2

> *500g cleaned cuttlefish (ask the fishmonger to do this for you)*
> *1 tbsp olive oil*
> *1 medium onion, finely chopped*
> *a few sprigs of celery leaf and/or flat-leaf parsley, torn*
> *2 or 3 tomatoes, peeled (see page 242) seeded and fragmented*
> *slither of lemon zest*
> *1 small glass of white wine (approx. 125ml)*
> *125ml water*

Wash the cuttlefish under running water in a bowl until they are thoroughly clean.

Next, prepare an appetising *sughetto* (little sauce). Heat the olive oil in a heavy frying pan and simmer the onion gently until it softens. Add the herbs, the tomatoes and the lemon zest. Now add the cuttlefish and the glass of wine and then the water. Cook on a lively heat for 10 minutes, then leave to cool. Eat with bread and black olives for lunch.

LA PIGNATA

In a chapter on 'Beans, Peas and Rustic Soups' Patience describes the use of *La Pignata,* a jug-shaped ceramic pot used in Apulia to cook chickpeas, peas, beans and broad beans on an open fire. The pot still exists, stacked on a shelf in the *cantina*. In her description of this pot and its uses, Patience manages to weave in history, a sense of place, an awareness of what the accompanying recipe says about the relationship between men and women in these parts and, buried within the text, the method of cooking, described in words that immediately make you want to make and eat the dish. So we learn not just how to cook beans, but also why the pot is called *La Pignata* (it resembles a *pigna* or pine-cone) and what the method reveals about Salentine life. Cooking beans in this way requires only a small fire, but it is a fire that must be watched. Wood is scarce in this stony landscape and, by demanding this dish, the man of the house (whether consciously or unconsciously) was ensuring that his woman was kept occupied and tied to the hearth for a large part of the day.

There is pragmatism too. After carefully describing the glazed hourglass pot with its two handles side-by-side (to aid removal from the fire), Patience goes on to deliver a droll whammy. This may be the traditional way to cook beans, but she cooks hers on a stove. She is too busy working to sit poking sticks into a fire all day. The stove in question still stands in her kitchen. It is a small, white four-ring cooker run on bottled gas. The oven was never used by Patience. Instead a small mouse lived there.

The picture painted by this recipe has romance: there are wild leeks from the vineyard and the musical lilt of words like *sprunzale* (onion shoots), but there is realism too. La Pignata created a protein-rich reward for hard physical work – work that had often only been sustained by a handful of dried figs at lunchtime. Added to which, the work involved in cultivating, threshing and drying these legumes was considerable and such a crop deserved careful cooking. This was a solitary life, but don't be fooled into thinking it was an unobserved one. Gray ends her piece with a description of the flat roofs of the Salento, which double as the drying platforms (*terraze*) of every grower and as observation points. Nothing goes undetected, and there is a hint of menace: 'No one ever goes anywhere unobserved.' But having made us aware of some of the hard facts of agricultural life in the Salentine, she steers the recipe back to the realms of myth: 'remember the Princess and the Pea; her mattress was, of course, made of pea-straw, as were many Apulian mattresses till recently'. It's a perfect slice of Patience Gray – one that acknowledges and honours the hard life of the peasant, but can't help but find a little fairy-tale magic in it too.

Chickpeas with Salsa Secca

The first room of the *masseria* that you step into at Spigolizzi is huge, with a curved ceiling. It was once Norman's studio and still holds some of his sculptures and artworks, including a striking geometric painting of red, gold and blue wooden pieces placed together in pleasing symmetry. Beside this piece is a tall wicker basket filled with the pale yellow dried pods of chickpeas, a crop that requires a considerable amount of attention at every stage of production. I would like to say that we laboriously podded them to earn our keep, but we didn't. We only idly popped a few of the pale beige-coloured pods at the dinner table, marvelling at the intense blackness of the pea.

This dish was cooked back in London with the addition of some Salentine *salsa secca*, bought in the market – this is tomato paste dried on plates in the sun and then massaged with olive oil to form a rich red paste that is added to beans, soups and sauces throughout the winter months.

Serves 2–3

> 200g dried chickpeas
> 2 tbsp olive oil
> 2 garlic cloves, peeled and crushed
> 1 small onion, sliced
> 4 hot peppers preserved in oil or 4 fresh red chillies, skinned (see page 242)
> 1 large tbsp salsa secca or tomato purée

Soak the chickpeas in water overnight. The next day drain them and bring to the boil in a large pan of fresh water and simmer until they are tender. Drain, reserving some of the cooking liquid.

In a frying pan large enough to hold the chickpeas, heat the olive oil, add the garlic and onion and fry until soft, then add the roughly chopped peppers and the *salsa secca* or tomato purée. Fry for another minute or so and then add the chickpeas, moistening the mixture with a little of the reserved cooking liquid. Let it bubble for a further 5 minutes or so, then serve.

WILD CHICORY

In the field opposite the house is an ancient stone threshing circle, around which a donkey would have pulled the oblong threshing stone which still stands on the terrace at the back of the *masseria*. The threshing circle has a lip of weathered stone, broken in two places to provide the donkey with access to the circle; in one of these gaps Norman Mommens placed a large stone head on a plinth. The head, which wears a pointed headdress, looks vaguely East African; he stares east and his name is Anatoli.

Above the surface of the threshing floor wave red seedheads of wheat, the grasses sprouting from grains that fell between the cracks long ago. In this field are pine trees and quinces, oleander and the majestic spiked leaves of pale grey-green agaves. And growing up amongst the rocks are wild fennel and chicory. I had in my bag the wooden-handled clasp knife that I use on the allotment and so, running the flat of the blade against the bottom of the plant, I cut a handful of chicory, making sure to take some of the root as well as the leaf.

Broad Bean Purée with Wild Chicory and Pancetta

Wild chicory grows abundantly around the *masseria* of Spigolizzi, but in Britain you could use fresh dandelion leaves (which do not require blanching) or cultivated chicory (boiled for five minutes and drained well) with equal success.

Serves 4

> 200g dried whole broad beans or dried split and halved broad beans which
>   don't need soaking
> shoots of 4 green onions or the green parts from a small bunch of spring
>   onions, sliced
> 1 tbsp olive oil
> a small bunch of mint leaves, or a garlic clove, peeled and crushed, and single
>   dried chilli, when mint is out of season
> sea salt and black pepper
> 4 dandelion heads (leaves not flowers) or 1 bulb of 'Rosso Treviso' chicory
> 50g pancetta, cut into strips

If you are using whole dried broad beans, bring them to the boil, cook until soft then drain them, reserving the liquid, and squeeze them out of their skins. Return them to the pan and cook to a purée.

If not, put the broad beans in a pan and cover with water, then bring to the boil and simmer until tender. Add more kettle-hot water if needed. When the beans are soft and most of the water has evaporated, stir well with a wooden spoon to form a purée.

While the purée is cooking, heat a skillet and fry the onion greens or spring onions in the olive oil, and then add the mint leaves (or garlic and chilli in winter). Cook until wilted, then add the broad bean purée with some of the liquor. Cook for a few minutes, then season well with plenty of salt and set aside.

Wash and pick over the dandelion heads. If using chicory, bring a small pan of salted water to the boil. Separate the leaves and blanch the chicory for 1–2 minutes, then drain.

Fry the pancetta in a griddle or frying pan and, when it is nice and crispy, add the drained dandelion heads or chicory. Toss in the pan for a minute or so. Pour the bean and onion mixture into a bowl and then arrange the leaves and pancetta on top. Add a dribble or two of olive oil and some black pepper. Eat with plenty of good bread.

Quince Jelly with Chilli

Makes approx. 1.5kg jelly, depending on the juiciness of the quinces

1.5kg quinces
juice of 1 lemon
2.5 litres water
approx. 1kg unbleached granulated sugar
5 or 6 dried red chilli peppers, plus 1 dried chilli per jar to decorate

Halve and quarter the quinces, leaving the skin on and cores in, and put them in a pan. Add the lemon juice and water and bring to a simmer. Cook slowly until the quinces have become very soft. Depending on how ripe the quinces are, you may increase (if they are very hard) or decrease (if they are very ripe) the amount of water.

Line a colander with muslin, place it over a bowl, and pour in the quinces and their liquid. Gather up and tie the bundle with string, and then suspend it over the bowl until all the liquid has dripped through.

Measure the liquid and then return it to the pan, adding 200g of the sugar for every 250ml of juice.

Bring to the boil and skim off any scum. Add the dried chillies now and simmer until setting point is reached. Use a jam thermometer or do the flake test (see page 214).

Pour the liquid into sterilised jam jars (see page 115). As the jelly cools and sets (about half an hour) add a dried chilli pepper to each jar, if you want it to look pretty. My jelly set hard, clear and rosy like amber, with a good fiery glow on the tongue. Seal the jars when still warm. Eat with cheese.

TO END

Writing this book has changed the way I think about food. The hours spent watching skilled and dedicated craftspeople producing high-quality ingredients has made me re-evaluate its cost. Handmade cheese is expensive, as is properly reared meat. They should be, for so much work goes into the production of both of them. I eat both these things less frequently now but, when I do, I don't mind paying a little more for them. By using up leftovers, preserving vegetables and making stock out of bones, I also try harder not to waste food. I eat more vegetables and pulses than I used to. When I can, I buy direct from the farmer or producer. Each of us is an important link in the chain of consumption. I also try harder to eat things like octopus and offal that look revolting raw, but repay careful preparation. And my fridge is never without some kind of fermented food now.

None of this has required drastic change, or many more hours spent in the kitchen. In fact, by having preserved foods to hand, I often have to do far less work to get a meal on the table. I have acquired some new skills, but acquiring them has been a gentle process. I have made lots of mistakes, but they have been the kind of mistakes that you learn from. This is the best thing I have discovered about producing more of my own food myself. Learning how to make a decent loaf or a jar of yoghurt may take a while, but you should not underestimate the balm that comes from undertaking practical tasks.

This is not an exhortation to return to domestic drudgery; more an understanding that, by embracing convenience so heartily, we have lost something else, something very important. There is great pleasure to be had from making something from scratch. The rewards go beyond the stomach, and doing work that is meaningful – however humble – is good for your spirit. Patience Gray quotes Stendhal's *Memoirs of an Egotist* in *Honey from a Weed*, in a chapter on chopping and pounding: 'Without work the vessel of human life lacks ballast.'

I have learnt so much in the last year, both from mastering unfamiliar techniques and from absorbing the practical know-how of the artisans described in this book, all of whom gave so freely of their time and knowledge. Their work may sometimes be repetitive, exhausting and physically demanding, but undertaking it sustains them and they are rightly proud of what they make. That pride and feeling of self-worth are something we all gain when we become, in Cobbett's words, 'a skilful person, a person worthy of respect'.

I sometimes suffer from feelings of restlessness and a desire to travel to distant lands; I am quite often dreaming of being elsewhere. When I read a Patience Gray recipe that tells me to light a fire and leave it to die down whilst I swim across the bay, I desperately want to escape to a little white stone house overlooking the Mediterranean, to dry tomato paste on its roof, pick olives and figs and make my own wine; but right now I can't. I have to stay here, in one of the world's largest cities, helping to shepherd our three children through education. It may not be as romantic as the Salento, but I can still keep a hive of bees, grow flowers for my table and pick dandelions to eat in a dish of wilted greens, chickpeas and pancetta. I can simmer down rhubarb into a spiced-fruit ketchup and eat it with sausages that I have made myself. Food is very far from being the only interest in my life, but anyone tempted to make light of the importance of this daily necessity would do well to remember Virginia Woolf's words in *A Room of One's Own*: 'One cannot think well, love well, sleep well, if one has not dined well.'

With the help of skilled artisans and trusted writers I have taught myself how to dine well every day and, in doing so, I have added another layer to my life. The city holds a wealth of skills and inspiration. If you look hard enough, you may find that your idyll lies closer to home than you think.

CONTACTS

E5 Bakehouse
Arch 395
Mentmore Terrace
London E8 3PH
020 8525 2890
www.e5bakehouse.com

St John Bakery
Arch 72
Druid Street
London SE1 2DU
020 7237 5999
www.stjohnbakerygroup.uk.com

Towpath Café
36 De Beauvoir Crescent, Hackney
Regent's Canal towpath, between
    Whitmore Bridge and Kingsland
    Road Bridge
London N1 5SB

Beehaus
Omlet Ltd
Tuthill Park
Wardington
Oxfordshire OX17 1RR
0845 450 2056
www.omlet.co.uk

Hackney Tree Nursery
Entrance off Marsh Centre Car
    Park, Homerton Road
London E9 5PF
info@hmug.org.uk

Neal's Yard Creamery
Caeperthy
Arthur's Stone Lane
Dorstone
Herefordshire HR3 6AX
01981 500 395 (phone and fax)
www.nealsyardcreamery.co.uk

Neal's Yard Dairy
108 Druid Street
London SE1 2HH
020 7500 7520
www.neals yard dairy.com.

Kappacasein Dairy
1 Voyager Industrial Estate
London SE16 4RP
www.kappacasein.com

Mary Holbrook
Sleight Farm
Nr Timsbury
Somerset BA2 7QU
01761 470620

Clean Bean
www.cleanbean.co.uk

Koya
49 Frith St
London W1D 4SG
020 7434 4463
www.koya.co.uk

Growing Communities
The Old Fire Station
61 Leswin Road
London N16 7NX
020 7502 7588
www.growingcommunities.org

Novella Carpenter
http://ghosttownfarm.wordpress.
 com

Hayes Valley Farm
450 Laguna Street
San Francisco CA 94102
California
www.hayesvalleyfarm.com

Spitalfields City Farm
Buxton Street
London E1 5AR
0207 247 8762
www.spitalfieldscityfarm.org

Franconian Sausage Company
Unit 1
Holyrood Court
Holyrood Street
London SE1 2EL
020 7407 5911
www.franconian.co.uk

Hansen & Lydersen Ltd
Unit 48
3–5 Shelford Place
London N16 9HS
07411 693 712
www.hansen-lydersen.com

BIBLIOGRAPHY

All places of publication are London, unless otherwise stated.

Acton, Eliza, *The English Bread Book*, Southover Press, Sheffield, 1990

——*Modern Cookery for Private Families*, 1845, new edition by Quadrille, 2011

Atwood, Margaret, *Oryx and Crake*, Bloomsbury, 2003

Baïracli-Levy, Juliette de, *As Gypsies Wander: Being an account of life with the Gypsies in England, Provence, Spain, Turkey & North Africa*, Faber, 1953

——*Wanderers in the New Forest*, Faber, 1958

Berger, John, *Pig Earth*, Writers and Readers Ltd, 1987

Braudel, Fernand, *The Structures of Everyday Life, Civilisation and Capitalism (15th–18th Century)*, HarperCollins, 1981

Carpenter, Novella, *Farm City – The Education of an Urban Farmer*, Penguin, 2009

Chang, David and Meehan, Peter, *Momofuku*, Absolute Press, Bath, 2009

Cobbett, William, *Cottage Economy*, 1822, reissued by Cambridge University Press, Cambridge, 2009

David, Elizabeth, *English Bread and Yeast Cookery*, Penguin, 2001

——*French Country Cooking*, John Lehmann, 1951

——*French Provincial Cooking*, Penguin, 1960

——*Spices, Salts and Aromatics in the English Kitchen*, Grub Street, 2000

de Mori, Lori and Lowe, Jason, *Bean Eaters and Bread Soup*, Quadrille, 2007

Der Haroutunian, Arto, *The Yoghurt Cookbook*, Grub Street, 2010

Gray, Patience, *Honey from a Weed*, Prospect Books, Devon, 2001

——*Work Adventures Childhood Dreams*, Edizione Leucasia, Italy 1999

Grigson, Geoffrey, *An Englishman's Flora*, Aldeine Press, 1955

Grigson, Jane, *Charcuterie and French Pork Cookery*, Grub Street, 2001

Hartley, Dorothy, *Food in England*, Macdonald, 1954

Henderson, Fergus and Piers Gellatly, Justin, *Beyond Nose to Tail*, Bloomsbury, 2007

Hopkinson, Simon, *The Vegetarian Option*, Quadrille, 2009

Kennedy, Jacob, *Bocca Cookbook*, Bloomsbury, 2011

Lanchester, John, *The Debt to Pleasure*, Picador, 1997

Larkcom, Joy, *The Organic Salad Garden*, Frances Lincoln, 2001

Lawrence, D. H, *Sea and Sardinia*, 1921, new edition Penguin Classics, 1999

Maeterlinck, Maurice, *The Life of the Bee*, Dover Publications, New York, 2006

Miller, Henry, *The Colossus of Maroussi*, Penguin, 1972

Olney, Richard, *Simple French Food*, Grub Street, 2003

——*The French Menu Cookbook* , 1970, new edition Collins 2011

Patten, Marguerite, *Jams, Preserves and Chutneys*, Grub Street, 2001

Pomiane, Edouard de, *Cooking in Ten Minutes*, Cookery Book Club, 1962

——*Cooking with Pomiane*, Cookery Book Club, 1969

Sahni, Julie, *Classic Indian Vegetarian Cookery*, Grub Street, 1999

Spyri, Johanna, *Heidi*, Penguin Classics, 1995

Thoreau, Henry David, *Walden: or, Life in the Woods*, Dover Publications, New York, 1995

Toklas, Alice, *The Alice B. Toklas Cookbook*, 1954, Serif Books, 2010

Waters, Alice, *Chez Panisse Menu Cookbook*, Random House, New York, 1982

——*Chez Panisse Vegetables*, HarperCollins, New York, 1996

ACKNOWLEDGEMENTS

Thank you first to Stephen. You are a wonder to love and be loved by. Also thanks to Beatrice, Hannah, Matilda, Lydia and Barbary for their appetites and good hearts; to my sister, Katherine, for encouraging me and for giving me the time to work; and to Tim Barnes for lots of things, but also for laying out my proposal (again). Thanks to my mum and dad, Sue and Bruce, for their support and for the example of energetic foraging in your seventies.

Thanks to Lynn Hatzius both for her extraordinary illustrations and for her enthusiasm for this book. Thanks to my friend, Lori de Mori, for inspiring me and for reading the manuscript and giving such good advice. Thanks also to Jason Lowe for spiriting me off to Apulia and for telling me about *Pig Earth*. Thanks to Laura Jackson for making our trip to San Francisco so much fun and for cooking me so many delicious meals. Thanks to David Cook likewise for the meals and for his taramasalata recipe. Thanks also to Fred Dickieson for taking me down to Mary Holbrook's farm and giving me that lovely slab of belly pork.

Thanks to Nick and Maggie Gray for their hospitality and generosity in showing me Patience Gray's letters, and also to Miranda Gray and Ashlyn Armour-Brown for sharing their memories of Patience. Thanks to Clara Farmer, Poppy Hampson, Beth Coates and Silvia Crompton at Chatto for believing in *The Modern Peasant*, and to my agent, David Godwin, for always being such a tonic.

The biggest thanks of all go to the craftspeople featured in this book, who inspired me with their knowledge, skill and dedication and so kindly gave up their time and let me clog up their days with annoying questions.

INDEX

Acton, Eliza, 20–1, 33, 34
  English Bread Book, 20, 21
  *Modern Cookery for Private
    Families*, 20, 21, 112
almonds: Beatrice's plum and
    almond tart, 258–9
America, 112–13
  see also San Francisco
anchovies
  onions with anchovies,
    black olives and thyme
    pizza topping, 44
  onions with walnuts and
    anchovies pizza topping, 44
Androuet, Pierre, 77, 82
  Guide du Fromage, 77
apples
  apple, pear and redcurrant
    compote, 265
  apple and date crumble, 270
  Apple Day salad with Roquefort
    and cobnuts, 260–1
apricot jam, 215
Apulia, 286

Spigolizzi farmhouse, 3–11, 213,
    285, 288, 289, 290
Arthur's Seat, 69
artichokes *see* globe artichokes;
    Jerusalem artichokes
Atherton, Jason, 154
Atwood, Margaret: *Oryx and Crake*,
    159
aubergine with walnut miso, 139
autolysis, 27
autumn recipes
  apple, pear and redcurrant
    compote, 265
  Apple Day salad with Roquefort
    and cobnuts, 260–1
  ricotta, dill and chard filo pie,
    262–3
Aylward, Wolf, 6, 7

back-yard paella with sorrel, squid
    and hot green peppers, 243–4
bacon
  dandelion and bacon salad with
    a hot vinegar dressing, 196

home-curing, 217–21
Baïracli Levy, Juliette de, 185
    As Gypsies Wander, 61
    The Herbal Handbook for Farm
        and Stable, 185
    The Illustrated Herbal Handbook,
        185, 188
baked ricotta with herbs, 99
bakeries, 22–31
baking, 17–51
Bampton, 185
basic chutney recipe, 203–4
Bateman, Michael, 3
bay boletes, 178
beans
    broad bean purée with
        wild chicory and pancetta,
        290–1
    ham hock and cannellini beans,
        266–7
Beatrice's plum and almond tart,
    258–9
Beehaus, 56–7, 295
beehives, 55–7, 59–60
bee-keeping, 51–62
beer, ginger, 114–16
bee space, 56
beeswax, 52
beetroot, 128, 129
    beet leaves, walnuts and raisins,
        269
    quick pickle, 206
Berger, John
    About Looking, 155–6

'Ladle', xiii
Pig Earth, 150, 153
Bermondsey
    Kappacasein Dairy (run by Bill
        Oglethorpe), 82–6, 295
    St John Bakery, 28–31, 32–3,
        295
Bermondsey Hard-pressed cheese,
    82–6
Bibendum, 164
Billingsgate fish market, 227
birch boletes, 178
black pudding, 170
blood-oranges see oranges
Bocca di Lupo, 279
Boletus edulis (ceps), 178
Borough Market, 83, 104
bottles, sterilising, 115
brains, 162–6
    calf's brains with a cream
        dressing, chives and celery
        (cervelles de veau froides à la
        crème), 164–6
brandy: sweet cherries 'pickled' in
    brandy, 207
Braudel, Fernand: The Structures of
    Everyday Life, ix, 136
bread, 19–40
    rye bread, 38–40
    sourdough loaf, 36–8
    thyme and bread soup, 282
    walnut and raisin bread, 38
bread oven, 22–3, 27
Brick Lane, 101

broad bean purée with wild chicory
and pancetta, 290–1
Bromiley, Mary, 185
Bunyard, Edward, 77–8
burdock: dandelion and burdock
cordial, 216
Burnley, 127
butchery, 147–56

cabbage
kimchi, 120–1
sauerkraut, 119
Café Oto, performance at, 153–6
Calçotoda (feast of the onion
shoots), 272–3
calçots (onion shoots), 272
salvitxada with *calçots*, 273–4
calf's brains with a cream dressing,
chives and celery (*cervelles de
veau froides à la crème*), 164–6
California, urban farms in, 133–8
Calocybe gambosa (St George's
mushroom), 178
Campbell, Thomas, 188
cannellini beans: ham hock and
cannellini beans, 266–7
capers: tomato sauce with capers,
Parmesan and mozzarella
pizza topping, 44
cardamom, 168
Cardo cheese, 87
Carpenter, Novella, 51, 134–7, 151,
296
Farm City, 135, 151

Carrara, 4
Catalonia, 4, 272
cauliflower fungus, 177
celery: calf's brains with a cream
dressing, chives and celery
(*cervelles de veau froides à la
crème*), 164–6
ceps (*Boletus edulis*), 178
Chang, David: *Momofuku*, 106
chanterelles on toast, 183
charcoal-burners (*Russula*), 178
chard, 128, 129
ricotta, dill and chard filo pie,
262–3
chargrilled squid and dandelion
salad with a lemon dressing,
248
cheat's sourdough pizza, 45
cheese, 68–9, 72, 76–100
Apple Day salad with Roquefort
and cobnuts, 260–1
baked ricotta with herbs, 99
how to make your own ricotta,
97–8
onions with blue cheese
and rosemary pizza topping,
44
potato, sage, taleggio and crème
fraîche pizza, 44
ricotta, dill and chard filo pie,
262–3
simple goats' cheese, 95
simple lactic cheese or cows'
curd, 92–3

tomato sauce with capers,
Parmesan and mozzarella
pizza topping, 44
watercress soup with ricotta
'dumplings', 100
'white' pizza topping of mozzarella or taleggio, 45
wilted leeks, lemon zest, thyme
and goats' cheese pizza
topping, 44
cheese-making, 68–9, 70–1, 77–91
at home, 92–3, 95–8
cherries: sweet cherries 'pickled' in
brandy, 207
Chesterton, G.K., 13
chestnut boletes (*Gyroporous
castaneus*), 178
chibolling, 272
chicken, 152–3
chicken and chorizo paella, 241–2
fairy pie (chicken-and-mushroom
pie), 180–2
grilled chicken with saffron and
lime, 246
roast chicken with chorizo, 268
chickpeas with salsa secca, 288–9
chicory, 143–4, 289
broad bean purée with wild
chicory and pancetta, 290–1
puntarelle and blood-orange
salad, 145
chilli peppers
added to basic chutney recipe,
204

back-yard paella with sorrel,
squid and hot green peppers,
243–4
kimchi, 120–1
parathas: Indian bread, stuffed
with winter greens, chilli and
coriander, 131–2
parathas stuffed with potato and
chilli, 133
pizzette with spicy chilli peppers,
pepper and sea salt, 45
quince jelly with chilli, 292
China, 103, 105
chives: calf's brains with a cream
dressing, chives and celery
(*cervelles de veau froides à la
crème*), 164–6
chorizo
chicken and chorizo paella, 241–2
chorizo and pea soup with
braised artichoke heart,
249–50
roast chicken with chorizo, 268
Chorleywood method, 19
Church's Butchers, 171
chutney
basic chutney recipe, 203–4
green gooseberry chutney, 210
pumpkin chutney, 141–2
spiced plum chutney with five-
spice, 211–12
Clean Bean, 101–5, 296
Neil's quick Clean Bean tofu
soup, 105

Clissold Park, 127–8
Clitocybe rivulosa
(false champignon), 178
Cobbett, William, 12–13, 14, 21–2,
68, 218, 236, 294
Cottage Economy, 12–13, 14,
21–2
cobnuts: Apple Day salad with
Roquefort and cobnuts, 260–1
cod, 221–4
Davo's taramasalata, 280
home-made salt cod, 223
salt cod with peppers and black
olives, 224
compote, 263–5
apple, pear and redcurrant
compote, 265
roasted rhubarb and blood-
orange compote, 278
Conisbee, Molly, 233
contacts, 295–6
Contigo, 254
Cook, David, 279
Davo's taramasalata, 280
cordial: dandelion and burdock
cordial, 216
coriander, 128, 140
parathas: Indian bread
stuffed with winter greens,
chilli and coriander,
131–2
Coriander Club, 140
cows' curd: simple lactic cheese
of cows' curd, 92

cream
calf's brains with a cream dressing,
chives and celery (*cervelles de
veau froides à la crème*), 164–6
strawberries and cream in the
style of Dorothy Hartley, 255
crème fraîche: potato, sage, taleggio
and crème fraîche pizza, 44
crêpes (pancakes), 275–8
perfect crêpes, 277–8
crumble: apple and date crumble, 270
curd, 68, 70, 72, 78, 79–80, 84, 85, 90
simple lactic cheese or cows'
curd, 92–3
cuttlefish: *polipetti, moscardini,
seppiole* (little cuttlefish), 285–6

damsons, 213
wild plum jam, 214
dandelions, 194–7
chargrilled squid and dandelion
salad with a lemon dressing,
248
dandelion and bacon salad with
a hot vinegar dressing, 196
dandelion and burdock cordial,
216
spring soup of Jerusalem
artichokes, lentils and
dandelions, 197
dates: apple and date crumble, 270
David, Elizabeth, 3, 162
English Bread and Yeast Cookery,
21

Davidson, Alan: *Oxford Companion to Food*, 79, 171
Davis, Irving, 273
    Catalan Cookery Book, 272
Davo's taramasalata, 280
Day of the Dead, 6, 7
Dean (tofu-maker), 102, 103
Delaunay, The, 168
Denmark, 187
dill: ricotta, dill and chard filo pie, 262–3
Donna (milker of goats), 93
Dorstone cheese, 71
Dorstone Hill, 69
Doyle, Conan, 53
dressings
    for Apple Day salad with Roquefort and cobnuts, 260–1
    for calf's brains with a cream dressing, chives and celery, 165–6
    for chargrilled squid and dandelion salad with a lemon dressing, 248
    for dandelion and bacon salad with a hot vinegar dressing, 196
    for tofu and tomato salad with shiso, 106

Eagle pub, Farringdon Road, 249
Edwin Tucker Seeds, 143
E5 Bakehouse, 22–7, 38, 295
Eglu, 56–7

Eiji, 138
elderberry shrub, 117–18
Ellen (dairy worker), 71
Ellory, Martin, 176–9
Emerson, Ralph Waldo: 'Nature', 244
Epping Forest Beekeepers' Association, 54–5
Epping sausage, 171
Evans, Tim, 59–60
Evelyn, John, 117, 142
Exmoor, 34, 38, 240, 245

faggots (gayettes), 160–1
fairy pie (or chicken-and-mushroom pie), 180–2
fairy ring champignons (*Marasmius oreades*), 177–8
    fairy pie (or chicken-and-mushroom pie), 180–2
false champignon (*Clitocybe rivulosa*), 178
Faroe Islands, 227
Fat Tuesday (Pancake Day), 275–6
fermented food, 65–121
    fermentation at home, 112–21
filo pastry: ricotta, dill and chard filo pie, 262–3
Finn cheese, 71
fires, cooking on, 238–40, 245
    recipes, 241–4, 246
fish *see* name of fish
Fisher, M.F.K., 162

five-spice
  pizzette with Bengali five-spice,
    45
  spiced plum chutney with
    five-spice, 211–12
flapjacks: honey flapjacks, 63
foraged food, 173–97
40 Maltby Street, 279, 280
France, 88, 167, 219, 257
Franchi Seeds, 144
Franconian Sausage Company,
    167–70, 296
Fred (author's friend), 86–7, 88, 93
frittata: nettle frittata, 190
fruit
  basic chutney recipe, 203–4
  fruit ketchup, 205
  see also name of fruit
fungi, 175, 176–84
  chanterelles on toast, 183
  fairy pie (or chicken-and-
    mushroom pie), 180–2
  kaki fruit salad with spinach,
    tofu and shiitake mushrooms,
    111–12
  potato and porcini gratin, 184

garlic
  garlic and pancetta with fresh
    herbs pizza topping, 44
  onions, garlic and mixed peppers
    pizza topping, 44
  onions with garlic pizza topping,
    44

gayettes (faggots), 160–1
Germany, 188
ginger beer, 114–16
Glasgow, 171
Gleaners and I, The (documentary),
    201
gleaning, 201
globe artichokes: chorizo and pea
    soup with braised artichoke
    heart, 249–50
goats, 88–9
  kid cooked in goats' milk, 93–4
goats' cheese, 68–9, 80, 87–8, 89–90
  simple goats' cheese, 95
  wilted leeks, lemon zest, thyme
    and goats' cheese pizza
    topping, 44
gooseberries
  gooseberry fool-and-jelly
    pudding, 256–7
  green gooseberry chutney, 210
gratin: potato and porcini gratin, 184
gravadlax, 229–30
Gray, Maggie, 4, 5, 9, 213
Gray, Miranda, 176
Gray, Nick, 3, 4, 5, 9, 213
Gray, Patience, 3, 4–8, 9, 10–11, 176,
    213, 272, 273, 285, 286, 287,
    294
  Honey from a Weed, ix, 3, 4–5, 8,
    9, 10, 11, 176, 294
  Work Adventures, Childhood
    Dreams, 7
Greece, 4, 88

Greek-style yoghurt, 75
green gooseberry chutney, 210
green manures, 130
greens, 125, 127–30, 142–4
    parathas: Indian bread stuffed
        with winter greens, chilli and
        coriander, 131–2
    see also names of greens
Grigson, Geoffrey, 188
    Englishman's Flora, 117, 187
Grigson, Jane, 167, 168, 256
grilled chicken with saffron and
    lime, 246
Grovely Ridge, 187
growing, 123–45, 237–8
Growing Communities, 125–6,
    127–9, 130, 296
Gypsy foragers, 185
Gyroporous castaneus (chestnut
    boletes), 178

Habermann, Donna, 167
Habermann, Jean-Paul, 167–70, 218
Hackney, 11, 27, 272
    E5 Bakehouse, 22–7, 38, 295
Hackney City Farm, 79
Hackney Marshes, 59, 128, 234
Hackney Tree Nursery, 59, 295
ham hock and cannellini beans, 266–7
Hampstead Heath, 177–9, 245
Hamsun, Knut: *Growth of the Soil*, 226
Hannah (author's daughter), 55, 87,
    88
Hansen, Ole-Martin, 226–8

Hansen & Lydersen salmon-
    smoking business, 226–8, 296
Haroutunian, Arto der, 67, 73–4
Harris, Henry, 164
Harrods Food Hall, 90
Hartley, Dorothy
    Food in England, 114–15, 208, 245,
        255
    strawberries and cream in the
        style of Dorothy Hartley, 255
Haydon (dairy worker), 71,72
Hayes Valley Farm, 136–8, 296
hazelnuts: tender tart, 49–51
Henderson, Fergus, 155, 219
Herbert, Matthew, 154, 156
herbs, 185
    added to soft cheese, 96
    baked ricotta with herbs, 99
    garlic and pancetta with fresh
        herbs pizza topping, 44
    herb soup, 281–2
    pizzette with herbs, 45
    see also names of herbs
Herefordshire: Neal's Yard
    Creamery, 68–72, 75, 92, 96,
    295
Herne Hill, 127
herring: sorrel and *matjes* herring
    smørrebrød, 251
Hilaire, 162
Hirneola auricula-Judae (Jew's ears),
    177
Hodgson, Randolph, 81
Holbrook, Mary, 87–91, 93, 218, 296

home-cured bacon, 220–1
home-made salt cod, 223
home-made sausages, 171–2
honey, 51–63
    honey flapjacks, 63
Hopkinson, Simon, 162, 164–5, 180, 229
hot dogs, 169
Hussain, Luftun, 139–40

Indian bread *see parathas*
Italy, 3–11 *see also* Spigolizzi farm-house

Jackson, Laura, 47–8
jam
    apricot jam, 215
    wild plum jam, 214
Japan, 103, 107, 108, 109–10
jars, sterilising, 115
Jennipher (assistant cheese-maker), 83–4, 85
Jerusalem artichokes: spring soup of Jerusalem artichokes, lentils and dandelions, 197
Jew's ears (*Hirneola auricula-Judae*), 177
Joyce, James, 77, 78

kaki fruit salad with spinach, tofu and shiitake mushrooms, 111–12
Kappacasein Dairy (run by Bill Oglethorpe), 82–6, 295

Kaspar (cook), 49
Katz, Sandor: *Wild Fermentation*, 113
Kennedy, Jacob: *Bocca Cookbook*, 224
Kentish Town, 127
ketchup: fruit ketchup, 205
Kettner's Book of the Table, 256
kid cooked in goats' milk, 93–4
kimchi, 120–1
King's Cross, 55, 57
Kirkenes, 226
Korea, 103
Koya, 107–10, 206, 296

labneh, 76
Lactarius deliciosus (orange milk cap), 176
lactic cheese, 79–80
    simple goats' cheese, 95
    simple lactic cheese or cows' curd, 92–3
Lactobacillus bulgaricus, 67
Lanchester, John: *The Debt to Pleasure*, 78
Langstroth, Rev. Lorenzo, 56
    The Hive and the Honey-Bee, 56
Larkcom, Joy: *The Organic Salad Garden*, 143
Lassco, 83
Lawrence, D.H.: *Sea and Sardinia*, 238–9
Lawrence, Frieda, 239
Lea, River, 234
leaven (starter/mother), 24, 30, 32, 34–5, 38–9, 41

leeks: wilted leeks, lemon zest, thyme and goats' cheese pizza topping, 44
Lee Valley nature reserve, 54
Leila's, 279
lemon
    chargrilled squid and dandelion salad with a lemon dressing, 248
    grilled chicken with saffron and lemon, 246
    making your own ricotta with, 97
    wilted leeks, lemon zest, thyme and goats' cheese pizza topping, 44
lentils: spring soup of Jerusalem artichokes, lentils and dandelions, 197
lettuces, 129
lime-flower tea, 186
living outside, 244–5
London
    bee-keeping in, 53–4, 55, 57, 58–60, 61–2
    Bibendum, 164
    Billingsgate fish market, 226
    Bocca di Lupo, 279
    Borough Market, 83, 104
    Café Oto, live performance at, 153–6
    Clean Bean, 101–5, 296
    Delaunay, The, 168
    Eagle pub, Farringdon Road, 249
    E5 Bakehouse, 22–7, 38, 295

40 Maltby Street, 279, 280
Franconian Sausage Company, 167–70, 296
Growing Communities, 125–6, 127–9, 296
Hackney Tree Nursery, 59, 295
Hampstead Heath, 177–9, 245
Hansen & Lydersen salmon-smoking business, 225–8, 296
Hilaire, 162
Kappacasein Dairy (run by Bill Oglethorpe), 82–6, 295
Koya, 107–10, 206, 296
Leila's, 279
lime trees, 186
Moro, 89, 93, 279
Neal's Yard Dairy, 68, 69, 81, 86, 90, 295
Racine bistro, 164
St John Bakery, 28–31, 32–3, 295
St John Bread and Wine, 29
St John restaurants, 11, 29, 89
Spitalfields City Farm, 139–40, 296
Spitalfields Market, 201
Spitalfields organic market, 104
Towpath Café, 46–8, 221, 272, 279, 295
vegetable growing in, 127–9, 139–40
see also Hackney; King's Cross; Stoke Newington
Lorne sausage, 171
Lowe, Jason, 3, 47

Luka, 28, 29–30, 31, 32
Lydersen, Lyder-Nilsen, 225–6

Mabey, Richard, 213
    Flora Britannica, 187
MacKinnon, Ben, 22, 23, 24, 25, 26, 27
McLennan, Neil, 101, 102, 103–5, 109
    Neil's quick Clean Bean tofu soup, 105
Maeterlinck, Maurice: Life of the Bee, 51–2
Manchester, 127
Marasmius oreades see fairy ring champignons
Margate, 127
Marilyn (bee-keeper), 58–9
Martin (baker), 28, 29, 30, 31
Matilda (author's daughter), 195
matjes herring: sorrel and matjes herring smørrebrød, 251
Max (chef), 31
meat, 147–72
    recipes see name of meat
Mehdi (baker), 28–31, 32
Mendip cheese, 90
Metchnikov, Dr Ilya, 67
Michael (employee at Koya), 108
milk, 70–1, 82, 96
    kid cooked in goats' milk, 93–4
    products see cheese; yoghurt
Miller, Henry: The Colossus of Maroussi, 10

miso: aubergine with walnut miso, 139
Moffat, 127
Mommens, Norman, 3, 4, 5, 6, 7–8, 9, 10, 285, 288, 289
Mori, Lori De, 46–7
Moro, 89, 93, 279
moscardini: polipetti, moscardini, seppiole (little cuttlefish), 285–6
mother (starter for breadmaking), 24, 30, 32, 34–5, 38–9, 41
mozzarella
    tomato sauce with capers, Parmesan and mozzarella pizza topping, 44
    'white' pizza topping, 45
mushrooms, 176–84
    chanterelles on toast, 183
    fairy pie (chicken-and-mushroom pie), 180–2
    kaki fruit salad with spinach, tofu and shiitake mushrooms, 111–12
    potato and porcini gratin, 184
Mycological Association of the Pyrenees, 179

'National Gardening Leave' (pamphlet), 233
Naxos, 4
Neal's Yard Creamery, 68–72, 75, 92, 96, 295

Neal's Yard Dairy, 68, 69, 81 86, 90, 295

Neil's quick Clean Bean tofu soup, 105

nettles, 186–93
  nettle and walnut pesto, 193
  nettle frittata, 190
  nettle porridge, 191–2
  spring pizza of spicy sausage and nettles, 43

New Economics Foundation, 233

nigari, 104

noodles, 107–8

nuts *see* names of nuts

Oakland, California, 134–6, 151

octopus
  octopus, pea and red pepper paella, 252–3
  octopus and potato *pincho* with piparras peppers, 254

offal, 159–61
  gayettes or faggots, 160–1
  see also brains

Oglethorpe, William (Bill), 82–6

okara, 103

Old Ford cheese, 87, 88, 89–90

olives
  onions with anchovies, black olives and thyme pizza topping, 44
  salt cod with peppers and black olives, 224

Olney, Richard, 162–3, 164, 196, 257, 275, 276, 277
  French Menu Cookbook, 239, 276
  Simple French Food, 162, 163

Omlet, 55, 56–7, 58, 295

'One Pig', performance of, 153–5

onions
  onions, garlic and mixed peppers pizza topping, 44
  onions with anchovies, black olives and thyme pizza topping, 44
  onions with blue cheese and rosemary pizza topping, 44
  onions with garlic pizza topping, 44
  onions with walnuts and anchovies pizza topping, 44
  onions with walnuts and griddled radicchio pizza topping, 44
  pickled onions, 208–9
  salvitxada with *calçots*, 273–4

orange milk cap (*Lactarius deliciosus*), 176

oranges
  puntarelle and blood-orange salad, 145
  roasted rhubarb and blood-orange compote, 278

Oxford Companion to Food, 79, 171

paella, 240
  back-yard paella with sorrel,

squid and hot green peppers, 243–4

chicken and chorizo paella, 241–2

octopus, pea and red pepper paella, 252–3

Pancake Day (Fat Tuesday), 275–6

pancakes (crêpes), 275–8

perfect crêpes, 277–8

pancetta

broad bean purée with wild chicory and pancetta, 290–1

garlic and pancetta with fresh herbs pizza topping, 44

panch phoran: pizzette with *panch phoran*, 45

parathas

parathas: Indian bread stuffed with winter greens, chilli and coriander, 131–2

parathas stuffed with potato and chilli, 133

Parmesan, 80

tomato sauce with capers, Parmesan and mozzarella pizza topping, 44

pastry, 51

Beatrice's plum and almond tart, 258–9

fairy pie (or chicken-and-mushroom pie), 180–2

ricotta, dill and chard filo pie, 262–3

tender tart, 49–51

Patchwork Gardens, 128–9

Paul, Johannes, 55, 56–7

tips from, 58

pears: apple, pear and redcurrant compote, 265

peas

chorizo and pea soup with braised artichoke heart, 249–50

octopus, pea and red pepper paella, 252–3

Pennell, Elizabeth Robins: *Guide for the Greedy by a Greedy Woman*, 167

peppers

how to skin, 242

octopus, pea and red pepper paella, 252–3

octopus and potato *pincho* with piparras peppers, 254

onions, garlic and mixed peppers pizza topping, 44

salt cod with peppers and black olives, 224

see also chilli peppers

Pepys, Samuel, 80, 191

perfect crêpes, 277–8

Perroche cheese, 71

pesto: nettle and walnut pesto, 193

PETA, 156

pickle: quick pickle, 206

pickled onions, 208–9

pies

fairy pie (chicken-and-mushroom pie), 180–2

ricotta, dill and chard filo pie,
262–3
pig feast, 153–6
pignata, la, 285–6
pincho: octopus and potato
pincho with piparras peppers,
254
pizza
cheat's sourdough pizza, 45
pizzette, 45
potato, sage, taleggio and
crème fraîche pizza, 44
sourdough pizza bases, 41–2
spring pizza of spicy sausage
and nettles, 43
toppings, 44–5
plain yoghurt, 73–4
plums, 212–13
Beatrice's plum and almond tart,
258–9
spiced plum chutney with
five-spice, 211–12
wild plum jam, 214
polipetti, moscardini, seppiole
(little cuttlefish), 285–6
Pomiane, Edouard de, 196
porcini mushrooms, 177
potato and porcini gratin,
184
pork, 89
rillettes – potted pork, 157–8
see also bacon; pig feast
porridge: nettle porridge, 191–2
Portugal, 88

potatoes
octopus and potato *pincho* with
piparras peppers, 254
parathas stuffed with potato and
chilli, 133
potato and porcini gratin, 184
potato, sage, taleggio and crème
fraîche pizza, 44
Potter, Beatrix, 188
preserved food, 199–230
preserves, 212–15
apricot jam, 215
quince jelly with chilli, 292
wild plum jam, 214
pumpkin chutney, 141–2
puntarelle, 143
puntarelle and blood-orange
salad, 145

queen excluder, 58
Queijo da Serra cheese, 87
quick pickle, 206
quince jelly with chilli, 292

Racine bistro, 164
radicchio: onions with walnuts and
griddled radicchio pizza
topping, 44
Ragstone cheese, 71, 96
raisins
beet leaves, walnuts and raisins,
269
walnut and raisin bread, 38
Rankine, Kerry, 128

Rashi (bee-keeper), 54–5
redcurrants: apple, pear and
    redcurrant compote, 265
rennet, 78–9, 92
rhubarb
    fruit ketchup, 205
    quick pickle, 206
    roasted rhubarb and blood-
        orange compote, 278
ricotta, 80
    baked ricotta with herbs, 99
    how to make your own ricotta,
        97–8
    ricotta, dill and chard filo pie,
        262–3
    watercress soup with ricotta
        'dumplings', 100
rillettes – potted pork, 157–8
roast chicken with chorizo, 268
roasted rhubarb and blood-orange
    compote, 278
Robinia (false acacia), 52
Roquefort: Apple Day salad with
    Roquefort and cobnuts,
    260–1
rosemary: onions with blue cheese
    and rosemary pizza topping,
    44
Ross (assistant cheese-maker), 89, 90
rotation, 129–30
Rubel, William: *The Magic of Fire:
    Hearth Cooking*, 240
Russula (charcoal-burners), 178
rye bread, 38–40

saffron: grilled chicken with saffron
    and lemon, 246
sage: potato, sage, taleggio and
    crème fraîche pizza, 44
St George's mushroom (*Calocybe
    gambosa*), 178
St John Bakery, 28–31, 32–3, 295
St John Bread and Wine, 29
St John restaurants, 11, 29, 89
salad
    Apple Day salad with Roquefort
        and cobnuts, 260–1
    chargrilled squid and dandelion
        salad with a lemon dressing,
        248
    dandelion and bacon salad with
        a hot vinegar dressing, 196
    puntarelle and blood-orange
        salad, 145
    tofu and tomato salad with shiso,
        106
salad leaves, growing, 127–30, 142–4
salmon, 226–30
    gravadlax, 229–30
salsa secca: chickpeas with salsa
    secca, 288–9
salt cod, 221–4
    home-made salt cod, 223
    salt cod with peppers and black
        olives, 224
salted food, 217–24
Salve, 7
salvitxada with *calçots*, 273–4
San Francisco, 51, 133–8, 254

Sanuki, 108
sauerkraut, 119
sausage, 167–72
    home-made sausages, 171–2
    spring pizza of spicy sausage and
        nettles, 43
Scotland, 188
scything, 235–7
seasonal ingredients, using,
    247–70
seppiole: polipetti, moscardini, seppiole
    (little cuttlefish), 285–6
shiitake mushrooms: kaki fruit
    salad with spinach, tofu and
    shiitake mushrooms, 111–12
shiso: tofu and tomato salad with
    shiso, 106
shrub: elderberry shrub, 117–18
Sicily, 88
Simms, Andrew, 233
Simon, André, 81
simple goats' cheese, 95
simple lactic cheese or cows' curd,
    92–3
Sleight Farm, 87–91
Sleightlett cheese, 87
Slip-cote cheese, 79
smoke (in bee-keeping), 55, 58
smoked food, 225–8
smørrebrød: sorrel and *matjes*
    herring smørrebrød, 251
Somerset, cheese-making in, 87–91
sorrel, 194
    back-yard paella with sorrel,

squid and hot green peppers,
    243–4
sorrel and *matjes* herring
    smørrebrød, 251
soup
    chorizo and pea soup with
        braised artichoke heart,
        249–50
    herb soup, 281–2
    Neil's quick Clean Bean tofu
        soup, 105
    spring soup of Jerusalem
        artichokes, lentils and
        dandelions, 197
    thyme and bread soup, 282
    watercress soup with ricotta
        'dumplings', 100
sourdough, 19–20, 24, 34–5
    cheat's sourdough pizza, 45
    sourdough loaf, 36–8
    sourdough pizza bases, 41–2
soya beans, 101–2, 103 *see also* tofu
Spain, 153, 269, 272
spiced plum chutney with five-
    spice, 211–12
spices
    in chutneys, 203, 204, 210, 211,
        212
    in ketchup, 205
    for *kimchi*, 120
    for pizzette, 45
    in sausages, 168
Spigolizzi farmhouse, 3–11, 213,
    285, 288, 289, 290

spinach: kaki fruit salad with spinach, tofu and shiitake mushrooms, 111–12

Spitalfields City Farm, 139–40, 296

Spitalfields Market, 201

Spitalfields organic market, 104

sponge (in breadmaking), 24

spring festivals: fat and lean, 271–82

spring recipes
  chargrilled squid and dandelion salad with a lemon dressing, 248
  chorizo and pea soup with braised artichoke heart, 249–50
  spring pizza of spicy sausage and nettles, 43
  spring soup of Jerusalem artichokes, lentils and dandelions, 197

Spyri, Johanna: *Heidi*, 76, 90

squid
  back-yard paella with sorrel, squid and hot green peppers, 243–4
  chargrilled squid and dandelion salad with a lemon dressing, 248

starter
  for breadmaking, 24, 30, 32, 34–5, 38–9, 41
  for ginger beer ('bee'), 114, 115, 116
  for yoghurt, 71

steak, 240

Steiner, Rudolf, 60–1

Stendhal: *Memoirs of an Egotist*, 294

sterilising jars and bottles, 115

Stoke Newington, 125, 126

strawberries and cream in the style of Dorothy Hartley, 255

Streptococcus thermophilus, 67

Stuart, Tristram: *Waste*, 201

summer recipes
  Beatrice's plum and almond tart, 258–9
  gooseberry fool-and-jelly pudding, 256–7
  octopus, pea and red pepper paella, 252–3
  octopus and potato *pincho* with piparras peppers, 254
  sorrel and *matjes* herring smørrebrød, 251
  strawberries and cream in the style of Dorothy Hartley, 255

Sussex, 176

Sweden, 183, 251

sweet baking, 45–51

sweet cherries 'pickled' in brandy, 207

Swiss Alps, 83

Sykes, Rosie, 154, 155

taleggio
  potato, sage, taleggio and crème fraîche pizza, 44
  'white' pizza topping, 45

taramasalata: Davo's taramasalata, 280

tart, 257
    Beatrice's plum and almond tart, 258–9
    tender tart, 49–51

tea, lime-flower, 186

tender tart, 49–51

terroir, 80

Theroux, Paul, 53

Thoreau, Henry David, 13, 175
    Walden, ix

thyme, 281
    onions with anchovies, black olives and thyme pizza topping, 44
    thyme and bread soup, 282
    wilted leeks, lemon zest, thyme and goats' cheese pizza topping, 44

toast: chanterelles on toast, 183

tofu, 101–10
    kaki fruit salad with spinach, tofu and shiitake mushrooms, 111–12
    Neil's quick Clean Bean tofu soup, 105
    tofu and tomato salad with shiso, 106

Toklas, Alice B., 45–6, 48, 49, 149, 151
    Alice B. Toklas Cookbook, 149, 151

Tolstoy, Leo, 235, 236
    Anna Karenina, 236

tomatoes
    how to skin, 242
    tofu and tomato salad with shiso, 106
    tomato sauce with capers, Parmesan and mozzarella pizza topping, 44

Tomme de Montagne cheese, 83

Towpath Café, 46–8, 221, 272, 279, 295

trompettes, 177

Tymsboro cheese, 87

udon noodles, 107–8

urban farms, 133–8, 139–40

Varda, Agnès, 201

vegetables, 123–45
    quick pickle, 206
    see also names of vegetables

vinaigrette, 106

vinegar
    dandelion and bacon salad with hot vinegar dressing, 196
    spiced (for pickled onion recipe), 208
    vinaigrette (for tofu and tomato salad with shiso), 106

walnuts
    aubergine with walnut miso, 139
    beet leaves, walnuts and raisins, 269
    nettle and walnut pesto, 193

onions with walnuts and
anchovies pizza topping, 44
onions with walnuts and griddled radicchio pizza topping,
44
walnut and raisin bread, 38
Wanstead, 55
Warré, Abbé Émile, 60
Beekeeping for All, 60
Warré hive, 60, 61
water (in breadmaking), 34
watercress soup with ricotta
'dumplings', 100
watering, 233–5
Waters, Alice, 134
Chez Panisse cookbooks, 134
Welsh borders, 34
Westhead, Charlie, 68, 69–71
whey, 85, 89, 90

wild plum jam, 214
winter recipes
apple and date crumble, 270
beet leaves, walnuts and raisins,
269
ham hock and cannellini beans,
266–7
roast chicken with chorizo, 268
Woolf, Virginia: *A Room of One's
Own*, 294

Ximena (gardener), 128–9

Yamasaki, Junya, 109, 110
yoghurt, 67–76
Greek-style yoghurt, 75
plain yoghurt, 73–4

Zimbabwe, 151–2

ABOUT THE AUTHOR

Jojo Tulloh is food editor of the current affairs magazine, *The Week*. She writes about food and gardens for a number of national newspapers and magazines and in her spare time works her allotment in Leyton, east London. Her first book, *East End Paradise,* was published in 2009. She lives in London with her family and a hive of bees.